The Nationality Question in Soviet Central Asia

edited by
Edward Allworth

 Published in cooperation with the
Program on Soviet Nationality Problems,
Columbia University

The Praeger Special Studies program—
utilizing the most modern and efficient book
production techniques and a selective
worldwide distribution network—makes
available to the academic, government, and
business communities significant, timely
research in U.S. and international economic, social, and political development.

The Nationality Question in Soviet Central Asia

PRAEGER SPECIAL STUDIES IN INTERNATIONAL POLITICS AND GOVERNMENT

Praeger Publishers New York Washington London

Library of Congress Cataloging in Publication Data

Allworth, Edward
    The nationality question in Soviet Central Asia.

    (Praeger special studies in international politics
and government)
    Bibliography: p.
    1. Minorities—Soviet Central Asia—Addresses,
essays, lectures. 2. Ethnology—Soviet Central
Asia—Addresses, essays, lectures. I. Title.
DK855.4.A63   1973   301.45'1'0420957
72-85986

PRAEGER PUBLISHERS
111 Fourth Avenue, New York, N.Y. 10003, U.S.A.
5, Cromwell Place, London S.W.7, England

Published in the United States of America in 1973
by Praeger Publishers, Inc.

Second printing, 1974

Printed in the United States of America

If this were a traditional study written by a single author it should be dedicated to two eminent scholars who until recently made extraordinary contributions to the Central Asian field, the philologist, Professor Janos Eckmann (August 21, 1905-November 22, 1971), and historian, Professor A. Zeki Velidi Togan (December 10, 1890-July 26, 1970). Perhaps more than any others in this era they instructed us in the West to appreciate Central Asia in its own terms. But, great teachers that they were, they would have understood that this new sort of interdisciplinary, group inquiry into contemporary developments should be inscribed to the impressively modern generation of Central Asians remaking their region, and to the young scholars there and outside the USSR who are rapidly transforming our knowledge respecting those vital people, their nationality-identities, and their homeland.

The contemporary focus predominant here is given perspective through a possibility for comparison of today's reality with the quickly changing situation in the Bukharan state around 1920-24, offered by several chapters treating each period. Although the chapters have been written by different authors, their combined analysis of the central theme—the present significance of nationality identity or ethnic relations in Central Asia—can be read as a single, integrated work. Wherever feasible, emphasis has deliberately been put upon research into current Central Asian newspapers and journals.

The volume is based in good part upon the work of the graduate Seminar in Soviet Nationality Problems in Columbia University conducted during 1971-72, eight of whose members appear as authors. That component, as well as the other major portion of the book, grew out of research and discussions connected with the Conference on the Nationality Question in Soviet Central Asia, held in New York April 7-8, 1972 and sponsored by the Program on Soviet Nationality Problems, Columbia University. Some of the many other scholars and specialists who joined in making that Conference a rewarding academic effort are named in Appendix B.

Both the calling of the Conference and the preparation of this volume as part of the Program's activity were made possible through the generous support granted by the Ford Foundation. Azamat Altay, Timur Kocaoglu, Machmud Maksud-Bek and Aman B. Murat contributed meaningfully to the investigations of several authors by scanning some of the recent Central Asian press. Ian M. Matley produced the ethnic map of Bukhara (Figure 11.1), Ralph Scott Clem the map of all Central Asia (Frontispiece), and Timur Kocaoglu also kindly provided the sketch of the Charjoy institute seal (Figure 13.1). John Hanselman advanced the research and writing of the manuscript in many ways, and the Columbia University Libraries' staff proved, as always, to be exceptionally helpful.

Throughout the book "Central Asia" includes Kazakhstan and "nationalities" exclude Russians.

New York City   E.A.
July, 1972

CONTENTS

Page

PREFACE

v

LIST OF TABLES

x

LISTS OF FIGURES AND MAPS

xiii

PART I: INTERDISCIPLINARY GROUP I

Chapter

1 REGENERATION IN CENTRAL ASIA
Edward Allworth

3

2 CONVERGENCE AND THE NATIONALITY
LITERATURE OF CENTRAL ASIA
Robert J. Barrett

19

3 THE IMPACT OF DEMOGRAPHIC AND SOCIO-
ECONOMIC FORCES UPON THE NATIONALITY
QUESTION IN CENTRAL ASIA
Ralph Scott Clem

35

4 ETHNIC INTERMARRIAGE AS AN INDICATOR
OF CULTURAL CONVERGENCE IN SOVIET
CENTRAL ASIA
Ethel Dunn and Stephen P. Dunn

45

PART II: INTERDISCIPLINARY GROUP II

5 AN AWARENESS OF TRADITIONAL TAJIK
IDENTITY IN CENTRAL ASIA
Barry M. Rosen

61

6 RECENT ASSIMILATION TRENDS IN SOVIET
CENTRAL ASIA
Ronald Wixman

73

7   WHO SHALL BE EDUCATED: SELECTION
     AND INTEGRATION IN SOVIET CENTRAL
     ASIA
     M. Mobin Shorish   86

          Appendix: "The High Cost of Marriage"   99

8   LEADERSHIP AND NATIONALITY: A COM-
     PARISON OF UZBEKISTAN AND KIRGIZIA
     John Hanselman   100

9   TAJIK AND UZBEK NATIONALITY IDENTITY:
     THE NON-LITERARY ARTS
     Eden Naby   110

          PART III: INTERDISCIPLINARY GROUP III

10   THE SEARCH FOR A HERITAGE AND THE
     NATIONALITY QUESTION IN CENTRAL ASIA
     Anna Procyk   123

11   ETHNIC GROUPS OF THE BUKHARAN STATE
     CA. 1920 AND THE QUESTION OF NATIONALITY
     Ian M. Matley   134

12   FĀRSĪ, THE VATAN, AND THE MILLAT IN
     BUKHARA
     William L. Hanaway, Jr.   143

13   THE EXISTENCE OF A BUKHARAN NATIONALITY
     IN THE RECENT PAST
     Timur Kocaoglu   151

14   NATIONAL CONSCIOUSNESS AND THE POLITICS
     OF THE BUKHARA PEOPLE'S CONCILIAR RE-
     PUBLIC
     Seymour Becker   159

15   THE TWO MODES OF ETHNIC CONSCIOUSNESS:
     SOVIET CENTRAL ASIA IN TRANSITION?
     Immanuel Wallerstein   168

Page

Appendix

A   REVISED DRAFT OF SOME THESES PRESENTED
TO THE CONFERENCE ON THE NATIONALITY
QUESTION IN SOVIET CENTRAL ASIA, APRIL
7-8, 1972
Edward Allworth   176

B   COMMENTARY UPON THE CONFERENCE
SUBJECT
Paula G. Rubel, Jonathan Pool, John W. Strong,
and others   181

NOTES   192

BIBLIOGRAPHY   215

SELECTED LIST OF RECENT (1951-71) BOOKS
IN ENGLISH ABOUT CENTRAL ASIA AND THE
GENERAL SOVIET NATIONALITY QUESTION

ABOUT THE EDITOR AND THE CONTRIBUTORS   218

ix

LIST OF TABLES

Table   Page

1.1   Central Asia's Younger Generation, 1959-70   11

3.1   Coefficients of Localization for Indigenous
         and Nonindigenous Ethnic Groups of
         Central Asia, 1959 and 1970   39

3.2   Correlation Coefficients, Percent Urban
         and Percent of Given Ethnic Group, 1970   41

3.3   Correlation Coefficients, Percent White
         Collar and Percent of Given Ethnic
         Group, 1959   43

4.1   Number of Ethnic Combinations in Mixed
         Marriages in Kirgizia, Turkmenia and
         Uzbekistan in 1936   48

4.2   Distribution of Ethnic Marriages in Central
         Asia in 1936   49

4.3   Proportion of Ethnic Marriages Among Urban
         and Rural Populations of Central Asia in
         1936   50

4.4   Number of Women Marrying Turkmens in the
         Cities and Settlements of Turkmenia in 1963   51

4.5   Number of Turkmen Women Marrying Men of
         Other Ethnic Groups   52

4.6   Comparative Data on Monoethnic and Inter-
         ethnic Marriages in Ashkhabad from 1951
         to 1965   53

4.7   Dynamics of Marriages in Ashkhabad   54

4.8   Length of Marriage from Registration to
         Factual Break-up of Family, Ashkhabad   55

4.9   Classification of Reasons for the Break-up
         of the Family, Ashkhabad   56

Table   Page

5.1   Ethnic Composition of Students in Higher and
Secondary Educational Institutions, 1966,
Tajik SSR   64

5.2   Marriage Rates of Tajik and Russian Women
in the Tajik SSR for 1959 per 1,000   65

5.3   Ethnic and Professional Affiliation of Tajik
SSR Deputies to the Eighth USSR Supreme
Soviet (1970)   67

6.1   Central Asian Minority Groups and Their
Assimilators   76

6.2   Population of Central Asian Minority Groups
1926 and 1959, in the USSR   77

6.3   Population of Selected Ethnic Groups Within the
Borders of Central Asia in 1959, by Native
Language   78

6.4   Titular Central Asian Nationalities in Central
Asia Outside Their Own Republics, by Native
Language in 1959   80

6.5   Percent of Russian Speakers Among Titular
Ethnic Groups in Their Own Republics in
Urban Areas and Capital Cities (1959)   81

6.6   Increase in Population Between 1959 and 1970
of Titular Nationalities   82

6.7   Percentage of Ethnic Groups Considering the
Language of Their Nationality as Native
Language in 1959 and 1970 in the USSR   83

6.8   Among Those Considering the Language of
Their Own Ethnic Group as Native, the
Percent With a Good Command of the
Russian Language in 1970   84

Table		Page
7.1	Selectivity Index of Russians, Tajiks, Uzbeks, and Turkmens in Higher Educational Establishments of the Soviet Union for the Years 1928, 1930, and 1933	87
7.2	Indexes of Selection in Higher Education of Tajik SSR, Uzbek SSR, Turkmen SSR, and Central Asia by Nationality, 1963-64 Academic Year	89
7.3	Selectivity Indexes of Selected Nationalities in the USSR Higher Educational Establishments, and Higher Education Enrollment per 10,000 Population, 1959 and 1970	90
7.4	Selectivity Indexes in Higher Education (Undergraduate) of Major Ethnic Groups (1968-69 Academic Year) in the United States	92
7.5	Graduates of Tajik Higher Educational Establishments According to Field of Specialization for Selected Years	94
7.6	Afghanistan: Population, Enrollment in Higher Education, and Higher Education Enrollment per 10,000 Population	95
7.7	Educational Levels of the USSR and the Central Asian Populations (Local and Outsiders Combined) Who Were Ten Years and Older in the Labor Force (1939, 1959, and 1970)	95
8.1	Distribution of Delegates to the 1971 Uzbek and Kirgiz Supreme Soviets by Occupation	104
13.1	Population of the Bukharan State Between 1909 and 1924, According to Local Sources	153
13.2	1917 Census Records of the Bukharan Government for Some of Its Eastern Provinces	154

LISTS OF FIGURES AND MAPS

Figure   Page

1.1   Friendship Symbol for Annual Meeting of
       Young Tajiks and Uzbeks   9

13.1   Seal of the Faizullah Khoja Teachers
       Institute of Charjoy, Bukhara, 1923   157

Map

       Soviet Central Asia: Ethnic Groups, 1964   xiv

11.1   The Ethnic Composition of the Population of
       Bukhara ca. 1920   136

Soviet Central Asia: Ethnic Groups, 1964

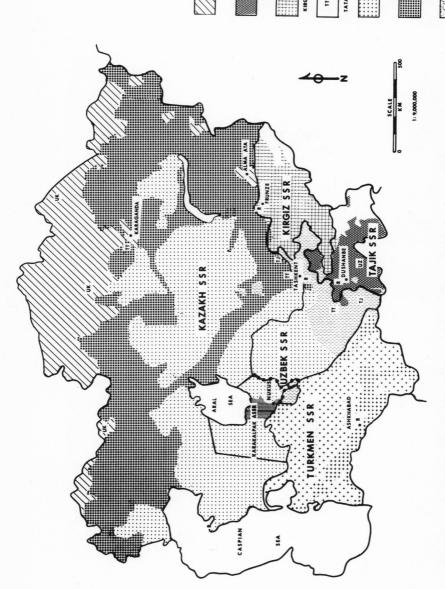

LEGEND

R — RUSSIANS	(hatched) — KIRGIZ
TJ — TAJIKS	TT — TATARS
(dark) — KARAKALPAKS	(dots) — TURKMENS
UK — UKRAINIANS	(grid) — KAZAKHS
	UZ — UZBEKS

N

SCALE
1:9,000,000
0 — KM — 500

Source: Prepared by Ralph Scott Clem from: Atlas narodov mira (Moscow: Institut Etnografii im. N. N. Mikhlukho-Maklaia Akademii Nauk SSSR, 1964), pp. 26-33.

CHAPTER

1

**REGENERATION
IN CENTRAL ASIA**
Edward Allworth

The Kirgiz and Kazakhs share a popular old saying with special
relevance to Central Asia today: "A nation regenerates itself in half
a century." (Elüü jïlda el jangïrat . . .),[1] which acknowledges both
the transient nature of contemporary reality—constantly assaulted by
inexorable renewal in human society—and the approximate span of
time in which the young generation physically and spiritually replaces
the old. This folk wisdom correlates mysteriously with the intellectual
history of developments in the region since the early 1900s. The
changing outlook of Central Asians has naturally been associated with
its younger men. Their attitudes toward ethnic identity or nationality
and toward the older generation and its values or beliefs presumably
differ to some degree from those of their senior countrymen or outsiders on the scene. These factors, of course, should have an important effect in Central Asia upon the evolving nationality question.
With reference to that question, it is worthwhile to undertake an assessment of the potential for significant change in terms of the relation
or conjunction between the youth and nationality problems of the area.

Central Asia is a region into whose society local innovations—
cultural, social, or political—of recent times seem to have been
introduced or transmitted mainly by its young men. The younger
generation, moreover, has sought at least twice within the twentieth
century to assume leadership of contemporary thought.

The first instance of this thrust embodied itself in the often
maligned reformist movement carried on from the first decade in
the twentieth century by the Central Asian Jadidchilar (Innovators).
An important phase of that Jadid development evolved in Bukhara and
Khiva, where the emphatic demarcation between traditional and modern, old and young, was dramatized by notably multiethnic groups
naming themselves the "Yash Bukharalilar" (Young Bukharans), who
exerted great influence, in all of southern Turkistan, and the "Yash
Khivalilar" (Young Khivans).

3

Perhaps their sophistication with respect to ethnic identity had been nurtured and confirmed in the cosmopolitan capital of Bukhara itself, well-known through the centuries for, among other ornaments, the thousands of students populating its many madrasas (seminaries). These young men were drawn from ethnic stock all over Central Asia as well as far beyond. In the 1800s Bukhara's students frequently participated in social and political life there, effectively supporting or opposing high-ranking clergymen or officials for important positions. Sadriddin Ayniy (1878-1954), Abdalrauf Fitrat (1886-1947), Osman Khoja (1878-1968), Mirza Abdulvahid Munzim (1877-1935) and many other Young Bukharan Jadids made up an unusually erudite corps of individuals who had in their time been among the students in the famed madrasas of this once renowned and newly reviving Muslim educational center. Those extraordinary young men initiated the transformation of Bukharan thought at the beginning of the twentieth century.

The 1924-25 partition of the Bukharan republic into Tajikistan, Turkmenistan, and Uzbekistan was paralleled by a parceling out of the multiethnic Bukharan intelligentsia and leadership to the new Central Asian "national" republics. They owe much of their early achievement in cultural and political fields to the contribution made by former Young Bukharans. Among them Abdulhekim Qulmuhammed became for a time the Soviet Turkmens' principal cultural leader. Sadriddin Ayniy laid the foundation for a separate "Tajik" literary establishment, and Abdalrauf Fitrat and Faizullah Khoja can be credited with major accomplishments as author-educator and politician, respectively, for the Uzbek SSR. The offspring of that remarkable generation in Bukhara and all Turkistan have already come of age.

An inheritance from Bukhara as valuable and lasting as the talents brought by these outstanding men was the legacy of esteem for modern enlightenment and for assimilation of currents of liberal thought, of easy receptivity to social change, of a sort of ethnic ecumenism and especially of selfless independent-mindedness among young intellectuals and activists in the application of all these qualities. This outlook combines with a clear sense of identification as youth contrasted with age, a strong attachment to place, and earnest engagement, amounting to a sense of mission, with what is promisingly new and might advance the society. Today's enlightened young men and women in Central Asia appear to share an aptitude for those traits to a remarkable degree. Government and party efforts contribute in many respects toward instilling or strengthening them in the rising generation of intellectuals.

Contemporary youth newspapers, especially 1971 issues of the Kirgiz-language Leninchil jash, Russian Komsomolets Uzbekistana, and Tajik Komsomoli Tojikiston, in addition to other recent sources, reveal how the authorities, at least outwardly, want to regard the subject of "youth and the nationality question" in Central Asia. An occasional, sometimes powerful youthful view emerges as well. Although strong, persistent emphasis is placed on youth's need to study and to learn, certain classes of young people evidently are not ordinarily expected to consider or discuss the Soviet nationality question as such. These classes include what seems to constitute the principal readership of the youth press—the large population of young manual, semiskilled and skilled laborers, military conscripts, secondary and technical-vocational school teachers, institute students, and the professional Young Communist leadership (Komsomol). A questionnaire specifically aimed at determining who among those of Uzbekistan's students beyond secondary school reads the communist youth paper Komsomolets Uzbekistana, was published September 15, 1971. It elicited responses from 1,037 individuals affiliated with 22 ethnic groups studying in 13 Uzbek institutions, including the Tashkent Institutes for Railroadmen, for Theater, for Agriculture, and for Irrigation; the Andijan Teachers' Institute; Tashkent Metallurgical Institute: Polytechnical Institute; Republic Institute for Russian Language and Literature; Institute of Foreign Languages; and Tashkent State University. The entire group taking part in the poll averaged 21.2 years of age. Nearly 64 percent of the 950 respondents who completed usable questionnaires were women.[2] Pollsters acknowledged that the 38 percent of those 950 who claimed to read the republic's Russian-language youth newspaper regularly and attentively comprised a regrettably small proportion of the thousands making up the student body of the republic's higher educational institutions. Interviews arranged to verify results of the poll were conducted with those attending one of the various institutes. The interviews disclosed that in the Tashkent Agricultural Institute alone 527 students subscribed to the competing Uzbek-language Komsomol paper Yash Leninchi (generally not available in the U.S.) and 791 to Moscow's Russian-language youth newspaper Komsomolskaia pravda. The fact that only 347 in the Institute acknowledged reading Komsomolets Uzbekistana, in addition to other data, including a survey of that paper's content, suggests persuasively that this Komsomol organ is neither aimed at nor reaching the young intellectuals of the Uzbek SSR, irrespective of nationality.

Recent efforts to inculcate young Central Asians outside the intelligentsia with the "right" views regarding nationality loyalty in the USSR have left Komsomol officials dissatisfied. In an extraordinary demonstration of priorities in the youth field, overemphasis upon work at the expense of ideology was severely criticized in the settlement of Ghijduvan, a Central Asian cattle market. Fifty kilometers northeast of Bukhara lies this small cluster of farms and service areas whose population of 10,850 (in 1959) had grown by only 679 since 1939,[3] leaving it still completely an agricultural area, as it was when a future Young Bukharan, Sadriddin Ayniy, was born there in 1874. Though contemporary Ghijduvan has since acquired running water, moving picture theaters, and other amenities of modern life, the present program of the Pakhtaabad Kolkhoz (with its 742 Komsomol members) for the upbringing of young people has been judged seriously behindhand by local authorities in at least two important respects. The large farm's plan consistently failed to allot time or attention to the military-patriotic training of young people, especially for the campaign to locate and designate local sites of memorable revolutionary, labor, or military events. It has been charged, moreover, that "affairs concerned purely with production overshadowed . . . the no less important side of bringing up youth in the revolutionary, militant traditions of the older generation. . . . "[4]

Paralleling the Komsomol authorities' dissatisfaction over the way young people in the Bukhara region are left ideologically untrained is the recognition that a great proportion of the yearly class of Uzbekistan's 150,000 unspecialized secondary school (sredniaia shkola) graduates "cannot find themselves" for long periods after receiving their diplomas, and remain uncommitted and isolated from the working society.[5] This understandable concern about the failure to direct and prepare many young people properly for Soviet adulthood has prompted a general reevaluation of youth education and Komsomol training efforts. The evident tension between intuitive doers and theoretical, scholarly analysts in this field has yet to be resolved, though the need for a fresh approach, emphasizing the quality rather than quantity of Komsomol activities, and the demand for interdisciplinary academic research into the whole scale of difficulty (problematika) associated with inadequate preparation of young people, is now being acknowledged and encouraged. In Uzbekistan's T. N. Kary-Niyazov Scholarly-Research Institute for the Teaching Disciplines, as in other institutes of the USSR, a special section was established in 1971 for studying, among other subjects, "the most effective conditions, routes and means for communist upbringing, taking account of the specific character of children's and youth organizations' activity and of the nationality peculiarities of the [Uzbek] republic."[6] The Bukharan Teachers' Institute, Qarshi Teachers' Institute, and Nizami State Teachers' Institute of Tashkent had all previously investigated aspects of these youth problems, but their work was considered inadequate. Pointing up this entire dilemma is the fact that " . . . [Uzbek] society still is obliged to exert huge efforts on educating people who are already adults. It is quite clear that these phenomena have their roots in the inadequate, ineffective training given by the school, the Pioneer, and the Komsomol organizations."[7]

If the schools, youth press, and youth organizations are not adequately reaching the young people, who is communicating with them—especially with intellectuals? The nationality question, when not entirely avoided, receives notably low priority in omnibus appeals directed to students and other young people.

There are many meaningful indications of this. At USSR-wide events like the rally of students held in Moscow starting on October 19, 1971 Soviet Communist party Secretary Leonid I. Brezhnev communicated the concern of the leadership for student contentment by promising the large audience better stipends and housing, but, in a speech touching many issues, never once referred to the nationality question. Uzbekistan's Komsomol Bureau responded to First Secretary Brezhnev's address to the students with a nine-point resolution in which only a minor subsection under Point 4 tersely noted the obligation of Komsomol committees to help authorities "strengthen the training of the student population in a spirit of Soviet patriotism, friendship among people of the USSR, and proletarian socialist internationalism."[8] Further indication that among the youth nationality problems are not officially a regular or casual topic of discussion came in the formal announcement by R. Alimov, Secretary of Uzbekistan's Komsomol Central Committee, issued well before the new year, that in 1972 Komsomol committees would create special "universities" under the slogan "My Fatherland is the USSR" and prepare talks about Soviet nationality policy and its success in Central Asia.[9] Finally, the almost complete absence of pointed articles about Soviet nationality affairs and policies from the youth newspapers of Kirgizia, Tajikistan and Uzbekistan for months on end further testifies to a studied official disinterest in combining youth and nationality problems into what may be regarded by the USSR's leadership as a potentially inflammatory mixture. One discussion of Soviet nationality policy, the exception that proved the rule that nationality and youth don't usually mix in the Uzbek case appeared in the Komsomol press only after a lapse of at least six months—and even then, significantly, from the pen of a "senior learned collaborator" in a central government institute of the USSR. Similar articles, never page-one material, were seldom published during that year for Tajik or Kirgiz Komsomol readers, and when they did appear focused carefully upon local application of nationality policy rather than on debatable principles.[10] This pragmatic approach centered either upon the multiethnic ("international") nature of personnel in factories and construction projects or upon the "triumph" of local progress in education or other fields—all insistently attributed to the party's nationality program.

There is an accepted local approach to the combination of youth and nationality, however, that with its low-key formality may be peculiar to the Soviet treatment of nationality relations in Central Asia in this period. This is the controlled visit or exchange of visits between selected representatives from two different ethnic groups,

devoid of spontaneity and reported routinely. These organized border
crossings between groups from neighboring republics contrast oddly
with the widespread intensive mixing encouraged between young Central Asians, as among many others, in a number of educational centers
or on certain multiethnic construction projects of the region. The
occurrence of what are essentially ritual contacts, however, supports
the idea that staged group confrontations involving only two nationalities—distinguished from highly varied mixing of individuals from a
number of ethnic pools in the Central Asian population—are either
given special significance or, once initiated, recur largely through
bureaucratic inertia or the need to report a quantity of routine activities to higher authorities. Under the heading of assigned "interna-
tionalist" and "friendship" activities, therefore, fall the joint meetings
organized in September 1971 between Tajik and Uzbek Komsomol
members from Khokand (Uzbekistan) and Koni Bodom (Tajikistan) and
held in that Tajik town just across the republic's border. A similar
contact, repeated for the ninth successive year between youths of
Panjakent (Tajikistan) and Uzbek Samarkand in September 1971, was
said by one of its participants both to show that " . . . the concept of
borderlines between fraternal Soviet republics has long since become
relative," and that the series of annual inter-ethnic meetings sustained
a tradition through which young people of the two groups carried on
the cooperation initiated by their fathers who had built a dam together
at Ravatkhoja in 1926. Hundreds of Komsomol members took part in
two days of meetings and festivities held in Samarkand marked at the
frontier by ceremonies at a large permanent stone obelisk erected
years earlier and bearing a representation of two clasped hands before shooting rays of the rising sun. Replicas of that Tajik-Uzbek
friendship symbol adorned the jackets of the participants.[11]

In addition to these occasions, a week-long visit of Turkmen
and Azerbaijanian delegates to Tajikistan, and a five-day youth festival
drawing Tajiks, Turkmens and people of many other ethnic origins
connected with branches of KID (Club for International Friendship)
to the Uzbek city of Namangan in July and August 1971, confirm the
impression that such organized interethnic gatherings of young people
occurred reasonably often in Central Asia during 1971 and involved
considerable numbers of individuals and substantial effort to arrange.[12]

For the younger generation especially the meaning of those
arranged contacts goes beyond bureaucratic inertia or meeting-prone
activism, of course. Present routine administrative arrangements in
Central Asia do not encourage casual meetings or natural contacts
among young intellectuals of the titular nationalities. For decades
interethnic mingling among intellectuals was regarded with particular
suspicion by authorities trained to detect "pan-ism" throughout
Central Asia in any form. The younger people, despite occasional

FIGURE 1.1

Friendship Symbol for Annual Meeting
of Young Tajiks and Uzbeks

Source: Komsomolets Uzbekistana, September 21, 1971,
p. 2.

visits to centers like Tashkent or Alma Ata, remain detached from
their counterparts in republics other than their own. While watching
for Bukharan or Turkistan nationalism, or when pan-Turkism or pan-
Islamism were the overriding concern, this ethnic insularity served
the regime rather well. Now, the divergence (Russian otdalenie,
Uzbek yiraqläshish) among nationalities, especially younger members of each group who did not experience the pre-1925 interaction,
has seemingly proceeded too far to harmonize with new policies that
give priority to the coming together (Russian sblizhenie, Uzbek
yäqinläshish, Tajik nazdikkuni) of nationalities. Young Central Asians
literally have to be taught to "come together" in the mass if large-
scale rapprochement is to be accomplished. As a step in this direction, novice Uzbek writers recently were explicity advised to revive
the catholic tastes and practices of their predecessors by cultivating
personal and working associations with young authors and poets which
could become "literary-social ties" throughout Central Asia.13
    As well as exhortations urging Soviet-style friendship among
the ethnic groups of the region youth hears persistent appeals like
those delivered at the Samarkand Komsomol meetings for Tajik-Uzbek
friendship in September 1971, to revere the heroic exploits of its
fathers, emulate their deeds, and follow their traditions and wisdom.
The appeals inserted regularly in the Kirgiz youth press direct attention not so much to the elders as a group, but persistently toward

the teacher,[14] who is held up as the proper, most important link between the generations

Both published and ceremonial expressions of Soviet policies and hopes for younger Central Asians serve to institutionalize a stratification of the population according to age groups in a manner unprecedented for the region as a whole, but undeniably comparable to the "self-identification" adopted 50 years earlier by idealistic "young" Bukharans. Educational and economic factors now combine to delay maturation among young Kazakhs, Kirgiz and other junior members of the society. Whereas the youngster of 13 or 14 had passed, directly, if ritually, into adulthood in the earlier twentieth century today's progeny of Central Asia graduates from childhood at about 14, only to remain a "youth" for his next 14 years. Komsomol organizers have recognized this newest, third stratum in Soviet and Central Asian society by creating an elaborate, pervasive organization that devotes itself exclusively to filling the gap caused by this prolonged passage to adulthood.

A natural offshoot of this stratification and organization by age level has been the creation of scores of institutions—social, artistic, educational, and the like—for and concerned with the young. One of the most recent additions to the field in Central Asia has been the State Theater for Youth (Teatri Davlatii Javonon) established in Dushanbe to serve both as an outlet for presenting the writings of young authors and for exposing youthful audiences to a specialized repertoire of interest to them. Young producer H. Abdurazzokov declared at the outset that his group in the new Tajik theater intended not merely to keep abreast of the times, but to move ahead of them in developing new theatrical and dramatic means for the region,[15] making the State Theater for Youth a kind of workshop for Tajik dramaturgy.

Focusing on budding dramatists, engineers, and their comrades as a special and distinct group undoubtedly creates the framework for a kind of counterculture with considerable status in contemporary society. As a result, present-day youth group leaders, mainly those of intellectual circles born after 1939, are strongly identified with a third, intermediate age stratum. That very numerous class (see Table 1.1 for the entire younger generation) exhibits confidence in its newly acquired powers of skill and learning and is aware of, but not traumatized or immobilized by the great territorial partitions, wars, purges, and upheavals that shook its parents in Soviet territory not long before its time. This group, moreover, seems comfortable in its improving material circumstances and, with some reservations, remains reasonably optimistic about its professional future. Press coverage, other published accounts, and reports of personal conversations with individual younger Soviet Central Asians, confirm

TABLE 1.1

Central Asia's Younger Generation, 1959-70

Ethnic Group	1959 Total USSR	Age 0-29	Percent of Own Ethnic Group	Age 0-34	Percent of Own Ethnic Group
Kazakh	3,621,610	2,229,300	61.6	2,456,296	67.1
Kirgiz	968,659	619,607	64.0	688,961	71.1
Tajik	1,396,939	920,137	65.9	1,017,589	72.8
Turkmen	1,001,585	607,287	60.6	672,550	67.1
Uzbek	6,015,416	3,896,606	64.8	4,313,301	71.7
(Russians	114,113,579	63,528,115	55.7	74,452,535	65.2)

Republic	1959 Total	Age 0-29	Percent of SSR Total	Age 0-34	Percent of SSR Total
Kazakh SSR	9,309,847	5,814,570	62.5	6,606,916	71.0
Kirgiz SSR	2,065,837	1,277,849	61.9	1,445,730	70.0
Tajik SSR	1,979,897	1,278,041	64.6	1,434,544	72.5
Turkmen SSR	1,516,375	959,453	63.3	1,079,304	71.2
Uzbek SSR	8,105,704	5,074,494	62.6	5,698,416	70.3
(RSFSR	117,534,315	65,387,798	55.6	76,490,710	65.1)

Republic	1970 Total	Age 0-29	Percent of SSR Total	Age 0-34	Percent of SSR Total
Kazakh SSR	12,848,573	7,747,254	60.1	8,896,905	79.2
Kirgiz SSR	2,932,805	1,819,764	62.4	2,028,056	69.5
Tajik SSR	2,899,602	1,825,035	63.0	2,017,661	69.6
Turkmen SSR	2,158,880	1,422,678	65.9	1,566,384	72.6
Uzbek SSR	11,960,000	7,790,000	65.1	8,589,000	72.7
(RSFSR	130,079,000	63,698,000	49.1	75,440,000	58.2)

Sources: Itogi vsesoiuznoi perepisi naseleniia 1959 goda. Svodnyi tom. (Moscow: Gosstatizdat. TsSU SSSR, 1962), pp. 211-225; Ibid., Kazakhskaia SSR (1962), pp. 30-31; Ibid., Kirgizskaia SSR (1963), pp. 22-23; Ibid., Tadzhikskaia SSR (1963), pp. 22-23; Ibid., Turkmenskaia SSR (1963), pp. 22-23; Ibid., Uzbekskaia SSR (1962), p. 22; Ibid., RSFSR (1963), pp. 62-63.
"Naselenie Turkmenistana. Soobshchenie tsentral'nogo statisticheskogo upravleniia pri Sovete ministrov turkmenskoi SSR," Turkmenskaia iskra July 11, 1971, p. 2; "Naselenie respubliki. Soobshchenie TsU kirgizskoi SSR," Sovetskaia Kirgiziia May 5, 1971, p. 3; "Sovetskii Kazakhstan: Biografiia rosta. Soobshchenie tsentral'nogo statisticheskogo upravleniia pri Sovete ministrov kazakhskoi SSR," Kazakhstanskaia pravda June 9, 1971, p. 1; "Naselenie nashei respubliki. Soobshchenie tsentral'nogo statisticheskogo upravleniia pri Sovete ministrov tadzhikskoi SSR," Kommunist Tadzhikistana May 6, 1971, p. 2; "Naselenie nashei respubliki. Soobshchenie tsentral'nogo statisticheskogo upravleniia pri Sovete ministrov uzbekskoi SSR," Pravda Vostoka April 28, 1971, p. 2; "Naselenie Rossii. Soobshchenie tsentral'nogo statisticheskogo upravleniia pri Sovete ministrov RSFSR," Sovetskaia Rossiia May 20, 1971, p. 2. Ralph Scott Clem kindly compiled some of the information included in this table.

these traits and disclose considerable disinterest among members of the age group in doctrinaire positions or old political arguments. These factors significantly differentiate the new educated youth from the young men of the Soviet past. As a consequence, identifiable contrasts in outlook, even tensions have begun to develop between one generation and the other.

Characteristic instances of generational disagreement arise especially among young, creative intellectuals. The management of the new "Yash Gvardiya" Uzbek youth theater in Tashkent has been accused of harboring the patronizing attitude that "contemporary Uzbek young people 'have not grown up enough' to understand Yash Gvardiya's aspirations . . . and [that] these youths don't want to see performances of the serious genres, preferring completely diverting comedies or melodramas which [merely] arouse the feelings."[16] A critic replied that young people also were not attending that same theater's less elevated entertainment, a new comedy, "Five-Day Bridegroom." The offering, by the recognized Uzbek author, Shuhrat, is described as a work about an amoral young couple who cooperate with two old connivers to dodge the labor laws through a fraudulently arranged marriage, a very funny play quite devoid of "principle" and absolutely lacking in positive characters. Its audience was composed primarily of "older people, exactly 'those who want to relax and be diverted . . . '" at the theater.[17]

The younger generation today responds actively to every important event and common problem in society or international and domestic politics. It is motivated by a common concern for service to humanity, strives for emotional commitment to a cause (romantika), works with interest and creativity, and seeks the love and esteem of those personally close to it, according to a "Social Portrait of Youth" sketched on the basis of sociological studies conducted by the Union-wide Komsomol organization. Surveys conducted among substantial numbers of youths to learn their theater-going habits have revealed an extraordinary frequency of attendance. None of the surveys so far apparently records the pattern in Central Asia itself, but an analogy for Tashkent (population, 1,385,000) with 15 higher educational institutions and 28 technical schools, may be offered by Ufa (in Bashrir ASSR) among whose population of 773,000 in 1970 indigenous nationalities also comprised much less than half the total), where 1,929 young male and female students reported an annual average of 29.6 trips to the theater. Young people in Ufa other than students attended 24.6 times a year on the average.[18] A lack of intellectual, artistic, or social regard for serious contemporary ideas and theater, therefore, can hardly be considered typical of the younger generation. It would also require an analysis of the nature and content of the plays they attended before such a finding could be declared conclusive.

Some prominently reviewed Central Asian dramas relating to the world of young people provide telling glimpses of differences between or among generations. But "Uzbek nationality" plays about youth—its life and aspirations—for example, are lamentably few, complain the critics, who rate theater very high in the work of ideological upbringing of youth.19

The Tashkent "Yash Gvardiya" (Young Guard) theater inaugurated its first season just before the Komsomol organization's fiftieth anniversary in 1968 (Central Asian Komsomol activity began in earnest in 1920-21)20 with the premiere presentation of a new Uzbek play Diydar ("A Longed-For Encounter"). One of the frequent propaganda lines of contemporary Central Asian Komsomol journalism—teaching the young esteem for the World War II elder-soldier-hero—was subtly invoked in "A Longed-For Encounter" by dramatist M. Karimov in what critics described as a most poetic way. In this lyrical mood, itself an idiom of today's younger creative intellectuals in Central Asia, Zilala, the protagonist daughter of such a fallen war hero touchingly idealizes him for years only to discover in an agonizing revelation that the protector and parent whom she never saw and whose self-sacrifice for all posterity she had been taught to revere was not only still alive, but remains the irresponsible character he had been when she and her mother were abandoned by him long before. In disillusionment Zilala now responds negatively toward her anything-but-heroic, real-life father and the pretense that sustained her idealized image of him. Although the drama critic approves the young heroine's rejection of the untrustworthy older generation, he nonetheless ignores symbolic and psychological implications in the work, defining the central theme of "A Longed-For Encounter" as an almost philosophical treatment of moral obligation and individual responsibility.21

An even sharper expression of divergence between the Central Asian generations has been occurring behind the scenes in the theatrical establishment. The "Young Guard" theater group that staged M. Karimov's play presented exaggerated contrasts among the younger and older players, the majority of the actors being young students in the Tashkent Theater Arts Institute.22 Such a combination of generations—not in similar proportion, perhaps—could be found recently in all the nearly 30 professional theater groups of Uzbekistan, although most were not youth-oriented. Customarily Central Asian troupes of recent decades have been dominated by a kind of apprenticeship system that has elevated to authority older directors and performers to whom younger personnel were expected to give patient attention and deference. Among those established producers and directors are Zaynab Sadiqova, Samarkand; Hashim Islamov, Khwarazm; Hajiqurban Nazarov, Khokand; and Ergash Musaffaev, producer for the controversial "Young Guard" theater in Tashkent. They, like the older generation (keksa ävlad) in Uzbekistan's important Hamza State Academic Drama Theater, are said to have shown affection, trust, and solicitousness in their dealings with "young growth" (yash nihal) in the theater. As the elders see it, the young generation (yash boghin) of actors is considered one wing of every group, the other comprising the middle and senior generations (orta va katta ävlad). At whatever theater you might attend in the capital or the provinces young theatrical people from the institutes are working with veterans in the field. To some extent the combination is functioning harmoniously, but there are indications that real strains have developed between the age groups. Uzbekistan's principal cultural newspaper has declared:

> We cannot say, however, that all our young people are responding in the same way to the concern of the producers and directors. Though we mention none of their names, young actors are to be found in every collective who have played one or two roles quite well, and, as soon as they become worth public approval, are unable to stand their own success. Among those very youths, having lost their heads over applause, and having put on airs, it is impossible not to say that . . . they are getting swell headed, making pretenses about pay increases, launching forays into heavy drinking, ruining their voice and authority among the people (el), even going around to party after party (toyma-toy) without appearing at shows or concerts at all, and are staining the honor of artistic mastery. Theater directors, the party, the Komsomol, and trade unions must put mass political training matters on the right track among such comrades.[23]

The elders habitually deplore what seem like the insufficiently respectful behavior and attitudes of their juniors, while praising, and often rewarding the most proper, compliant young. Independent-mindedness seems to threaten a system built on conformity and seniority. The discontented young Central Asians in the dramatic and performing arts share with their peers in other humanistic or technical fields a restiveness toward the system of elders and the conventions of the recent past plus an understandable fascination with new methods and independent ideas.

The new spirit seems to find an echo within political ranks. Local Young Communist leader, Uktam Alimov, originated in the severe environment of the Hungry Plains' Jizzakh region—the area that produced Sharaf R. Rashidov, since 1959 secretary of Uzbekistan's Communist party. Said to have inherited the strong character of his plainsmen ancestors, Alimov is described as a young Uzbek whose calmness, deliberateness, and, above all, thorough, analytical mind, distinguish his actions and words. Educated in the agricultural faculty at Samarkand after secondary school and navy service in the Far East, Alimov finished a dissertation "born," as it is noted with some emphasis, "in the field and not behind a laboratory table."[24] Alimov is called highly productive in his professional work as well as innovative in the youth field through which he has risen to the position of secretary of the Komsomol organization of the Agricultural Institute in Samarkand. Known as the initiator of new Institute traditions, as the author of many serious or popular writings, as the founder of the "international" club "Orbit," and as a devotee of using the questionnaire to keep Komsomol officials informed of student opinion and life, Alimov himself emphasizes that "The main thing in Komsomol work . . . is to get away from the clichés, to search out and find new means and new methods constantly. . . . A spirit of competition must reign in the Komsomol, for without it, it is impossible to move ahead."[25]

Equally devoted to discovering or creating something new are leading young writers and artists of Central Asia. Just as Alimov's demeanor and actions reflect his deep roots among ancestors in the harsh Jizzakh plains, the poets today articulate harmonious esteem for their own heritage. Based on this, the new lyrical mood is inquisitive, repeatedly probing the numerous group identities into which almost every individual fits—among family, friends, peers, professions, nationality, hometown, homeland, etc. With Central Asia's rising creative generation, these artistic circles or universes now define themselves in terms of the radius and circumference of the poet's personal experience, visionary or physical. Verses devoted to the union, the republic, oblast or other political-administrative convenience would fail—in those bureaucratic dimensions—by their impersonality, to interest the young writer. "Homeland" is another matter. It connects with the self. Partly for that reason and mainly because "homeland" in the new usage applies almost mystically to any piece of town or terrain with which an individual is linked by ties of kinship or affection, contemporary verse returns to the exploration of "homeland" again and again.

One of Cholpan Ergash's poems, "Recognizing the Homeland" (Vätänni tänish), recently printed in a thin pamphlet of his verse issued by Uzbekistan's Komsomol Central Committee, analyzes the substance of his personal homeland:

> . . . So that my generation (näslim) would comprehend
>   the Homeland's worth,
> Men were always transformed to dust, it seems.
> The Homeland is the remains of our forefathers
> Who turned into dust for this precious soil.

... Bilsin deb Vätänning qädrini näslim,
Adämlär tupraqqä äylänär ekän.
Shu äziz tupraq deb tupraqqä ketgän
Atä-babamizning khakidir Vätän.26

Born in 1941 in the village of Saribulak, Kirgizia and educated at the
Kirgiz State University by correspondence, a young Kirgiz poet, Turar
Kojomberdiev, was made a laureate by the republic's Komsomol in
1971, and now works on the Kïrg̈izstan pioneri newspaper for young
people. This new poet and youth leader speaks of a homeland (meken)
more primal than the maternal breast: " . . . Remember, even before your mother's milk / You drank the milk of the homeland." (. . .
Ënekengdin sütünön da murdaraak, / Emgeningdi bilgin sütün mek-
endin).27 Lyric poetry of this order has become enormously popular
in Central Asia within the past several years. Regardless of grumbling
from official critics that these evocative literary media, still suspect,
might attend more profitably to the obligations of citizenship in the
USSR,28 new verse in surprising quantity, versatility, and craftsman-
ship continues to be composed and published by indigenous Central
Asians. In this intense new literary, dramatic and artistic communication must lie the basis for the response to the question posed earlier:
Who is reaching the young intellectuals if the recognized youth establishment is not? The implicit answer: They are reaching each other.
     While young writers explore the significance of their esthetic
and intellectual world, offering fresh definitions of Soviet reality,
activists among their coevals forward programs already formulated,
contributing additional momentum to the youth movement in Central
Asia through an admirable division of labor with the new thinkers
within the educated class of junior citizens. Gulsum Rahmat has been
publicly described as an "ordinary" Central Asian girl. Yet she compiled an exceptional grade record in her three years at the Tashkent
Institute for Irrigation Engineers and Agricultural Mechanization,
was elected to the Institute's Komsomol committee, and made head
of its section for activity among young women from "the local nationalities." Since her arrival from the tiny Krasnogvardeisk settlement
in the Galla Aral region, Samarkand oblast, Ms. Rahmat has won successive fellowships and was designated in 1971 as a delegate to the
Union-wide student rally held in Moscow. She is described as a person
of "stubbornness, persistence, responsiveness, and high principles,"
by a newspaper feature regarding her.29
     If Gulsum Rahmat were indeed "an ordinary girl," or if the
young poets, agricultural specialists, and dramatists were ordinary
men, Central Asia would possess a huge, dynamic resource in all
those approximately within the official Komsomol age range— 14 to 28.
The numbers of males and females between 16 and 29 (the census age

bracket closest to Komsomol years) populating the Uzbek SSR alone
by 1970 had reached 2,156,000, in Kazakhstan 2,673,138, in the Kirgiz
SSR 533,998, in Tajikistan 516,100, and in Turkmenia 411,158—all
told over 6,290,000 people of about Young Communist age.30 These
figures represent all ethnic groups, including outsiders, in each republic total. When young age groups are considered in Table 1.1,
which also distinguishes major titular nationalities from other groups
for 1959 (1970 age cohort data remain unavailable for individual ethnic
groups), we find that an unusually high proportion—well over 60 percent of indigenous Central Asians, led by Tajiks and Uzbeks—fell into
the group under 30 years of age and almost 70 percent under 35 in
1959. Continuing high birthrates since then probably assure that this
youthful proportion will have increased significantly by 1970, disre-
garding unforeseen developments.

Age group figures in Table 1.1 representing the entire ethnic
spectrum in the Central Asian republics cannot in most cases distinguish even by inference between the effect on indigenous youth
percentages of the presence or absence of numbers of old or young
outsiders. For 1959 it is evident that in the Turkmen SSR, for example,
63.3 percent of all the inhabitants were under 30 years of age, yet
only 60.6 percent of all Soviet Turkmens, 92.2 percent of them concentrated in Turkmenistan, belonged in that 0-29 age cohort.31 Whether
the higher, ethnically heterogeneous republic percentage reflects the
presence of compensatory numbers of young "outsiders," of a dispersion of older Turkmens beyond republic borders, or some other
variable cannot be determined exactly from available information.
Whatever the explanation, the fact of the general population's definite
lack of age remains highly suggestive. In the Central Asian indigenous
population, the preponderance of youthful, educated individuals has
been attested by Soviet statistical reports. (See also M. Mobin Shorish,
chapter 7). The attitudes of that articulate young majority, therefore,
especially with respect to questions as crucial as youth and nationality,
become of vital importance to the society.

Though aloof from the elders as a class, the young freely express sincere esteem individually for the human qualities of their
own parents or a particular teacher, but not necessarily for their
beliefs or ideas. Characteristically, Halima Khudayberdieva, cate-
gorized as one of Central Asian poetry's "latest arrivals" (kenjä
ävladi), devotes her new elegy, "When the Golden Apples Ripened,"
to her deceased father, Ummatqul Khudayberdi-oghli,32 without a
hint of didacticism or cant. Unconsciously, this new generation appears to be on the way to revolutionizing Central Asia's views regarding the question of nationality for the third time since 1900. The
first clamorous, overt effort of the early Jadids, notably the wing of
the movement calling itself the "Young Bukharans," attempted to

institutionalize multiethnic nationality and statehood but was thwarted in 1924 and 1925. For about a decade thereafter, tendencies grew toward what might be termed ethnic "national communism" in each Central Asian republic, only to disintegrate noisily during Stalin's terror and the devastating purges of 1937-38. Now there is a quiet, organic change underway, and, unlike the two previous developments, largely independent of politicians.

This latest shift of attitude among intellectuals toward nationality reflects the emergence of a new society with its own imperatives. These blend the typical young person's involvement in his immediate environment and disinterest in the recent, toilsome past, with an invulnerability among the educated to stereotypes provided by patriotic slogans about zealous internationalism, official "friendship" between ethnic groups, or insistent claims of older generations about the felicity of regional bilingualism, classless comradeship, and the unshatterable union of nationalities.

In a positive sense, perhaps the fact that the young Central Asian majority is not saying anything—at least not anything couched in the old vocabulary—about the nationality question, is the principal new message. Downgrading recently introduced nationality conceptions, they deemphasize the nationality principle (ethnic, multiethnic, or other), while radically redefining the country in "love of country" and the land meant in "homeland." If this change of heart works by chance to limit the universe of each individual to the confines of one present "administrative unit," it would be accidental, and the seeming divergence of one group from neighboring units an unintended by-product of such separateness. This third stage in the intellectual evolution of modern Central Asia and its nationality question has, without fanfare, nevertheless been reached in almost exactly the five decades foreseen in the Kirgiz-Kazakh proverb cited at the beginning about national rejuvenation. The new view deemphasizes administrative or political nationality by widening the distance in the USSR between the old (conservative, Russian?) and young (innovative, Central Asian) generations into the primary social and intellectual cleavage affecting the region, giving local preeminence to personal identity once again.

2

CONVERGENCE AND THE NATIONALITY LITERATURE OF CENTRAL ASIA

Robert J. Barrett

Five decades of Soviet nationality policy, as implemented in Central Asia—an ethnically heterogeneous, supranational Muslim area in the recent past—have led to the crystallization of specific ethno-linguistic groups—Karakalpak, Kazakh, Kirgiz, Tajik, Turkmen, Uzbek, and others. These groups have become highly conscious of and attached to their present nationality identities. The communist party of the Soviet Union, however, considers further movement along the lines of national divergence with regard to the titular nationalities detrimental to its long-range aims of the convergence, or merging (Russian: Sblizhenie i sliianie) of nations into a single Soviet nationality.

Using mainly Soviet Central Asian sources, this chapter examines the central formulation of Soviet literary policy vis-à-vis the Central Asian republics, certain aspects of the implementation of that policy, and the reaction and resistance of Central Asian writers and intellectuals to that policy as reflected in the local press and literature. Concentrating principally upon literary relationships between the Uzbeks and Russians, the inquiry attempts to evaluate, in a case study pertinent to the entire area, the results of this cultural confrontation in terms of their possible long-range implications for the nationality question in Central Asia.

In 1961 the Twenty-Second Congress of the Communist party of the Soviet Union declared that all Soviet citizens, regardless of their nationality, "possess a single socialist Homeland, . . . a common social class structure, a single world-outlook of Marxism-Leninism, and a common goal—the building of communism."[1] In addition, the various nationalities of the Soviet Union were expected to share a single socialist ideology; devotion to the cause of communism; love for the Soviet Motherland and concern for its well being; a feeling of fraternal unity; a desire for mutual aid in all areas of social life;

a profound feeling of proletarian internationalism; an esteem for the national dignity and rights of other nations; and a common spiritual and psychological outlook.[2]

From the resolutions of the Twenty-Second, Twenty-Third, (1966), and Twenty-Fourth (1971) party congresses, it is clear that the party leadership is charging the numerous branches of multinational Soviet literature with the promotion of these character traits desired for the new Soviet man. In the view of party leaders, literature must bend its efforts to the task of facilitating "an ever closer fraternal cooperation and mutual aid, consolidation and converging in all areas of life."[3]

There is considerable evidence that part of the attention presently given to promoting ideological convergence stems from the party's concern over the possibility of the continued divergence among the nationalities as a result of the earlier Soviet policy of creating separate ethnic-linguistic groups in a once ethnic conglomerate such as Muslim Central Asia.[4] Continued movement along the discernible lines of national divergence with regard to the titular Central Asian nationalities—Karakalpak, Kazakh, Kirgiz, Tajik, Turkmen, and Uzbek would be detrimental to the attainment of the professed, long-range Soviet goals of the convergence and merging of nations (sblizhenie i sliianie natsii) into a single Soviet nationality.

Faced with this possibility, the CPSU leadership has opted to proceed along a subtle but slippery course between attempts to halt national divergence without promoting an unwanted side result the converging and merging of major Turkic and Iranian groups in the area and attempts to promote convergence solely among Central Asian groups and the Russians. To insure success in implementing such a delicate policy, the party calls first for the successful attainment of ideological convergence in the belief that a successful convergence of nationalities will follow—hence the present importance assigned to the various units of nationality literature in creating the new Soviet man, the embodiment of the approved character traits of the "multinational Soviet people."

To promote its ideological goals the party calls on the literary establishments among the nationalities to accelerate "the converging of the national artistic and creative processes based on unified socialist and communist content."[5] In the eyes of the party, each nationality literature is important in the ideological upbringing of the new Soviet man; each, therefore, must make its contribution to the party's goal of seeing that every nationality is able organically to combine its own national and international interests in the desired manner.[6] The nationality forms will "constantly change, improve, and be freed from everything obsolete; and they will draw closer among themselves".[7] In this converging process the party will determine which of the forms are obsolete and which are "progressive," and therefore to be retained for the general culture. As a Soviet specialist on the nationality question has put it:

> Everything valuable from the nationality cultures passes into the common culture of the Soviet people which will come into being and develop as a historically ordained synthesis of the nationality cultures. Gradually there is formed the culture of communist society as the highest stage of human culture.[8]

According to the same party spokesman, this internationalization of Soviet culture does not mean that the nationality form will disappear overnight. It will slowly change and be made to reflect the socialist-communist content which, compared with the aspect of nationality, is considered the more important of the two elements. As another Soviet scholar sees it:

> The international element synthesizes the true richness and diversity of the national element. Becoming an inalienable part of the lives of the people, the inter-national element gives new and progressive direction and development to the national processes. Thus, the inter-nationalization of social life under socialism does not at all imply "denationalization."[9]

As expressed explicitly and implicitly in various Soviet sources, then, the policy of the Russian-controlled literary center, the Communist party of the Soviet Union and the All-Union Writers Union, vis-à-vis the nationalities of Central Asia and Kazakhstan, may be summed up as follows: Proceeding from the premise that the national literary intelligentsias of the nationalities in Central Asia and Kazakhstan play a vital role and exert a profound influence in the business of creating desired nationality images, Soviet literary authorities charge them with promoting convergence by propagandizing and popularizing in works of literature approved character traits and standards of behavior of an ideal prototype of the new Soviet man as the representative of the future multinational Soviet culture in Central Asia, including Kazakhstan; developing "multinational" local language branches of literature that will become fully interchangeable and understandable among the various nationalities with respect to ideological and social content, differing only in language and certain acceptable, deep-rooted local customs and traditions; promoting the Russian language as a necessary international language and medium of communication among all Soviet nationalities; extolling the

leadership role of the Great Russian people and their literature in
the economic, social, and cultural achievements in the area; preventing
further literary development along narrow and exclusive nationalistic
lines; and blocking the coalescence of any grouping of nationalities
or cultures that could challenge Russian cultural and literary hegemony.

Efforts at implementing this policy proceed mainly through the
formalized, interlocking literary hierarchy, the centralized Union-
wide Writers' Union and affiliated writers' unions in the constituent
republics and through officially sponsored and approved exchanges
of literary festivals and multinational writers' meetings among the
republics.

The Russian-dominated USSR Union of Writers and its Union-
wide congresses serve as a sounding board and fountainhead of
literary directives that must be heeded by members of the central
body and those affiliated with it through their republic writers' unions.[10]
Pronouncements and criticism emanating from the authoritative
USSR Union of Writers are considered to make up the official literary
policy sanctioned by the Communist Party of the Soviet Union. Union-
wide writers' congresses—attended by literati from all the republics—
serve as transmission belts for this policy from the center to the
periphery. The Sixth Uzbekistan Writers' Congress held in April
1971, for instance, elected 19 delegates to the Fifth Congress of
Soviet Writers held in Moscow in June and July 1971. Among these
delegates figured the prominent Uzbek writers and officials Uyghun,
Laziz Qayumov (editor of Ozbekistan mädäniyäti), Mirmuhsin, Asqad
Mukhtar, and Kamil Yashin, chairman of the Uzbekistan Writers' Union
Governing Board.[11] Similarly, other republic writers' unions elected
delegates to the Moscow congress. Such a centralized hierarchy of
writers' organizations ensures the priority of the same writing tasks
before the writers of all the nationalities, thereby aiding convergence
in socialist content.[12] At the Fifth Congress of Writers in Moscow,
the Central Asian and Kazakhstan delegates heard G. M. Markov,
party spokesman on literary matters, criticize their literature for
inadequately reflecting contemporary Soviet industrial life.[13]

In considering the role of writers' congresses and similar mass
activities, one should keep in mind the socio-political, activist role
of the writer in the Soviet Union. Central Asian authors such as
Sharaf Rashidov, Kamil Yashin, and others, are intimately involved
in party political work. Rashidov's political position as first secretary
of the Uzbekistan Communist Party Central Committee undoubtedly
adds gravity to his pronouncements on literature, both publicly and
in private.

Kamil Yashin served as a delegate both to the Twenty-Fourth
Party Congress and to the Fifth Congress of Soviet Writers. After
the Union-wide Party Congress in March and April 1971, he returned

to Tashkent, where he reported to the Uzbekistan Writers' Union. Speaking of the tasks the party was placing before writers in "the period of the building of communism," Yashin said:

> The role of literature and art in the formation of the new man is exceedingly great. This being so, let us never forget that we must always resolutely serve the Leninist principles of party loyalty in our creative endeavors. It is necessary to struggle not for the volume of our works but for their quality. In them we must strive for a bright and complex portrayal of the image of the communist, the industrial worker, and the simple toiler. . . . This is the basic obligation and duty of all the writers' cells of our republic.14

Not satisfied with the considerable convergence apparent in ideological content, the literary establishment calls upon Central Asian writers to emulate more closely the works of the approved, recognized leaders of the various branches of nationality literature. Approved examples for the Uzbeks include such diverse works as Gorky's Mother, Mayakovsky's Vladimir Ilich Lenin, Sholokhov's Virgin Soil Upturned, Fadeev's Young Guard, Ostrovsky's How the Steel Was Tempered, Aybek's Sacred Blood, Mukhtar Awezov's (Kazakh) Abäy, Hamid Alimjan's Zaynab and Aman, Sharaf Rashidov's Stronger Than the Storm and Powerful Wave, and Yashin's Guiding Star. According to Soviet critics, these works possess the following characteristic traits in common:

> Their main hero is the people, and they correctly show the people's historic role, the vitality and greatness of our socialist society. In them is propagated the great social creative force which creates all of the material and spiritual wealth of human society.15

Having marked out the general lines of permissible literary development, the authorities look to mass participatory activities to popularize their aims and to generate enthusiasm for their implementation. The periodic ten-day literary and art festivals (dekada) and other literary exchanges held at irregular, but frequent intervals among the nationalities meet this need.

Since the 1930s, the party and the Soviet government have encouraged and sponsored literary festivals and cultural exchanges among Russians and the various nationalities as a forum for generating determined support for party and government directives and goals in various sectors of the country's planned economic, social, artistic, and literary life. For the nationality writers and their literature these highly publicized, periodic events—especially those held in Moscow—mean the opportunities for publicity and international exposure. These events also give those in charge of enforcing literary policy an opportunity to review and evaluate progress along party lines and to ensure, through the process of criticism and self-criticism, adherence to literary orthodoxy.[16] Between 1936 and 1960 25 republic and nine autonomous republic festivals took place in Moscow, while between 1957 and 1969 14 republic and three autonomous republic festivals were held in Uzbekistan. Since 1960 11 such Uzbek festivals have taken place in nine other republics.[17]

In the present drive for convergence and merging, exchanges of this nature take on an added significance. They are supposed to accelerate the process of removing harmful, divisive, and "narrowly nationalistic" customs and attitudes and to promote the generalization and popularization of new "positive" nationality traits that may be shared by all of the nationalities of the USSR as a single family of nations. According to the recently published Uzbek Soviet En-cyclopedia:

> The festivals increase the influence of the fraternal people's literature and art upon each other, and they strengthen the creative cooperation among the writers and artists of the various nationalities. In connection with a festival the republic and central publishing houses print many original and translated works, biographical sketches of the participants in the festival, theater and concert programs. . . . Participants in the festival discuss and evaluate the literary works, representative samples of art, and theatrical productions. On the basis of these discussions and criticisms, the lines for the future development of literature and art are marked out.[18]

At the 1959 Moscow festival of Uzbek literature and art an Uzbek literary historian criticized Uzbek writers for being out of touch with life, preferring to research other writings rather than life itself. Too often he said, they chose the cool comfort of Tashkent's Writers' Club instead of excursions to hot, dusty collective farms, noisy factories, and construction sites where one could get meaningful, firsthand impressions of Soviet life in Uzbekistan. He also declared that Uzbek dramatic themes were too narrow in scope, that dramatists were not developing new and innovative methods quickly enough, and that dramatic situations were obsolete and hackneyed. Significantly, but not unexpectedly he urged his fellow writers and critics to study

Russian masterpieces and the successful works of Uzbek literature in order to eliminate these shortcomings.[19]

Sharaf Rashidov did not miss the opportunity to join in this paean to Russian literature:

> The works of many of our writers in recent years give
> proof of their growing literary maturity. . . . They are
> mastering the rich experience of the Russian and world
> classics. . . . Russian literature with its revolutionary
> traditions, deep love of humanity, and its true popular
> spirit is considered the real university where Uzbek
> writers attain their literary expertise and mastery.[20]

It is not only at the festivals scheduled in Moscow that Central Asian writers praise Russian literary leadership and call for support of party aims in literature; the story is similar in the Central Asian republics. On September 28, 1971, after months of intense preparation, a gala ceremony staged in Tashkent's Alisher Nawaiy Opera Theater officially opened the 1971 10-day Festival of Kazakh Literature and Art in Uzbekistan. Present at the opening—sharing the spotlight on stage and lending the occasion the aura of an important social event—were top-echleon party, government, military leaders, numerous writers and other artists from both republics.[21]

The first speaker of the evening, the chairman of the Uzbek SSR Council of Ministers, N. J. Khudoiberdiev, warmly welcoming the Kazakh guests and congratulating them on Kazakhstan's economic, social, and cultural achievements, expressed the hope that the festival would bring the two people even closer together in bonds of strengthened friendship. He continued:

> The Uzbek people and the Kazakh people have been friends
> since ancient times. This friendship united them in the
> struggle against the oppression of local exploiters and the
> Tsarist officials and against backwardness. . . . Through-
> out the years of the Soviet government Kazakhstan has
> blossomed and thrived thanks to . . . the indestructible
> friendship and the fraternal cooperation of the people of
> the Soviet Union under the leadership of the Great
> Russian people.[22]

In his response, B. A. Ashimov, chairman of the Kazakh SSR Council of Ministers, noted that the festival was a great holiday in Uzbekistan. Such festivals, he said, have become "a wonderful Soviet tradition." He added:

This present festival gives us the possibility of becoming better acquainted, to benefit from each other's creative experience, and to discuss the present problems in the development of literature and the arts in our republics. . . . The achievements of Kazakhstan and Uzbekistan are due to . . . the fraternal help from all the people, but first of all from the Great Russian people.[23]

Ashimov then called on the writers and intellectuals to help develop in every possible way the "process of convergence of the nationalities and tribes" (millät wä elätlärning yäqinläshuw protsessi).[24]

The literary portion of this festival opened on September 29 in Tashkent's Hamza Drama Theater. Kamil Yashin greeted the guests and praised the accomplishments of Kazakh poets and songwriters of the past: "These heralds of friendship for our people . . . in their verses and songs . . . dreamed of that bright day when the people would unite in a great friendly family; the people are now uniting in such a family."[25]

In his response, Anwar Alimjanov, first secretary of the Kazakhstan Union of Writers Governing Board, asserted that the meeting of writers of the two republics took on a special meaning in light of the decisions of the Twenty-Fourth Congress of the CPSU and the subsequent Fifth Congress of Writers of the Soviet Union. According to Alimjanov, these congresses rightly emphasized "the beneficial influence, the mutual enrichment" and profitable exchange of ideas that take place at such meetings and subsequently make themselves felt in the creative work of the writers. "Such meetings and festivals," he added, "successfully carry forward the cause of cementing the fraternal relationships among the people."[26]

Centrally inspired endeavors like the festivals, designed to advance official literary policy and control literary development among the nationalities, seem to have generated efforts by certain Central Asian writers to side-step the stereotypes and maintain a modicum of literary independence. Given the nature of the controlled Soviet literary world, resistance to party and union dicta on the subject is difficult, often resulting in banishment from the literary establishment with the concomitant loss of the right to be published in the state-controlled publishing houses.[27] Despite the considerable pressure for conformity, subtle resistance does make itself felt from time to time.

At present Central Asian writers, who claim a right to develop their talents and their nationality literature as they would like, seek refuge in the writings of Lenin or in the works of the approved Russian literary figures and critics: Vissarion Belinskii, Anatolii Lunacharskii, Alexander Herzen, Nikolai Chernysevskii, Maxim

Gorky, etc. A recent article in the journal <u>The Social Sciences in Uzbekistan</u> will serve to illustrate this new resistance tendency.[28] Entitled "Leninist Teachings About Friendship Among the Nationality Literatures," the article cites Lenin's thoughts about the equality between the nationalities in literature and how there should be co-operation among the writers of the various nationalities on an equal footing. The author also cites Lenin's criticism of Great Russian chauvinists who felt that the Russian nation deserved a status above the other nationalities of the Russian Empire. The author, writing in Uzbek, quotes the Uzbek-language edition of Lenin's <u>Works</u> (Äsärlär) in order to bolster his own position that the nationalities are, or should be, really equal with Russia and with each other. Quoting Lenin's admonition that it was not necessary to have a single, obligatory state language, he repeatedly stresses the Bolshevik leader's concern that relations among the various nationalities develop "on the basis of equal rights." With specific regard to the equality of literary relations, the Uzbek author enlists Maxim Gorky's aid to shore up his own view and that of Lenin. This equality the author takes to mean that each nationality and each people should develop the democratic and socialistic elements from their own culture and literature.

The Uzbek writer then skillfully resorts to quoting Lenin for a defense against the wholesale Russification of nationality languages: "We are corrupting the Russian language. We are using foreign words out of place and improperly; we just do not use these foreign words correctly at all. Has not the time come to announce a struggle against corrupting the Russian language?" The author seems clearly to be saying to his Uzbek readers that, given the equality of languages and literature as sanctioned by Lenin, what is true for the Russian language should also be true for the others: Why should Central Asians employ foreign (Russian) words when their own nationality languages, such as Uzbek, possess the adequate lexical wealth to express all shades and concepts of meaning?

An even more subtle and effective form of resistance is manifested by a number of the more talented Central Asian literati who consistently avoid utilizing official priority literary themes in their works. Concerning this maneuver, an Uzbek critic has complained:

> . . . a good many aspects of our contemporary social life
> remain outside the attention of our prose writers. There
> are still very few short stories, sketches, tales and
> novels which present in a true and interesting manner and
> by means of real conflict and clear characters the lives
> of our innovative workers and leading engineers in our
> plants and factories, of our doctors who selflessly guard
> the health of the Soviet people, of our creative

intelligentsia laboring to develop Soviet sciences and culture.29

Merely a casual glance at recent Uzbek literary output as published in the journal Shärq yulduzi throughout 1970-1971 substantiates this assertion. A preponderance of the stories, novels, and sketches published there in this period have as their main theme rural life with a village or collective-farm setting, deal with the ever-popular romantic love motif, or concern themselves with the Uzbek (Central Asian) past.30

While neglecting themes of contemporary, industrial life dominated by machines and production plans, Uzbek, Kazakh, Kirgiz, and other Central Asian writers appear to be obsessed—as are many of their Russian counterparts—with the rediscovery of their own ancient past, a theme until so recently restricted to exposures of earlier political tyranny and social stagnation. This renewed interest in the past and the reaching back to it for spiritual and intellectual inspiration has been observed as a Union-wide phenomenon.31 "If Russia's past is an approved theme for literary and historical investigation," the Central Asians seem to ask, "Why can we not have, on the basis of equal nationality rights, the same prerogative to explore our own splendid ancient civilization?"

It is difficult to say how much of this bold, new attitude stems from, on the one hand, the post-Stalinist thaw, "the restoration of socialist legality," and the feeling that things can never again be as bad as they were, or on the other hand, how much is due to Central Asia's—especially Uzbekistan's—growing international contacts and the end of the relative isolation of the area up to the 1950s and 1960s. Today Tashkent is a mecca for Asian and African delegations and tourists; the Uzbek capital now possesses the atmosphere of a convention center. Heads of state have met there, and it has been, and soon again will be, the site of conferences of writers from Asia, Africa, and Latin America. Moreover, Uzbek writers have literally roamed the globe in the past two decades. In 1947, Aybek visited England; in 1949, he and the Tajik poet, Mirza Tursunzada, visited Pakistan; the poetess Zulfiaya visited India in 1956; Abdullah Qahhar was there in 1955; Hamid Ghulam, S. Akbariy and Mirmuhsin have visited the Arabian countries; and Asqad Mukhtar has been to Japan and China.32

These growing international contacts expose Central Asian intellectuals and writers to new political and literary currents and ideas from non-Soviet sources and to a broader world view. Under these new, more open circumstances, it would be embarrassingly difficult for the Soviet authorities to silence a new Cholpan or Abdullah Qadiriy, both victims of the purges of the nationalists in the 1930s,

without damaging the image they seek to promote among the intellectuals and writers of the Third World.

The influence of non-Soviet Oriental literature, especially Indian
and Arabic, has definitely begun to make itself felt in Central Asian
writings, to the chagrin of official Soviet literary critics who from
time to time feel compelled to issue caveats against this dangerous
trend away from an approved adherence to Soviet Russian literature
and its formula of socialist realism. "Some of our writers," an
Uzbek critic recently complained,

> have endeavored to create works imitating foreign
> Oriental literature, and they ended up imitating only the
> sentimental, romantic treatment in them. Naturally, this
> writing method produces no positive results, but only
> creates great difficulties in presenting the image of our
> contemporaries. This method does not at all correspond
> to the present degree of development of our literature,
> and to a certain extent it leads away from socialist
> realism. This had happened in T. Jalalov's Altin qäfäs
> (The Golden Cage), D. Nuriy's Aqsham qoshiqläri (Songs
> of Evening), and in the works of a considerable number of
> young writers.[33]

According to this complaint, the works of some such writers
were almost indistinguishable from translations of sentimental Indian
and Arabic tales. One short story, Jawab (The Answer) by B. Daminov,
the critic said, "is so far from (Soviet) life that were it not for such
words as institut, kolkhoz, räis (chairman), and partkom (Russian/
Uzbek abbreviation for "party committee"), it would be difficult
to understand where the story is taking place. The nationality image
of its characters is completely distorted and unreliable."[34]

On the positive side of the ledger, the same critic cites Asqad
Mukhtar's novel, Tughilish (The Birth), as a good specimen of the
desired new literature, because the author shows Soviet workers of
various nationalities harmoniously toiling side by side on the construction of a hydroelectric station in Uzbekistan. He finds a positive point
in Mukhtar's deliberate playing down of the sharp nationality distinctions in the speech and dress of his characters. Such a muted treatment
of the usual identifying nationality traits, aside from being the currently approved one, is supposed to be a true reflection of life and
labor at a typical Soviet "international" construction site.[35]

In their concern for the past, in preference to "contemporary"
themes, the critic accuses other Uzbek writers of neglecting the
approved task of depicting the evils of old Muslim customs and
traditions (bride price, enforced marriage, polygamy, religious

fasting, and the like) and the parallel obligation to promote the acceptance of new "communist traditions" (<u>kommunist än″änälär</u>). "Old mental attitudes and customs," he wrote,

> set young brothers in competition with their older brothers, they taint true love with shame, embarrass lovers, sow discord between husband and wife, between the groom's mother and the bride, between mother and child; and they lead to grave tragedies. The writer must not only expose old customs and mental attitudes, but he must also see and accept the new forces in life that are fighting against them.[36]

Finally the critic concludes that the most successful Uzbek works have been those in which the authors kept in mind the rich experience of Russian and "progressive" world literature. This is because, it is said, Russian literature gave the Uzbeks and the other people of Central Asia the tested, reliable literary method, socialist realism.[37]

The preoccupation with the past that is beginning to permeate the writings of certain Uzbek writers deserves closer examination. A most illustrative example of this phenomenon is contained in the following extract from the short story, "Listen to Your Heart!" by the young writer, Otqir Hashimov:[38]

(On a snowy winter evening in Tashkent, Yadgar, a young architecture student is escorting home his girlfriend, Charas, an art student. During their walk, the pair lament the fact that they know so little about Central Asia's ancient cultural heritage, which in some respects seems to them superior to that of the Christian West. Yadgar suddenly says in an agitated manner:)

> I don't know whether it's because they teach history badly in school or whether we study it badly . . . Nawaiy, Ibn-Sina, Ulughbek . . . And who else? We don't even know the names of the others, do we? Why, I just recently found out that from the eighth century until the sixteenth century Central Asia was one of the centers of world culture. I also recently learned that four and a half centuries before Columbus set off on his chance voyage to America, Biruni had said that a large land mass existed on the far side of the earth; he had even drafted an approximate map of America; and he had accurately measured the diameter of the earth.

(In praising the architecture of Khiva's ancient buildings, Yadgar said:)

> One can hardly believe that such rare architectural ensembles could have come into being in that period of history. That science and art should have been so well adapted to each other! And even now they just cannot pin down the chemical composition of the glazed tiles. Those thousand-year-old tiles remain like new, while decorations covering the newly restored areas have turned into scab-like patches. In other words, chemistry in those times must have been quite advanced. . . .

(Speaking of her chosen field of art, Charas interjects:)

> All of the specialists agree that the artist Behzad and his apprentices were superior to their contemporaries in the West. In the Timurid period while artists in the West took a religious ideal as the basis of their works, Behzad's miniatures depict real events of life: hunting excursions, trips, and scenes of nature. In other words, he stood close to the real life of the times.

(Continuing their chat, the pair bemoan the neglect that has fallen upon many of the architectural and artistic monuments of Central Asia. Yadgar concludes:)

> It seems that it is necessary to be able to tie the past to the future in every field. We must not lump all of our wise ancestors together as illiterates, but we must study their wisdom.

(The young lovers move on into the night, excitedly discussing the possibility of applying some of Central Asia's ancient architectural designs and decorations in the construction of modern buildings.)

In poetry, too, there are clear signs—the first since the 1920s and the early 1930s—that Central Asian poets are daring once again to attribute a local significance to the revered concept of vätän (homeland), a word until so recently used almost exclusively with regard to the Soviet Union as a whole. The Uzbek poet Jamal Kamal has written:

> . . . . In the end whatever fate is your choice,
> Oh, Homeland, you are the fountainhead of happiness . . .
> When you are well there is such joy and contentment
>   in my heart;

When you are well the radiance of the world dances in my
soul.
When the sun lowers its head toward your evening horizon,
With a tear of gladness in my eye I place my head against
your bosom . . .
How happy the moment when I understood your pride,
And in the world of my heart I enclosed your love.
Your love became a melody unto my heart,
And without this melody, how sad, so forlorn my soul . . .

(Ey Vätän, sensän säadät bashi!—deb qildim khitab.
Sen amansänki, yuräkdä shunchälär shävqi-shuur,
Sen amansänki, jähanning jilväsi konglimdädir.
Ul quyashkim, kechälär ufqing uzrä qoygändä bash,
Bash qoyärmän men ayaghinggä, sevinchdän kozdä yash . . .
Ne mubaräk lähzäkim, men iftikharing änglädim,
Häm kongil dunyasidä mehringni mumtaz äylädim.
Häm bu konglim, ta buyuk ishqingdän etmishdir näva,
Shul nävasiz benävadir, benävadir, benäva! . . .)39

Kamal elsewhere defines the terrain of his homeland as well:

    . . . Oh Jamal, look at your land,
       And you shall ever see
On one side, sunny Bukhara,
       On the other, dawn in Ferghana valley.
(Ey, Jämal, Bäqsäng diyaringgä,
       korärsän här zäman
Bir taman—kungäy Bukhara,
       bir taman—Färghanä kun . . .)40

    Thus, the wheel has turned full circle; Central Asians are
appropriating the literary right, long enjoyed by the Russians,
to explore their rich cultural heritage, to assign artistic value where
it is due, and to pay allegiance to a homeland according to their own
inclinations. Given the intensified nationality awareness of certain
Central Asian writers, it is evident that the potential for significant,
low-keyed tension exists within Central Asian-Russian literary
relations and in the general area of nationality policy. This may
not be an uneven battle in which Central Asian literary and cultural
forces are doomed from the outset to eventual defeat. In reality,
there are advantages and disadvantages—pluses and minuses—on each
side which enter into the situation and bear upon the outcome. An
audit of these pluses and minuses in the present accounts between the
Central Asian writers and the Russian-dominated, centralized literary
establishment may reveal where the balance lies.

Central Asian literature, as an instrument of the official literary policy for the CPSU, plays and probably will continue to play an increasingly important role in popularizing and inculcating party-approved character traits of the new Soviet man in Central Asia and Kazakhstan. Such literature also continues to promote the adoption of the new customs, traditions, and mores of a multinational Soviet culture. At the same time, literature is expected to wage a more relentless campaign against the disapproved Muslim traditions and customs of the past. Success in the promotion of the "international," Soviet prototype in the literature will eventually weaken the image of the local nationality prototype. For the Central Asian nationalities and their endeavors to maintain and develop their independent nationality image, this represents a minus.

The official writers' organizations, like the republic writers' unions, continue to follow the lead set in Moscow by the CPSU and the USSR Union of Writers and to serve the central organizations as transmission belts for the outward flow of literary dicta and pronouncements. The locally elected representatives of the literary hierarchy may be expected to continue their verbal support of the centrally formulated policy. This, too, results in a minus for the local nationalities.

Overt or active literary resistance must remain difficult if not impossible where approved themes are dictated from the center and where membership in the literary hierarchy—and the right to publish—carries along with it the obligation to abide by the rules and by-laws of a literary establishment pledged to support the Communist Party's political goals. Yet another minus for the Central Asians.

Under these circumstances, considerable passive resistance may continue to manifest itself in the willful neglect of certain approved, contemporary industrial themes and in a stubborn adherence to historical or rural and folk themes in historical novels and in biographical works about great figures of Central Asia's past. Success in this subtle ploy on the part of the Central Asians falls on the plus side of the ledger for them.

The Central Asians are continuing their efforts to resist the Russification of their languages first by resort to Lenin's writings about the equality of the nationality languages; also through the skillful extrapolation and extension of his remarks concerning the necessity of keeping the Russian language pure and free of inappropriate foreign terms; and finally by recalling Lenin's admonition against rigidly instituting a single, official state language. Success in this area represents another plus for the Central Asians.

Given the present alignment of cultural and artistic forces in Central Asia, an equilibrium in the nationality question seems to have been reached. The Central Asian nationalities want and insist on continuing the existence of their present separate ethnic identities, and the Russians are unwilling or unable to force a further Russification of the Central Asians. This is because of the resilience of the nationalities themselves and perhaps too because of the repercussions such a step would have among members of the intelligentsia in the Third World.

Considerable convergence in the ideological sphere has already been attained; and undoubtedly the central literary authorities—the Russians—will continue to press for complete convergence here. To their minds, such a denouement will mean a step toward convergence between themselves and the Central Asian nationalities, for in the terms of the dialectic, at a given point of development in modern, industrial society, cultural content must become manifest in form as well.

Those Central Asian writers and other intellectuals concerned for their future ethnic identity continue with the limited means available to them to ward off their complete absorption into the diluting stream of a colorless, conformist, multinational culture. They surely recognize that in such a potpourri the prevailing hue must come from the dominant ingredient, the Soviet Russian culture. Their desire to avoid this eventuality is enhanced daily by the developments in the former colonial areas outside the Soviet Union where nationalism is holding sway. Seeing the swelling list of United Nations membership, now bursting at the seams with new states and once-forgotten nations, and observing the birth of Bangladesh which the Soviet Union attended as a midwife, can they not but harbor the hope that their time will someday come? If by analogy such a hope began to move Central Asian writers and fellow intellectuals toward attempts at active realization of the desire for genuine cultural sovereignty, the apparent balance in the present nationality arrangements would most likely slip off center into disequilibrium. This further divergence would introduce another marked change into the nationality question of Central Asia.

3

THE IMPACT OF DEMOGRAPHIC AND SOCIOECONOMIC FORCES UPON THE NATIONALITY QUESTION IN CENTRAL ASIA
Ralph Scott Clem

Recent scholarly work in the social sciences has been concerned with the effects of the socioeconomic milieu on the behavior of society.[1] It is apparent that individuals are influenced by a variety of socio-economic or demographic forces, and that these forces operate across cultural lines. Socioeconomic forces and trends influence the national-ity situation in contemporary Soviet society, and nowhere as dramat-ically as in Central Asia. It is our intent to identify certain of these forces and to substantiate the hypothesis that for the most part these forces and trends have worked to the disadvantage of the indigenous Central Asian nationalities. By "disadvantage" we mean that the ethnic mixing characteristic of this area, and particularly the large influx of Russians, has reduced opportunities for the indigenous nationalities to gain the social and economic advancement to which they aspire through higher education and skilled employment. One major assump-tion implicit throughout this work is that the indigenous nationalities actually aspire to higher socioeconomic levels. In light of the expe-riences of ethnic minorities, immigrants, and other generally disadvan-taged groups there would seem to be no basis for rejecting this assumption.

In the broader sense we attempt to answer the question: How and to what degree have socioeconomic trends with their attendant disadvantage influenced the nationality question in Soviet Central Asia, and what are the implications for the near future? One very interesting aspect of these socioeconomic forces is their frequent assumption of ethnic dimensions: status, as evidenced by occupation, income, and

---

The author expresses his appreciation to Professor Robert A. Lewis, Columbia University, for his valuable comments.

education, is divided along nationality lines. Thus the influence of the disadvantage experienced by indigenous Central Asians on the nationality question in Central Asia is related to the differentials in socioeconomic forces and trends. The nationality question as viewed in this inquiry concerns the relationships, including mutual attitudes and expressions, as well as more administrative or physical arrangements between indigenous nationalities and nonindigenous groups. Nationality and nationality problems are inherently difficult both to define and to work with. Clearly, relationships among the Central Asian nationalities and between them and outsiders are also complicated and often difficult to define operationally, and even then they do not constitute the nationality question in its entirety.[2]

We have examined these internationality relationships through an analysis of demographic or socioeconomic data balanced with information available from the Central Asian press. In this analysis we have confined ourselves to the period 1959-70, the time-span between the last two Soviet censuses, from which the majority of the data in this study are drawn. Other data have been cited from various Central Asian statistical handbooks.[3] Reports found in the Central Asian press were taken from Pravda Vostoka and Kazakhstanskaia pravda, which were surveyed for the year 1971.

In the first part of this analysis we examine the spatial distributions of the Russians and the other nationalities throughout Central Asia, including measures of concentration and dispersion and socioeconomic status. In the second part hypotheses are coined from the background data and tested against data from the censuses.

Prior to undertaking the analysis, however, it is important to consider the modern historical events that have created the contemporary demographic scene in Soviet Central Asia. The first of these events was the Russian military conquest of Central Asia and the migration of large numbers of Russians and other Europeans to the newly won lands.[4] Land shortages, archaic agricultural practices, and low productivity in central Russia, combined with the attraction of land in the plains of Kazakhstan, resulted in a substantial migration into the region.[5] The new arrivals were mainly agriculturists, particularly in Kazakhstan. In southern Central Asia the Russians tended to be more urban and engaged in business, industry, and trade, because the irrigated agricultural system largely excluded rural settlement by migrants.[6] The consequences of receiving this large settlement of outsiders were not long in coming. With the fall of the czarist regime the Russian minority in Central Asia became a fifth column of sorts, providing a means of introducing the revolutions of 1917 into the area and resisting Muslim separatist movements.[7]

The industrialization that commenced in Central Asia following World War II, and particularly the almost explosive growth of heavy and extractive industry in Kazakhstan, has attracted the second major wave of outsiders to Central Asia. These outsiders, primarily Russians, have been drawn mainly to the urban-industrial centers, and these same centers have become Russian "islands" in a largely Central Asian "sea."[8] Recent in-migration of Russians and Ukrainians to rural areas during the development of the Virgin and Idle Lands scheme has increased the nonindigenous rural population, but on a limited geographic basis (being confined primarily to northern Kazakhstan).

The other major demographic event of recent Central Asian history has been the population explosion occurring among the indigenous nationalities. Central Asians have been growing at the phenomenal average annual rate of well over 3 percent. The high birth rate in the predominantly indigenous rural areas, together with a low death rate, combine to give Central Asians what must be one of the highest rates of natural increase in the world.

Thus, these demographic trends have resulted in the following contemporary situation: a large, nonindigenous population has been superimposed upon the indigenous Central Asian population, with the newcomers dominating the cities and industrial areas, and providing what probably amounts to a substantial proportion of the local rural-to-urban migrants from their older agricultural settlements. Combined with continuing in-migration of nonindigenous population is the extraordinary increase among the predominantly rural indigenous nationalities. This scenario portrays what could prove to be the major problem of the coming decades in the Soviet Union.

In this analysis we first examine the geographic distribution of the nationalities in Central Asia, both in the spatial and urban-rural contexts. Secondly we discuss the effects of this distribution upon the socioeconomic status of nationalities, and conclude with tests of hypotheses derived from these data. In the quantitative analysis we considered the Russians and the following seven nationalities for study: Kazakhs, Kirgiz, Tajiks, Turkmens, Uzbeks, Tatars, and Ukrainians. This sample represents all indigenous and nonindigenous ethnic groups of significant size in Central Asia, and accounts for 90.7 percent of the regional population in 1970. Other indigenous groups, such as the Karakalpaks and Uyghurs, were not considered because they were not enumerated in a sufficient number of administrative units for any meaningful statistical analysis. Administrative units utilized in this study were the smallest territorial units for which nationality data were presented in available sources. In most cases this would be the oblast or autonomous republic level, but in some republics (Kirgiz, Tajik, and Turkmen) nationality data have not yet been presented in units below republic size for 1970.

To delimit the spatial distributions of the nationalities accurately, we computed an index of concentration and/or dispersion.

The coefficient of localization (Table 3.1) describes the distribution of a particular group relative to the distribution of the total population, unit by unit. Values of the coefficient range from zero to one, with values approaching zero indicating that the group is distributed similarly to the total population, and values nearing one indicating concentration in a few units. This coefficient indicates that the Russians and Tatars are quite evenly distributed throughout the region, and that the Ukrainians, Kazakhs, and Uzbeks are somewhat more concentrated but still fairly evenly distributed compared to the Kirgiz, Tajiks, and Turkmens, who are heavily concentrated.

An examination of data indicating the proportion of a given nationality enumerated in each unit of the nationality total for the region as a whole revealed some interesting shifts in population between 1959 and 1970. The Russians became significantly more concentrated in the following units during this period: Bukhara oblast of Uzbekistan and Gur'ev, Kustanay, Pavlodar, Karaganda, and Alma Ata oblasts of Kazakhstan. Without exception these are areas that have undergone considerable industrial development in the last decade.[9] In these units not only did the proportion of total Russians in the region increase, but the Russians increased their share of the unit's population at the expense of the indigenous nationalities, whose share generally decreased (with the exception of Alma Ata, where the Russians' share of the population shrank in spite of a large absolute gain and the Kazakhs' share increased, and Kustanay, where both Russians and Kazakhs increased—the Kazakhs only slightly). But the indigenous population did not decline; indeed, the fact that the indigenous population increased at a dramatic rate illustrates the attraction these industrializing areas exert upon outsiders. For instance, in Bukhara oblast the Uzbeks increased by 57 percent during the period 1959-70, or an average of 4.2 percent per year, but the Russians increased by 139 percent, or 8.2 percent per year, making the Uzbeks' share of the oblast's population decline from 74.2 to 71.9 percent, while the Russians' share increased from 7.5 to 11.1 percent. The other nonindigenous nationalities, the Ukrainians and Tatars, also shifted toward the industrializing areas.

Examples of such movements of outsiders into the industrial areas are often noted in the local Central Asian press. One recent article described in detail how two Ukrainians came to Kazakhstan to work on the construction of the Sokolovsko-Sarbaiskii ore concentrating combine at Rudnyi.[10] Another article in the same vein described a Belorussian and his role in a major urban development project, the new Sovetskii Prospekt in Karaganda.[11] The individual articles, interesting though they may be, are not important in themselves, but viewed collectively they indicate that such in-migration of skilled industrial workers from European areas of the Soviet Union is at least

TABLE 3.1

Coefficients of Localization for Indigenous
and Nonindigenous Ethnic Groups
of Central Asia, 1959 and 1970

Ethnic Groups	Coefficients[a]	
	1959	1970
Russians	.272	.285
Tatars	.239	.221
Ukrainians	.434	.431
Uzbeks	.487	.485
Kazakhs	.468	.490
Tajiks	.705	.710
Kirgiz	.793	.812
Turkmens	.879	.883

[a]Low values of the coefficient indicate mixing, whereas higher values indicate concentration in a few units.

Sources: Data for 1959 are from Itogi vsesoiuznoi perepisi naseleniia 1959 goda (Moscow: Gosstatizdat), Kazakhskaia SSR (1962), pp. 168-173; Ibid., Kirgizskaia SSR (1963), pp. 132-133; Ibid., Tadzhikskaia SSR (1963), pp. 122-123; Ibid., Turkmenskaia SSR (1963), pp. 132-133; Ibid., Uzbekskaia SSR (1962), pp. 144-146. Data for 1970 are from Soviet Geography: Review and Translation, XII, 7 (September 1971), 447-453.

tolerated if not encouraged by the Soviet government. It is just such in-migrants who come equipped with the necessary skills and take jobs for which most Central Asians would have to be trained.[12]

The indigenous nationalities, on the other hand, demonstrated mixed trends in population shifts during 1959-70. The Kazakh population shifted toward Alma Ata, and the Uzbeks underwent no significant shifts during this period. Kirgiz, Tajiks, and Turkmens became more concentrated in their titular republics.

In addition to spatial distributions, the distribution of nationalities is characterized by an urban-rural dichotomy. "Urban" in the Soviet context is a good surrogate for the attributes of an advanced society: industrialization, higher education institutions, skilled employment and services. Thus, the participation of a group in urban life is a good measure of its mobilization or degree of participation in the advantages of technically advanced society. Russians and Tatars are predominantly urban in Central Asia, the indigenous nationalities are predominantly rural, and the Ukrainians stand midway between the two groups. In Central Asia in 1959 the Tatars were 67.7 percent urban, Russians 65.9 percent, Ukrainians 45.2, Turkmens 25.1, Kazakhs 24.7, Uzbeks 21.5, Tajiks 20.1, and Kirgiz 10.4 percent. The Russians, Tatars, and Ukrainians each constituted a higher proportion of the urban population than of the total population of Central Asia in 1959, whereas the Central Asians had a disproportionately small urban share.[13]

The predominantly rural nature of the Central Asians is a reflection of their lack of participation in modern industrial society. The Central Asians are underrepresented in all sectors of the economy of their titular republics with the exception of agriculture.[14] Within their own republics the indigenous nationalities are underrepresented in institutions of higher education.[15] Education data from the 1959 Soviet census showed that in all cases the level of education for the indigenous population was below that of the republic average, whereas the Russians, Ukrainians, and Tatars were in all instances above the average.[16]

There can be little doubt that by Western standards and in a material sense Soviet society has greatly improved the lot of the average Central Asian. Dramatic declines in mortality, increased literacy, increased skilled employment, and increased school and university enrollments for Central Asians have clearly been significant accomplishments under the Soviet government. Certainly there is a case to be made for viewing the Central Asian situation in terms of progress expressed in trends in education and skilled employment in particular. Yet the contemporary Soviet situation is still characterized by lower levels of education, urbanization, and skilled employment for the indigenous Central Asians. One must consider that it is the contemporary situation that will influence the individual Central Asian, and the past achievements under the Soviet regime will seem of little importance to the individual if he finds that he cannot secure suitable employment in his own national republic because Russians, perhaps more highly skilled, have preempted the better jobs.

The Central Asians have not yet been mobilized into advanced sectors of society within their own nationality areas to the extent that their numbers warrant. The major nonindigenous ethnic groups, Russians, Tatars, and Ukrainians, occupy a disproportionately large share of the urban, educated, and skilled-employment sectors of Central Asian society. Having determined this from the background data, we proposed two hypotheses for testing with census data ordered into the various political-administrative units of Central Asia. The first test was designed to measure the relationships between the various nationalities and the level of urbanization, since urbanization subsumes many of the attributes of an advanced society. Accordingly, we ranked

TABLE 3.2

Correlation Coefficients, Percent
Urban and Percent of Given Ethnic Group, 1970

Ethnic Group	Coefficients	Number of Units
Russians	.697*	30
Tatars	-.075	30
Ukrainians	.461*	27
Uzbeks	-.818*	18
Kazakhs	.412*	26
Tajiks	-.377	12

*Asterisk indicates significance at the .05 level.

Sources: Nationality data are from Soviet Geography: Review and Translation, XII, 7 (September 1971), 447-453. Urban data are from Narodnoe khoziaistvo SSSR v 1969 g. (Moscow: Statistika, 1970), 17-18.

all oblasts and units of an equivalent level for 1970 by percentage urban and percent of each nationality, and measured the relationships by Spearman rank-order correlation (Table 3.2). Correlations could not be computed for Kirgiz and Turkmens because they were not enumerated in enough units for meaningful correlational analysis. The category of "urban" in all instances follows the Soviet census definition.

Russians and Ukrainians were positively correlated with the level of urbanization, the Russians highly so. In other words, high levels of urbanization will most often be accompanied by high percentages of Russians and Ukrainians. Figures for Uzbeks and Tajiks showed predictable results, being negatively correlated with urbanization. Thus, high levels of urbanization are accompanied by low percentages of Uzbeks and Tajiks. Patterns for the highly educated, highly urbanized Tatars and the less urbanized, less educated Kazakhs are anomalous. The Tatar figure can probably be explained by the fact that several highly urbanized areas, primarily in Kazakhstan, report low percentages of Tatars. The positive relationship of the Kazakhs with urbanization can be attributed to the fact that they are coincidentally related to areas of high urbanization, insofar as eight of the ten most urbanized oblasts in Central Asia are located in Kazakhstan. This same correlation, computed for Kazakhs and percentage urban in Kazakhstan only, was .146 and was not significant at the .05 level, indicating that in their own republic the Kazakhs are not related to urbanization.

The second hypothesis to be tested in this fashion concerned the relationship of the nationalities to some index of skilled employment. The index chosen was the percentage of the work force in each unit classified as "white collar" (sluzhashchie). Despite certain limitations this index was available for 32 census units of Central Asia in 1959. Again, Kirgiz and Turkmens could not be included in this test because they were not enumerated in a sufficient quantity of units. Ranking the units by percentage white collar and percentages of each nationality, we arrived at the same pattern found by the first test (Table 3.3). The Russians and Ukrainians were positively associated and the Uzbeks were negatively associated with the white-collar work force, but the Tajiks demonstrated no association. Again, the positions of Tatars and Kazakhs relative to this index were anomalous, probably because of the peculiar distribution of these two groups relative to the main urban-industrial centers.

The tests necessarily utilized surrogate variables and resorted to measures of association and probability approximations rather than the more desirable direct evidence; one must recognize the limitations arising from the so-called "ecological fallacy." Measures of association do not imply that within a unit all the Russians will be urban white-collar workers and all the indigenous nationalities rural workers. Taken together with our background data, which indicate that the outsiders do hold the bulk of skilled jobs and constitute significant portions of the urban population, the tests indicate that it is more than coincidence that wherever one finds high levels of urbanization and skilled employment one also finds Russians and other outsiders. Given the scarcity of Soviet data, we believe that these results confirm our hypothesis concerning the disadvantage of Central Asians vis-à-vis the outsiders.

There are, in effect, two separate spheres of Central Asian population, indigenous and nonindigenous. These are characterized by dichotomous levels of urbanization, dispersion, education, and skilled employment. Clearly, this division must influence the nationality question in Central Asia.

The aim of eliminating differences between urban and rural life reflects an important Soviet policy.[17] However, despite material improvements in the standard of living in the rural areas, rural life is apparently still quite different in the material and/or cultural sense from life in the urban areas. The exodus of young people from rural to urban areas throughout the Soviet Union testifies to this fact. One recent study reported in the Central Asian press attributed the greater aspirations of rural young people for continued education to their desire to use education as a means of moving from rural to urban areas.[18]

TABLE 3.3

Correlation Coefficients, Percent
White Collar and Percent of Given Ethnic Group, 1959

Ethnic Group	Coefficients	Number of Units
Russians	.651*	32
Tatars	-.302	32
Ukrainians	.512*	32
Uzbeks	-.574*	20
Kazakhs	.435	26
Tajiks	.029	10

*Asterisk indicates significance at the .05 level.

Source: Itogi vsesoiuznoi perepisi naseleniia 1959 goda (Moscow: Gosstatizdat), Kazakhskaia SSR (1962), pp. 63, 168-173; Ibid., Kirgizskaia SSR (1963), pp. 39, 132-133; Ibid., Tadzhikskaia SSR (1963), pp. 39, 122-123; Ibid., Turkmenskaia SSR (1963), pp. 40-41, 132-133; Ibid., Uzbekskaia SSR (1962), pp. 44-45, 144-146.

The cities of Central Asia are with a few exceptions Russian in all but geographic location. The rural character of the Central Asians remains alien to the urban environment and thus is subject to change when they enter it. Clearly, the historical Central Asian cities have a long and brilliant past, but the vast majority of Central Asians are rural folk, and their culture to a large degree must be based on rural values and customs. Thus, it is our contention that this urban-rural dichotomy has influenced the nationality question by reinforcing the rural aspects of Central Asian culture, which in turn must reinforce Central Asian nationality.

Historically, it has been noticeable that when people perceive that they are not receiving their fair share of the benefits of society they have resorted to identification with some group through which they can redress their grievances. Being disadvantaged in education, employment, and general mobilization into advanced society, the Central Asians would look to their respective ethnic nationalities or other appropriate groupings as a means of exerting their demands for higher socioeconomic status. The Central Asian "problem" is rapidly approaching a critical juncture in this regard, because the tremendous growth of indigenous population will of necessity force many Central

Asians into the city for employment. If no employment, skilled or otherwise, awaits them, because it has been preempted by Russians, this could be another reason for resorting to their nationality as an interest group. For the present and near future, unless the Soviet government recognizes the problem and takes steps to alleviate it in short order, the disadvantages still shared by all of the Central Asian nationalities can only strengthen nationality ties.

Relationships between nationalities often assume socioeconomic dimensions, and Central Asia is apparently no exception. The historical facts of Central Asian life have not coincided with the present reality of modern Soviet society, at least in the socioeconomic context. The Central Asians, a predominantly rural people still largely unengaged in modern industrial society, have not yet been assimilated into that system. Yet pressures on the land occasioned by tremendous population growth will most likely force them into the advanced society and, by definition, into more intense socioeconomic rivalry with the Russians. Furthermore, competition for more desirable jobs in the advanced sector may well mitigate against supranational groupings because each nationality may find it necessary to claim certain privileges within its own republic. Socioeconomic disadvantage has and will probably continue, barring major calamities, to strengthen the ethnic nationality consciousness of the different Central Asian peoples until these dichotomies are no longer a feature of life in Soviet Central Asia.

4

ETHNIC INTERMARRIAGE
AS AN INDICATOR OF
CULTURAL CONVERGENCE
IN SOVIET CENTRAL ASIA
Ethel Dunn and Stephen P. Dunn

When an important Soviet article about cultural convergence
and its effects on the family life of the people of Central Asia appeared
in 1962, it carried in a footnote the following interesting statements:
"No special studies on the extent of mixed marriages have yet been
made among the people of Central Asia. . . . The ethnographic data
at hand are extremely fragmentary. Systematic collection of such
data is to begin in the immediate future. . . ."[1] The purpose of our
present study is to describe the data that have appeared in the decade
since this article was published and to draw some tentative conclusions
from the data.

In assessing the situation regarding ethnically mixed marriages,
several factors must be kept in mind. According to commentaries
on Muslim law, "marriage between Moslems and women of the
'Kitabi'—i.e., those who recognized Scripture and the prophets (including Christians and Jews)—was permitted. However, the Moslem
clergy instilled in the working people of the local nationalities the
conviction that marriages with persons of other faiths were a gross
violation of the shariat [Muslim religious law]. Those who entered
into such marriages were persecuted."[2] Although such persecution
often reflected the disapproval of local religious communities, in
fact the law of the Russian Empire until the beginning of the twentieth
century expressly forbade marriages between persons of differing
religious faiths. However, no such obstacle existed if the person
converted to Russian Orthodoxy in areas where this faith was ethnically
or politically dominant, or, in much rarer instances, to Islam.[3]
When conversions to Islam occurred they most frequently involved
women, although men were sometimes accepted as well. It is
interesting that one of the few cases of a contemporary marriage of
a Russian man to a Turkmen woman noted for a rural population in

the Turkmen SSR also includes the piquant detail that the man involved
is known by a Turkmen name as well as a Russian one.[4] The man
had married a Turkmen girl six years earlier (the basic field work
was done in the early 1960s). Their daughter has a Turkmen name.
However, in other Turkmen-Russian families the children frequently
have two sets of names, Russian and Turkmen. This practice is
apparently widespread throughout Central Asia. It is noted for the
Kirgiz[5] and for the Uzbeks.[6]

Marriages among the various Central Asian people—those of
Islamic faith—were much more common, although the rate of such
marriages in pre-1917 times seems to have been inhibited by a number
of economic and customary factors, chiefly the necessity to pay the
bride price (higher for a girl from another ethnic group, who might be
considered more desirable in some cases), and also by the distinct
preference for marriage either to close relatives or only among
certain tribal groups. In most instances tribal affiliation was reckoned
from the father. An exception has been noted for a group known as
Chalakazakhs (half-Kazakhs), whose ancestors were Tatars.[7] In this
case, since a Tatar father lacked tribal affiliation, descent was
reckoned through the mother.

That these preferences continue to the present day can be seen
from a study of the Beluchis in Turkmenia. The population of the
kolkhoz studied for this previously nomadic group is really ethnically
quite diverse, although there are few "Europeans" in it. Besides the
Beluchis there are Turkmens, Kazakhs, Uzbeks (locally known as
Tats), Afghans, Persians, Jemshids, Russians (the smallest group),
Berbers, Khazars.[8] Nevertheless, these ethnic groups continue to
maintain their separateness. Relatively few interethnic marriages
occur: the same study shows, for example, that in the central settlement, of 40 marriages, 4 (12 percent) were between persons of various
ethnic groups, including three not involving Beluchis. In the central
settlement for the first and second brigades, of 140 marriages 17
(12 percent) were interethnic. There is a distant preference among
the Beluchis for marriages to close relatives and to peoples with
whom the Beluchis had had social relations in the past, such as the
Afghans.[9]

In general, the data on ethnic intermarriage from ethnographic
sources are far from impressive. One of the reasons for this is
methodological: the ethnographer generally concentrates on a single
population, or at most a region. Very often his impressions are
dramatic and nonstatistical, since he is concerned with social groups
rather than with numbers. Secondly, until very recently ethnographers
have concentrated on rural populations, and although ethnic changes
have occurred in the rural setting they are by no means as intense
as in the cities. Another Soviet scholar, who ordinarily documents her

research with loving care, has only this to say about mixed marriages: that they are generally concluded among people who do not have large and tightly knit family groups. However, such marriages are no longer rare, even though they usually take place most frequently in the cities and settlements of urban type and among young people who have served in the army or have gone on to higher educational institutions.[10] Furthermore, it is evident from the rest of her discussion, involving cultural factors, that the situation among the Turkmens is still in flux.

A study of the Uzbeks in the middle Zerafshan Valley also fails to reveal very significant rates of ethnic intermarriage: in the kolkhoz "Communism" in 1962 there were 16 mixed marriages, 10 of them Uzbeks with Tatar women; only three of these 10 men worked in the kolkhoz but all the women did. One marriage involved an Uzbek man and a Uyghur woman, one an Uzbek and an Azerbaijanian woman, and one an Uzbek and a Ukrainian woman; in two families the man was Arab and the woman Russian. In these two cases one couple were both teachers while in the other the man was a worker and the woman a kolkhoz member. In one family the Uzbek was a railroad worker and the Russian woman belonged to the kolkhoz. In the qishlaq (village) of Baimak, of 42 families studied the majority were Uzbek with a few Tajik. It was found that the fewest mixed marriages occurred with non-Muslim groups.[11]

If the ethnographers have had to be content with isolated instances or general statements, sociologists working in Central Asian cities have been able to present quite another picture. Ethnically mixed marriages, even in 1936, occurred in a great variety of combinations throughout Central Asia (see Tables 4.1 and 4.2), although the percentages of such marriages were markedly lower in rural areas (see Table 4.3). The Turkmens show statistically one of the lowest rates of intermarriage, and perhaps for this reason sociologists in recent years have paid considerable attention to the Turkmen SSR. One such inquiry notes that from the data of the 1959 census, of every 1,000 families in Turkmenia 85 were interethnic; among the Uzbeks, 82.[12] According to the 1970 census, 48 percent of the population of Turkmenia was urban.[13] This represents only a 2 percent growth since the 1959 census, when 25 percent of the urban residents of Turkmenia were Turkmen. The flow of rural population to the cities has since slowed down. However, the flow of population between cities in Turkmenia appears to be intense, and under these conditions it is interesting that 80 percent of the migrants from the rural areas are male. Some women are said to be attracted to the Turkmen SSR because they know that they can find employment in the textile industry, which suffers from a labor shortage. These migrants, both within the republic and from outside it, are in the 16-34 age bracket.[14] About 2,000 women were gained through in-migration and more than 8,000

TABLE 4.1

Number of Ethnic Combinations in Mixed Marriages
in Kirgizia, Turkmenia, and Uzbekistan in 1936

| | Number of Ethnic Groups Represented in Mixed Marriages | | | | | |
| | Uzbek SSR | | Kirgiz SSR | | Turkmen SSR | |
Ethnic Group	Male	Female	Male	Female	Male	Female
Kazakhs	14	11	5	4	3	4
Uzbeks	40	31	12	14	10	6
Kirgiz	9	7	11	12	—	—
Turkmens	7	5	1	1	14	17
Tajiks	11	16	14	6	—	—
Tatars	20	21	8	10	9	12
Chuvash	3	5	1	1	1	4
Uyghurs	10	6	7	8	1	—
Russians	20	47	17	30	16	33
Ukrainians	11	18	11	16	10	14
Germans	4	10	3	8	4	6
Jews	10	10	4	2	4	10
Poles	5	7	4	5	3	6
Armenians	9	10	4	2	7	7
Mordvins	5	9	2	3	4	7
Iranians	8	6	—	—	12	11

Source: N. P. Borzykh, "Rasprostranennost' mezhnatsional'nykh brakov v respublikakh srednei Azii i Kazakhstane v 1930-kh godakh," Sovetskaia etnografiia No. 4 (1970), p. 90.

men during the 1958-68 period considered by the author. Another scholar mentions a considerable exchange of population between Turkmenia and the other Central Asian republics, chiefly the Uzbek SSR. However, during the 1963-67 period, the exchange favored the Uzbeks.[15] The North Caucasian region (still largely Muslim) also attracts Turkmen out-migrants,[16] as do other regions of the Russian SFSR to varying degrees.

A Turkmen author has pointed out that Turkmen men more frequently marry women of another ethnic group than the reverse, with the men exercising a wider range of choice (Table 4.4 and 4.5). Let us note again that nationality is usually determined through the

Distribution of Ethnic Marriages in Central Asia in 1936

Ethnic Groups	Total Marriages						Interethnic Marriages						Percent of Interethnic Marriages				
	Uzb. SSR	Kaz. SSR	Kirg. SSR	Turkm. SSR	Taj. SSR	Total	Uzb. SSR	Kaz. SSR	Kirg. SSR	Turkm. SSR	Taj. SSR	Total	Uzb. SSR	Kaz. SSR	Kirg. SSR	Turkm. SSR	Taj. SSR
Men																	
Russians	7,662	17,125	2,349	2,672	1,147	30,955	697	1,700	399	236	126	3,158	9.1	9.9	12.4	8.8	11.0
Ukrainians	836	4,759	812	339	188	6,934	695	1,820	392	289	149	3,345	83.9	40.7	45.0	85.3	79.3
Uzbeks	34,734	621	1,234	558	1,085	39,232	2,185	72	115	79	380	2,831	6.3	14.5	9.1	14.2	18.8
Kazakhs	1,176	16,114	80	279	71	17,720	207	774	21	18	11	1,011	17.6	14.6	26.3	6.5	15.5
Kirgiz	535	—	3,030	1	114	3,680	90	—	134	—	16	240	11.8	—	4.2	—	14.0
Turkmens	210	—	1	4,746	18	4,974	36	—	1	284	5	326	17.1	—	100.0	6.0	25.6
Tajiks	2,324	—	55	7	5,225	7,611	511	—	22	6	483	1,022	22.0	—	37.7	85.9	9.2
Tatars	1,222	907	146	189	124	2,588	200	174	47	76	36	533	16.4	17.0	31.5	40.0	29.0
Others	3,682	2,081	495	902	473	7,633	1,603	852	221	412	150	3,238	43.5	40.8	46.6	45.6	31.7
Total	52,381	41,607	8,202	9,693	9,445	121,328	6,224	5,362	1,352	1,400	1,356	15,694	39.6	34.1	8.7	8.9	8.7
Women																	
Russians	8,639	18,139	2,455	3,127	1,338	33,698	1,674	2,714	505	691	317	5,901	19.4	14.9	21.0	22.1	23.7
Ukrainians	589	4,500	784	220	120	6,231	448	1,561	364	170	81	2,624	76.1	34.8	49.0	77.3	67.5
Uzbeks	33,663	592	1,274	535	1,891	37,955	1,114	43	155	56	186	1,554	3.3	7.0	12.1	10.5	9.8
Kazakhs	1,070	15,492	83	278	68	16,991	101	122	24	17	8	272	9.4	0.8	29.0	6.7	11.8
Kirgiz	494	—	2,971	1	138	3,604	49	—	75	—	40	164	9.9	—	2.5	—	29.0
Turkmens	205	—	1	4,512	14	4,732	31	—	1	50	1	83	15.1	—	100.0	1.2	7.2
Tajiks	2,402	—	58	1	4,948	7,409	589	—	25	—	206	820	26.2	—	43.1	—	5.1
Tatars	1,904	1,197	159	237	181	3,678	882	464	60	124	93	1,623	46.3	38.7	37.7	52.3	51.4
Others	3,145	1,687	417	782	747	7,048	1,336	458	143	292	424	2,653	39.1	27.1	34.3	37.3	56.8
Total	52,381	41,607	8,202	9,693	9,445	121,328	6,224	5,362	1,352	1,400	1,356	15,694	39.6	34.1	8.7	8.9	8.7

Source: N. P. Borzykh, "Rasprostranennost' mezhnatsional'nykh brakov v respublikakh srednei Azii i Kazakhstane v 1930-kh godakh," Sovetskaia etnografiia No. 4 (1970), p. 91.

TABLE 4.3

Proportion of Ethnic Marriages Among Urban and
Rural Populations of Central Asia in 1936

	Uzbek SSR	Kazakh SSR	Kirgiz SSR	Tajik SSR	Turkmen SSR	Total
Urban Population						
Total marriages	15,459	11,427	1,920	1,585	4,163	34,554
Interethnic marriages	2,685	2,010	479	397	1,062	6,633
Percent of interethnic marriages relative to total	17.3	17.6	25.0	25.0	25.5	19.2
Rural Population						
Total marriages	36,922	30,180	6,282	7,660	5,530	86,774
Interethnic marriages	3,539	3,452	873	959	338	9,162
Percent of interethnic marriages relative to total	9.6	11.4	13.9	12.2	6.1	10.6
Total Population						
Total marriages	52,381	41,607	8,202	9,445	9,693	121,328
Interethnic marriages	6,224	5,462	1,352	1,356	1,400	15,794
Percent of interethnic marriages relative to total	11.9	13.1	16.4	14.3	14.4	12.9

Source: N.P. Borzykh, "Rasprostranennost' mezhnatsional'nykh brakov v respublikakh srednei Azii i Kazakhstane v 1930-kh godakh," Sovetskaia etnografiia No. 4 (1970), p. 92.

father. When Russians and other non-Central Asians marry, their children most frequently designate themselves Russian regardless of whether it is the father's or the mother's identity.[17] In the city of Ashkhabad during 1950-62 only 162 Turkmen girls chose mates from other ethnic groups; however, 50 such marriages occurred during 1964-65.[18] This increase in the tempo of interethnic marriages is noted also for Charjoy, where there were 316 mixed marriages in 1967, 36.4 percent of the total registered.[19] There had been 542 mixed

TABLE 4.4

Number of Women Marrying Turkmens in the Cities
and Settlements of Turkmenia in 1963

Ethnic Group	Cheleken	Krasnovodsk	Nebit-Dag	Mary	Ashkhabad	Bairam-Ali	Gaurdak	Kizyl-Arvat	Bezmein	Karki	Total
Russians	7	15	9	13	50	6	1	2	7	2	111
Ukrainians	4	1	3	3	6	—	—	—	3	1	21
Tatars	15	5	11	11	16	5	—	2	4	1	70
Uzbeks	—	1	—	—	5	1	—	—	—	6	13
Azerbaijanians	—	—	1	1	5	2	—	—	1	—	9
Bashkirs	—	1	1	1	2	—	—	—	—	—	6
Moldavians	—	—	1	—	1	—	—	—	—	—	2
Belorussians	—	—	—	2	1	—	—	—	—	—	3
Gagauz	—	—	—	1	—	—	—	—	—	—	1
Germans	—	2	—	—	—	1	—	—	—	—	3
Armenians	—	1	1	—	—	—	—	—	—	—	2
Jews	—	—	1	—	—	—	—	—	—	—	1
Greeks	—	—	—	1	—	—	—	—	—	—	1
Uyghurs	—	—	—	—	—	1	—	—	—	—	1
Ossetians	3	—	—	—	—	—	—	—	—	—	3
Latvians	—	—	—	—	1	—	—	—	—	—	1
Bulgarians	—	—	—	1	—	—	—	—	—	—	1
Mordvins	—	—	—	—	2	2	—	—	—	—	4
Chuvash	—	—	—	—	3	—	—	1	—	—	5
Arabs	—	—	—	—	—	1	—	—	—	—	1
Lakhs	—	—	—	—	1	—	—	—	—	—	1
Koreans	—	—	—	—	—	1	—	—	—	—	1
Poles	—	—	—	—	1	—	—	—	—	—	1

Source: Sh. Annaklychev, Byt i kul'tura rabochikh Turkmenistana (Ashkhabad: Izdatel'stvo "Ilim," 1969), p. 389.

TABLE 4.5

Number of Turkmen Women Marrying Men of
Other Ethnic Groups

Men of Non-Turkmen Ethnic Group	Nebit-Dag, 1963	Krasnovodsk, 1963	Bairam-Ali, 1963	Ashkhabad, 1964	Mary, 1963	Bezmein, 1963	Karki, 1963	Total
Russians	3	1	1	13	—	—	—	18
Ukrainians	—	1	—	—	2	—	—	3
Kazakhs	—	1	—	—	—	—	—	1
Uyghurs	—	—	1	—	—	—	—	1
Azerbaijanians	1	—	—	3	2	—	—	6
Uzbeks	—	—	—	2	7	—	9	18
Armenians	—	—	—	2	1	—	—	3
Chuvash	—	—	—	—	—	1	—	1
Tatars	—	—	—	1	—	—	—	1
Belorussians	—	—	—	1	—	—	—	1

Source: Sh. Annaklychev, Byt i kul'tura rabochikh Turkmenistana (Ashkhabad: Izdatel'stvo "Ïlïm," 1969), p. 391.

marriages registered in Charjoy during 1950-62.[20] This appears higher than the rate for Ashkhabad as detailed in the source for Tables 4.6 and 4.7, which reports that during 1961-65 ethnically mixed marriages accounted for 31.6 percent of the total registered in Ashkhabad. The same author adds that the rate of dissolutions for the 1951-55 period was 6.2 percent for monoethnic marriages and less than 6 percent for interethnic; in 1956-60 the corresponding rates were almost 8 and 9.5 percent. It would seem from Table 4.6 that interethnic marriages are not as stable as ethnographers like Vasil'eva, Abramzon, and Vinnikov assume, though the case in rural localities (which are much more conservative) may be different. In one instance, a Kazakh kolkhoznik abandoned plans to divorce his Russian wife in favor of a Kazakh woman under pressure from his parents and public opinion.[21] Margulan and Vostrov state that divorce

in the Kazakh aul (village) is rare. Marriages in Ashkhabad have also
been analyzed in terms of length of marriage prior to dissolution and
reasons for the dissolution (Tables 4.8 and 4.9). Although nothing is
said about the ethnicity of the parties to these marriages, the tables
are interesting in view of Musaev's assertion that the stability of
monoethnic and interethnic marriages is approximately the same.

By way of comparison with the Turkmens, we may cite a study
of mixed marriages in Dushanbe from 1946 through 1966, where, of
55,000 marriages, 22,000 were mixed.[22] The largest ethnic groupings
were Russian, Tajik, and Uzbek, followed by the Tatar, Ukrainian,
Jewish, Mordvin, Ossetic, and other ethnic groups. Men entered into
mixed marriages more frequently than women. The authors found
that the difference between the theoretical probability of interethnic
marriage and its observed frequency (the first being significantly
higher) was greater in the case of marriages involving Russians than

TABLE 4.6

Comparative Data on Monoethnic and Interethnic
Marriages in Ashkhabad from 1951 to 1965

Year	Monoethnic Marriages	Disso- lutions	Interethnic Marriages	Disso- lutions
1951	1713	110	647	34
1952	1477	96	610	29
1953	1308	82	481	29
1954	1504	84	544	29
1955	1500	98	522	44
1956	1525	103	506	46
1957	1612	105	559	44
1958	1680	129	665	60
1959	1520	128	579	66
1960	1715	171	740	75
1961	1726	193	779	85
1962	1556	169	716	75
1963	1395	169	622	120
1964	1283	274	620	108
1965	1354	295	655	169

Source: O. Musaev, "Nekotorye rezul'taty issledovaniia
mezhnatsional'nykh brakov i semei v Turkmenistane," Izvestiia
Akademii nauk turkmenskoi SSR, Seriia obshchestvennykh nauk, No. 5
(1969), p. 22.

TABLE 4.7

Dynamics of Marriages in Ashkhabad

Year	Total Registered Marriages	Interethnic Marriages	
		Number	Percent
1920	381	81	21.26
1921	502	93	18.52
1922	501	93	18.56
1923	444	71	15.94
1924	596	90	15.10
1925	525	95	18.09
1930	919	145	15.77
1933	966	267	27.63
1934	1011	244	24.13
1935	1325	369	27.84
1939	1455	374	25.70
1940	1297	401	30.91

Source: O. Musaev, "Nekotorye rezul'taty issledovaniia mezhnatsional'nykh brakov i semei v Turkmenistane," Izvestiia Akademii nauk turkmenskoi SSR, Seriia obshchestvennykh nauk, No. 5 (1969), p. 19.

for those involving only members of different Central Asian ethnic groups. In addition, when the mother was Russian and the father Tajik, 82 percent of the children declared themselves Tajik when applying for a passport; in cases in which the father was Tajik and the mother Uzbek, more than 74 percent of the children declared themselves Tajik.[23] The authors conclude that this "shows a definite stability of ethnos among the Tajiks, Uzbeks, and Russians." In the case of the Central Asians they attribute this in large part to the influence of Islam.

Although Soviet scholars are unquestionably closer to the problem than we, it seems questionable to place the onus on Islam. The influence of Islam centers around the fact that religious observance is equated with national tradition. This confusion in the popular mind arises because "religion" and "way of life" were once synonymous, and although the Soviet regime has done much to destroy this equation it has not been completely successful. An American author has suggested that Leninist nationality policy was based on czarist religious policy stripped of religion.[24] A reading of both scholarly and popular

materials by Soviet writers on the sociology of religion gives some
ground for supposing that religion will not be eradicated as long as
the theoretical formulations laid down by Lenin (and Stalin) go unaltered.

Islam may be considered as the organized expression of national
consciousness, since many Central Asians even today appear to feel
that it is precisely Islam that contains the essence of their cultural
tradition. In fact, the folk religion is replete with practices not
sanctioned by Muslim clergy, and the stubbornness of these pre-
Islamic survivals does not argue well for a strong Muslim religious
organization. Current Soviet studies of Islam document an attempt
by the Muslim clergy to influence women, even to the point of insisting
on their equality in a religious and social context (and social groups
with a Muslim heritage are still strongly male-oriented). In this
connection it is asserted that Turkmen males preserve the survivals
of the past in social relations.[25] This (perhaps feminist) view is
sharply at variance with the case among Christian groups, where women
are repeatedly said to be the guardians of tradition and conservatism.
However, one fragmentary study of religiosity among urban Turkmens,
for example, indicates that levels of religiosity are about equal between

TABLE 4.8

Length of Marriage from Registration to Factual
Break-up of Family, Ashkhabad
(in percent)

Length of Marriage	1964	Years 1965	1966
Up to six months	8.5	12.5	13.0
6 mos.-1 year	8.0	10.5	8.0
1-2 years	20.0	16.0	14.0
2-4 years	26.0	23.0	23.0
4-8 years	26.0	25.0	24.0
8-16 years	10.0	10.5	12.0
Over 16 years	1.5	2.5	5.0

Source: Ia. Modzhekov, "K voprosy o brachno-semeinykh
otnosheniiakh v usloviakh Turkmenistana," Izvestiia Akademii nauk
turkmenskoi SSR, Seriia obshchestvennikh nauk, No. 6 (1967), p. 23.
Five hundred marriages were studied, 400 in the Supreme Court and
100 in the Sovetskii Raion court in Ashkhabad.

TABLE 4.9

Classification of Reasons for the Break-up of the
Family, Ashkhabad
(in percent)

Reasons for Break-up	1964	1965	1966
Antisocial behavior of one or both spouses expressed in crime, hooliganism, parasitism, drunkenness, feudal-bai relationship to women, etc.	21.0	19.5	19.0
Marital infidelity	19.0	16.0	11.0
Jealousy	4.0	2.5	4.0
Marriage without love	3.0	2.0	3.0
Conflicts because of abnormal attitude toward parents of spouses	11.5	11.5	7.0
Small everyday quarrels in the family	4.0	5.0	7.0
Short premarital acquaintance	4.0	5.5	6.0
Marriage for material reasons, material difficulties, difficulties in everyday life	1.5	2.0	2.0
The presence of children from other marriages	3.0	0.5	4.0
Loss of respect and trust between spouses	7.0	11.0	8.0
Prolonged absence of cohabitation	1.5	2.5	6.0
Differing characters and differing views	9.5	5.0	7.0
Egotistical attitudes towards family life	3.0	5.5	5.0
Great age differences	1.0	—	5.0
Survivals of nationalism	0.0	1.0	—
Physiological reasons (inability of wife or husband to produce children, nervous diseases, sexual dissatisfaction, etc.)	7.0	10.5	12.0 (Sic)

Source: Ia. Modzhekov, "K voprosy o brachno-semeinykh otnosheniiakh v usloviakh Turkmenistana," Izvestiia Akademii nauk turkmenskoi SSR, Seriia obshchestvennikh nauk, No. 6 (1967), p. 23.

the sexes, with women having a relatively slight edge. After attempting a study of 6,146 persons in Tashauz,[26] its author somewhat ruefully admitted that the questionnaire method must be supplemented by direct observation. Interestingly enough, he considers the main objection to circumcision not its threat to health but the fact that it marks very young children as Muslim; some people answering this questionnaire stated that they considered it a national custom that should be performed medically. Another study, involving a rural group in Kohna-Urganch raion, Turkmen SSR,[27] indicates that the opinion of one's face-to-face group is a highly important factor in religious observance. For instance, a man who professes indifference to religion submits to various forms of religious taxation in order not to be thought miserly. In both the urban and the rural setting ritual observances such as circumcision and funerary feasts, far from causing economic harm to the families whose rites of passage they are, in present-day Turkmenia obviously enhance the solidarity of the group, since all those attending contribute to them. The people in the rural community have the interesting idea that although the observance of religious rituals such as prayers and fasting are desirable in the young, they are not as important for them as for those over forty, since the sins of the young are written in clay and can be altered, but those of the over-forty are chiseled in stone. Furthermore, it is sufficient if only one person in the family observes the rituals. Another work includes a comparison of Tashauz, the only city in northern Turkmenia, and Kohna-Urganch, the largest and most isolated raion.[28] Religiosity is higher in the countryside, but the spread does not seem as marked as in European Russia.

Women, being most directly concerned with family matters, are undoubtedly more susceptible to social and religious pressure, but it is no longer religion as such that hinders ethnic intermarriage. These marriages are occurring at an ever-increasing rate, and the reasons why they take place predominantly among Muslim populations should be sought elsewhere. The ethnographers approve of inter-ethnic marriages, because, they say, such marriages are watched very carefully and sooner or later their best features are adopted. These marriages greatly facilitate the acceptance of new life-styles and social relationships. But, the scholars warn, the process must not be forced.

It is hard to see just how the element of force could be read into this situation. We assume that Soviet ethnographers are reacting to Western skepticism about the prevalence of ethnic intermarriages in Central Asia, or they are trying to reassure their Central Asian colleagues who are sensitive to any hint of Russification. Alexandre Bennigsen stated at a conference on religion and atheism in communist countries (held in Ottawa in April 1971) that marriage between a Muslim girl and a Russian man "appears to be totally impossible even today." The same sources used in this paper were presumably available to him, and his over-statement suggests that he considers the ethnographic data to be insignificant.

Soviet sociologists like Kozenko and Monogarova seem genuinely surprised by their own findings: that in their most intimate social relations Soviet people prefer to remain with people of their own cultural traditions, people of often the same educational and social status. In 1967 we were roundly criticized for suggesting that urbanization under Soviet conditions had to follow the Western model, but that there might be a Central Asian variant of Soviet culture.[29] Our judgment in the first proposition now seems over-hasty, but on the basis of the data presented above we must at least tentatively reassert that there appears to be a Central Asian variant of Soviet culture emerging.[30] Its "Soviet" elements can best be suggested by data on bi- and trilingualism (including Russian as lingua franca in the cities), and by emerging educational and professional patterns.[31] These topics are beyond the scope of this paper, but they should be included in future discussions of Soviet nationality policy.[32]

PART

II

**INTERDISCIPLINARY
GROUP II**

AN AWARENESS OF
TRADITIONAL
TAJIK IDENTITY
IN CENTRAL ASIA
Barry M. Rosen

This investigation will attempt to show why the traditional
identity of a distinct Central Asian ethnic group, the Tajiks, remains
virtually unaffected by the process of urbanization occurring in its
republic and also why this strong identification has a definite effect
upon the general nationality question in Central Asia. With this
purpose in mind we will consider whether the policy of sblizhenie
(converging) and sliianie (merging) introduced by means of industrialization has revealed a distinct Central Asian unity or rather an urban-
rural ethnic polarization, traditional patterns in the local elite, and
a Tajik cultural identity.

Soviet statistics, the Russian-language press, recent Western
periodicals, and the following four Tajik-language newspapers and
journals for the year 1971 have been surveyed for these purposes:
Maorif va madaniyat, the cultural newspaper, and Tojikistan Soveti,
official bulletin of the Central Committee of the Communist Party,
the Supreme Soviet, and the Council of Ministers of Tajikistan; Sadoi
Sharq, the literary journal of the Writers Union of Tajikistan, which
usually includes stories, plays, and essays; and Kommunisti Tojikston,
the journal of the Central Committee of the Communist party of
Tajikistan.

In considering nationality we avoid the recent Soviet definition,
which describes a nation as "a social-ethnic community of people
(liudi) characterized by a unity of industrial economy, territory,
literary language, national character, and culture."[1] According to
our own definition, a nation must evidence an identity, a subjective
group bond, in addition to being economically and politically independent. The Tajiks, as well as the other Central Asian nationalities,
do not possess the above prerequisites except for ethnic identity.

Also, although the large Uzbek population in the Tajik Soviet
Socialist Republic seems to be undergoing the same demographic

processes as the Tajik majority, we cannot draw further parallels concerning other trends among the Uzbeks. This is explained by the relative lack of Tajik press and journal coverage directed toward the Uzbek minority in Tajikistan. With the exception of references to the Uzbeks as "ancient friends" who have contributed to Tajik culture, or Tajik gratitude towards the Uzbek SSR for its assistance in constructing the Nurek Hydroelectric Plant, and the celebration of Tajik-Uzbek literature during a literary festival in the Vakhsh raion,[2] from available sources the actual internal relationships existing between these two ethnic group cannot be described.

For the Tajiks now to attain a position in which their tradition experiences an integration with Soviet culture, allowing for geographical variants, there must be an effacement of those ethnic distinctions that are termed the "private" aspects of culture, including family relationships, religion, and world-view. Some American anthropologists maintain that the Russians in their relationship with Central Asia have avoided a direct confrontation with the old social structure and are concentrating on the indirect attack via industrialization and its corollary, urbanization.[3] The process of urbanization for our purposes takes place in a definite territorial unit and is defined as response to specific avenues of social mobility, such as education, technical skill, and a good knowledge of the Russian language. Whether these openings are available or not to the ethnic Tajik is a significant question because such availability reveals the general processes of the nationality policy, which tend to isolate nationalities, thereby solidifying the "private" culture and its traditional identity.

What then is the position of the Tajiks in relation to their proportion of the total population of their republic vis-à-vis their share in some indicators of an industrialized-urban society? Some figures available from the 1970 Soviet census reveal a high rate of natural population increase for the Tajiks. This growth has raised the Tajik percentage of the republic population in comparison to the Russian.[4] But the 1959 census provides a basis for a finer analysis with its ethnic breakdown of our indicators. The composition of Tajikistan's population according to the 1959 census shows that among the three major ethnic groups within the republic—Tajiks, Uzbeks, and Russians—there is a discrepancy between the percent of each in the population and the general picture of urbanization. The Tajiks in 1959 constituted 53.1 percent of the population, but only 19.5 percent of the total Tajiks were considered urban. The Uzbeks made up 23 percent of the republic's inhabitants and revealed the same trend, with 16.5 percent of their total given as urban. Although the Russians reached a total of 13.3 percent of the republic's population, their share in the urban population rose to an outstanding 86.9 percent.[5]

Along with the recent high rate of Tajik natural increase, calculated at 4 percent annually, the high fertility rates, which if the
1964-65 rates remain constant will result in an average of 5.3 children
per woman in Tajikistan, and the 36.6 percent increase in rural
population since 1959, the in-migration of Russians has reached an
absolute increase of 30,000.[6] As a result, even though there happens
to be a labor surplus in Tajikistan concentrated in the rural areas,
there is a negligible flow of the rural population into the towns of the
Republic. The urban areas of Dushanbe and the conglomerates of
people in the Leninabad oblast have become Russian occupational and
linguistic enclaves, while the rural areas are left with an overexpanding
and culturally separate local work force.

From educational indexes we know that the student population of
Tajikistan is drawn mainly from the urban, non-Tajik areas. Moreover, the educational system leading up to higher education is more
advanced in the city than in the countryside; therefore, a Russian bias
toward technology (Table 5.1) overbalances a Tajik inclination for
fields such as education, where teachers must be in public contact
with pupils of their own language group. A review of the doctoral
candidates studying chemistry in Dushanbe in 1971 revealed that
approximately 50 percent were Russian,[7] a rate substantially higher
than that for Russian scientists in Tajikistan in 1960 (40.5 percent).[8]
In rural areas there are establishments such as the kolkhoz "Pobeda"
in the Lenin raion, where schools are planned to accommodate a
student body of 640, and qishloqs (villages) in Orjonikidzeobod raion
where libraries are expanding;[9] but one cannot ignore the lengthy
catalog of kambudho (shortcomings), ranging from poor teaching to
shortages of experienced teachers, textbooks, libraries, and films.[10]
Moreover, according to the 1970 census only 15.4 percent of the
Tajiks were found to be proficient in Russian as a second language
and 98.5 percent regarded the Tajik language as their mother tongue.[11]
Some of the reasons for this are the shortage of Russian-language
teachers in nationality schools, lack of methodological literature and
textbooks in rural areas, and presence of local teachers with an
extremely poor command of Russian.[12]

A Soviet study of the personnel policy at specific industrial
projects in Tajikistan, the Nurek Hydroelectric Plant and the Dushanbe
Integrated Textile Mill, found that ethnic factors interfered with the
entrance of Tajiks into these enterprises. The Nurek Hydroelectric
Plant, part of one of the largest irrigation networks in Central Asia
and nearing completion in 1972, was situated in a densely populated
area almost exclusively settled by Tajiks. But, according to the
study, only one-fourth of the construction workers were Tajiks. In
the Dushanbe Integrated Textile Mill the ethnic ratio of the Tajiks
was almost identical with their proportion of the population in

TABLE 5.1

Ethnic Composition of Students in Higher and Secondary
Educational Institutions, 1966, Tajik SSR

Ethnic Group	Total	Percent
Higher education	38,819	
Tajiks	14,658	37.8
Russians	12,624	32.5
Secondary education	49,568	
Tajiks	15,222	30.7
Russians	20,279	40.9

Source: Narodnoe khoziaistvo srednei Azii, v 1963 godu
(Tashkent: Izdatel'stvo "Uzbekistan," (1964), p. 332.

Dushanbe—15.2 percent. With the exception of the additional factor
of early marriages among Tajik women (Table 5.2), which inhibited
hiring of females, factors contributing to the Tajik employee shortage
at the Mill include lack of a knowledge of Russian, lack of technical
qualifications, and the administrative transfer from Russia of both
skilled and unskilled workers. Although the Soviet report claims
ethnic "merging" was proceeding rapidly, it called for a reduction of
the Russian influx, an improvement in the teaching of Russian, a
step-up in vocational training, and institution of job quotas for the
Tajiks.[13]
    Soviet authorities encouraged the process of Tajik urbanization
in the mid-1960s, but in Central Asia the Russian and local-language
press and journals between 1969-71 reveal no change in the urban-
rural disparity. In January 1969 a Party periodical complained:
" . . . while there is a surplus of manpower in the countryside, there
is an acute shortage of workers in industry and construction. Insufficient attention is paid to training workers from the indigenous
population; there are notably few Tajiks among the industrial production personnel at enterprises in the chemical industry, machine
building, and metal processing. . . .[14]
    The Tajik Party Central Committee also cited the mismanage-
ment of agriculture, where, despite an increase in technical equipment, low labor productivity characterizes the operation of collective
and state farms. Agricultural agencies, moreover, were similarly
reminded of the poor use of machinery and the drawbacks of manual
labor on farms. Concerning educational and cultural facilities in

TABLE 5.2

Marriage Rates of Tajik and Russian Women
in the Tajik SSR for 1959 per 1,000

	Age		
	16-19 yrs.	20-24 yrs.	25-29 yrs.
Tajik	384	869	822
Russian	86	465	798

Source: Itogi vsesoiuznoi perepisi naseleniia 1959, goda.
Tadzhikskaia SSR (Moscow: Gosstatizdat, 1963), p. 128.

rural areas the Party's resolution stated that a large proportion of
villages were not equipped with clubs, libraries, and motion picture
theaters. Stressed was the need for "the voluntary study of Russian,
which has in effect become the common language among all the USSR's
nationalities."[15]

Considering the absence of a rural migration to the cities, we
cannot expect any real change in economic or social relationships in
Tajikistan. According to a recent American study concerning Central
Asia, population movements are decisive in destroying the traditional
patterns of a culture.[16] When population shifts occur change can be
anticipated in the "private" or primary social institutions; but the
Tajiks apparently prefer not to move within their republic, and the
Russians are not likely to take up residence in the villages. Soviet
efforts to draw Russian migrants into the urban centers by offering
incentives such as scholarships and bonuses[17] primarily act to isolate
both outside and local culture and extend the life of traditional Tajik
identity.

Some Western studies maintain that throughout the period from
about 1945 to 1965 a definite Tajik-Russian model of political participation in Tajikistan was discernible.[18] According to them, the model
operated to maximize the political control of the Russians and at the
same time dissipated Tajik demands for political responsibilities.
This effect was produced by the active participation of a compact
elite representing the Tajiks but not controlling the machinery of
power.

Can this earliest model be substantiated at all today by an
analysis at the Union-wide and republic level of some state and Party
agencies? An examination of the ethnicity and professional affiliation

of Tajik SSR deputies to the Eighth USSR Supreme Soviet in 1970 (Table 5.3) shows that although the Tajiks were in the majority, the Russian contingent contained the greater share of administrators, technicians, and specialists. In the Supreme Soviet of the Tajik SSR not only is the overwhelming numerical representation of the Tajiks striking but the Russian representation in the commissions of the agency is impressive. In its presidium 13 out of 15 members are Tajiks, and the Russians make up only 10.5 percent of a total of 255 deputies; but they exercise control as first deputy committeemen in six out of fourteen key commissions, including those handling legislation, budget and planning, youth affairs, construction, and irrigation.[19]

In the Council of Ministers of the Tajik SSR, the most important state body, A. Qahhorov, a Tajik, is chairman, but the first deputy and fourth deputy, G. V. Zubarev and V. E. Novichkov, are Slavs. Moreover, Slavs represented 31.9 percent of the Ministries' Staff and Committees attached to the Council, and held the senior post in State Security, a position whose functions transcend the borders of the republic.[20] In analyzing the composition of the Bureau of the Tajikistan Communist Party Central Committee, the power base of the republic, it becomes evident that while the Russians number four out of nine Bureau members, none is noted as "candidate members" of the Bureau. The first secretary is a Tajik, providing local participation, but the second and third secretaries' positions are filled by Russians.[21]

Given the privileged position of the local political leadership, can it be said that this group is assimilating Marxism-Leninism and transmitting it throughout the hierarchy, whether political or administrative? Assimilation is both external and subjective where there is not only the outward acceptance of an ideology but the internalization of it as well.[22]

In an effort at "self-criticism" the Central Committees of the CPSU and the TCP have emphasized the inadequate concern shown over increasing and organizing Party cadres. These and other problems are stigmatized as remnants of "traditional attitudes." In 1969 city and district committees in Dushanbe, Leninabad, Qahinbadam, and Qairaqqum were censured for not drawing "workers" into the activities of Party life. The Central Committee of the CPSU went so far as to reprimand the TCP Central Committee and the Gorno-Badakhshan oblast committee for neglecting the selection, assignment, and the indoctrination and training of personnel. There are said to be those who "violate Party and state discipline"—people who do not possess the necessary political qualifications, lose their sense of responsibility, and "take the path of deception and falsify records in order to conceal their shortcomings and create an impression that all is well."[23] In fact, in 1969 Party committees were accused of covering up the corruption of managers and certain ministries, such as the Ministry

TABLE 5.3

Ethnic and Professional Affiliation of Tajik SSR Deputies
to the Eighth USSR Supreme Soviet (1970)

Position	Ethnic Affiliation
Chairman of Supreme Soviet of Tajik SSR	(CA)
Teachers	(CAF)
Farmers	4 (CA) 2 (CAF)
Brigade leaders (farms)	5 (CA)
Miners	(CA)
Mill operators and mechanics	4 (CA) 2 (CAF) 2 (S)
First Secretaries from City Party Committees	2 (CA)
Chairman of Tajik SSR Council of Trade Unions	(CA)
First Deputy Chairman of Tajik SSR Council of Ministries	(S)
Member of the Academy of Sciences USSR	(S)
Editor-in-Chief of Izvestiia	(S)
Minister of Power and Electrification	(S)
Secretary of Union-wide Central Council of Trade Unions	(S)
Chairman of USSR Council of Ministers State Cinematography Committee	(S)
Chairman of Board of USSR State Bank	(S)
	Total 23 Total 9

Key: (S) Slav; (CA) Central Asian Male; (CAF) Central Asian Female.

Source: The Current Digest of the Soviet Press, XXII, 27, pp. 18-19.

for Building-Materials Industry, in which "kind protectors" reduced and altered plans in order to ease responsibilities. It is the "bureaucratism" of the general Party administration, according to I. Koval, a member of the Secretariat of the TCP Central Committee, that causes a manager to " . . . incur several penalties for one and the same piece of negligence. Furthermore, these penalties are immediately forgotten! Almost the next day the penalized manager is given a bonus or promoted to more responsible work."[24]

Although there is a call to increase Party indoctrination seminars in city committees in 1971-2, the first secretary of the TCP, Rasulov, admitted that party chairmen are doing a poor job in checking the work of personnel.[25] In such raions as Jirgatol, Komsomolobod, Yovon, Shahtuz, and Nov village committees were cited for "neglecting executive procedures in the administration of plans."[26]

Another indication of strength in traditional attitudes is provided by the weak effort to direct atheistic propaganda. According to the CPSU Central Committee the TCP's "atheist propaganda has slackened of late, and the priesthood and religious sects have stepped up their activity. Persistent struggle is not being waged against the survivals of the past in people's minds, in their way of life, and in family relations. . . ."[27]

In answer to this criticism the TCP Central Committee has committed itself to an effort at instilling the public with Soviet patriotism in opposition to the customs and habits of Islam; but the Committee admits that its agitators cannot reach the public. A recent report reveals a novel attempt by officials to undermine the local cult of mazors (sacred tombs). Archeologists were brought into the village of Chilhuja, near the city of Uroteppa, to prove to the inhabitants that the giant Qahgaha was not buried under a mazor. Legend has it that Imam Ali came to Chilhuja and defeated the giant with the aid of his mule Duldul. Apparently the historical evidence proving the impossibility of Ali's ever having reached Tajikistan was rejected by the villagers, and so was the archeological evidence of the absence of a giant.[28]

The proportion of Tajik women in the TCP is declining, and throughout the city and district committees very few are promoted to executive positions.[29] No doubt this reflects the traditional attitude toward seclusion, which the political hierarchy unofficially tolerates. An example of this attitude is found in the pamphlet Qurbon va zanon (Victims and Women), which cites the case of a girl in a kolkhoz named Katinini located in the Hisor raion who was forced to relinquish the position of brigade leader because the kolkhoz threatened to disgrace her. Clear evidence of complicity is related concerning the Panjakent Party organization which was well aware of a case of wife abuse but would not interfere in "a husband's rights."[30] It might also be asked why, if the political organization is so interested in attracting women to its work, it would encourage them to produce large families by awarding one Russian and 90 Tajik women the honor of Qahramon, or hero, for bearing ten or more children each.[31] The persistence of under-age marriages, the payment of the bride price, and the general existence of Islamic culture are confirmed by a writer for the Tajik Party journal Kommunisti Tojikiston, who states that indoctrination is impossible so long as women remain outside the productive sectors of the economy. The mountainous regions of Tajikistan, the separation of urban and rural inhabitants in their living conditions, and the consequent strength of Islam within villages, according to that writer, can be overcome only if the outlook and beliefs of the woman, the receptacle of religious inculcation, is changed.[32]

While women's rights play a changing role in Tajik society, it is the definition of culture that is presently affecting the nature of the Tajik and his historical outlook. Culture is described by Lenin as having both "progressive" and "feudalistic" elements.[33] At the Congress of Journalists' meeting in Dushanbe on October 30, 1971, the aims of the cultural policy in Tajikistan—"national in form and Soviet in content"—were stressed in order to "oppose to bourgeois ideology the patriotism of the Soviet Union, the internationalism of the workers, and a love for Soviet life."[34] This means that the terms "feudalistic" and "bourgeois ideology" are considered synonymous with attempts to produce a culture that not only utilizes a specific language spoken by a self-aware ethnic group but fosters a definite heritage distinct from the Sovietwide model.

A significant result of the cultural policy in relation to the Tajiks is reflected in the Soviet division of the former Bukharan and Turkistan areas. In effect, the Soviet authorities are responsible for transforming the historical events of the area, such as the integral relationship of Uzbeks and Tajiks. Consequently, when one reviews a selection of "Tajik" folkplays such as Rais (The Chief) or Zani eshon (The Wife of the Ishan), the striking feature is the attempt to adapt Islamic life in the bazaar and at home—which actually takes place in the geographical surroundings of Bukhara—into a specific Tajik heritage.[35] This is all the more notable when it is found that these plays are also known in "Uzbek" versions.

Not only in folk literature but also in great medieval literature do we see critical analysis delineating separate "Tajik" poetic and historical contributions. Rudaki (b. 858), who is considered by Iranians as the first Islamic-Iranian poet to write in Persian, is characterized by Soviet Tajiks as an undisputed national hero of Tajikistan. Today's hero worship offers a striking contrast to the strong negative criticism Tajiks incurred in 1927 when they cited certain tenth-century verses of Rudaki, such as those praising the Emir of Bukhara.[36] According to a Tajik professor of Tajik philology, Rudaki is credited with stimulating patriotism during the period of the Samanids (A.D. 875-999), the first "Tajik" dynasty in Transoxania. This presentation does not treat the Samanids as an organic part of Tajik ascendancy both culturally and politically. The Samanids are described in terms of their centralized government, although they are also described as characteristically feudal and aristocratic.[37]

That Soviet interpretation of history fits into the Tajik idea of their linguistic development and the attempt to solidify Tajik as a language free from any outside accretions as early as the eleventh century. A Tajik author writing in the journal Sadoi Sharq discusses a treatise by a scholar named Roduyoni who lived in the eleventh century and was apparently the first person to analyze Tajik poetry scientifically and prove its advanced level. The writer claims that Roduyoni's work is conclusive proof of the fact that the Tajik language was then a rival to Arabic in its poetic forms.[38]

Interesting treatment is given in current Tajik criticism to literary-historical figures who are constantly quoted by Tajiks, Firdausi (d. 1020-21) and Hafiz (d. 1389). Writing at the end of the Samanid period and during the reign of Mahmud of Ghanza (999-1030), Abul Qasim Firdausi is judged by present-day Iranians to be the poet linked with the preservation of Persian national sentiment. The Shah Nama (Book of Kings) of Firdausi presents the epic of the Iranian empire from the creation of the world to the Muslim conquest. How-ever, the Tajik press calls the poet Tajikistan's own. A local essayist refers to Firdausi's poetry as an inspiration for Tajik patriotism, citing his lines that "it is necessary to love one's soul but it is more honorable to love one's country." This modern Tajik admits at the same time that during Firdausi's era the meaning of vatan, "homeland" or "fatherland", was limited and was principally understood as one's village. Today, on the other hand, he says, the meaning of vatan has changed to include the entire Soviet Union. This allegiance, however, does not change one's love for his birthplace, village, city, or repub-lic. In fact, he continues, the most fundamental (ibtido) love relates to a part of the vatan, to one's birthplace, Tajikistan. It is clear, according to the essay, that when one does not love his birthplace he is "like a bird without a nest to return to in the evening."[39]

The 650th anniversary of the birth of Shamsiddin Muhammad Hafiz occasioned visits from both Iranian and Afghan educators to Dushanbe in 1971 and prompted the writing of several articles about the poet in the journal Sadoi Sharq. Although Hafiz lived in Shiraz and can only be termed Iranian, the Tajiks assume a shared jurisdic-tion over the poet because of his Farsi-Tajik language and the temporary political control of Shiraz by the Timurids during Hafiz's day. What is reflected in an article about Hafiz and folklore is the protest value of the poet's work. The article points to Hafiz's techniques of sarcasm and allusion, and says that the poet was able to counter the cruelty of his age by these means and for that reason is loved to this day by both literate and illiterate Tajiks.[40] Although Hafiz is pictured as a libertarian, he is also singled out in Tajik culture and elevated to the status of an international figure represent-ing Soviet ideals.

This tension between loyalty to Tajikistan and to the whole Soviet Union is a theme elaborated in a new Tajik play called <u>Bevatan</u> (Without a Homeland) written by Sulton Safar. Although the drama's original period is World War II, the audience is confronted with the contemporary situation of a Tajik-Muslim <u>vatan</u> contrasted with the Soviet Union. The main character, Kamol, finds himself a prisoner in a German military camp, where he meets Ayub, a fellow Tajik. Ayub learns that Kamol's father was branded "an enemy of the people" because of his Basmachi (anti-Russian partisan) affiliations in the early 1920s, and attempts to persuade Kamol to help "the Germans free our homeland from the Bolshevik <u>kafirs</u> [unbelievers]." Ayub describes a future to Kamol in which Tajikistan will take its place in a larger Islamic brotherhood, but does not provide the audience with any further details.[41]

Another contemporary author, the poet Gulrukhsor, expresses the intimate feelings of a Tajik for his republic in verses entitled "Vatan." His allusion to a rural setting accents a local identity with its limited geography. Gulrukhsor writes:

Nadoram yod, ka bori nakhustin man Vatan guftam,	I don't remember the first time I said <u>Vatan</u>,
Diyoram, kishvaramro bo muhabbat "joni man" guftam,	With affection I called my land, my country "my soul,"
Baroyash bori avval bayt guftam. . . .	For it, I recited a verse for the first time. . . .
Hamon ruze, ka bar domoni modar cakht chaspida. . . .	That very day when I clung to my mother's apron. . . .
Nakhustin bor mavji kishtzoronro bididam man,	The first time I saw the waves of the sown fields.
Nakhustin bor az gulhoi yoboi shumardam man,	The first time I counted wild flowers.
Ajab ne, bo farah bori nakhustin man Vatan guftam. . . .	It's not surprising that I uttered <u>Vatan</u> with joy for the first time. . . .[42]

New Tajik literature like other evidence, has shown that industrialization and urbanization have influenced the general nationality question by providing the Tajik with a self-identification that will affect relationships between Central Asians and outsiders, mainly the Russians. The features in Tajikistan such as (1) a dichotomy created by separate urban Russian and rural Tajik societies, (2) a

Tajik political-administrative leadership that assumes a token representative role but does not negate traditional patterns of culture, and (3) a cultural policy of "national form and socialist content," which produces a Tajik identity, lead us to maintain that this republic is not proceeding toward (a) a converging or merging among Central Asian nationalities and/or between them and the Russians, or (b) a return to any previous supraethnic divisions or movements favoring new ones. Rather, there is a tendency to diverge both from other Central Asians and the Russians.

In terms of the nationality question Tajikistan represents a situation that is equally noticeable in much of Central Asia: the general deficit, so far as the indigenous ethnic groups are concerned, of rewards, representation, and recognition in the Soviet system. This situation encourages and insulates the local cultures, helps to maintain the rural nature of the region's population, and to a certain extent puts demands on the dominant group, the Russians, to narrow the distinctions between themselves and these Central Asians. The authorities are therefore in a dilemma, for to grant the responsibility that goes along with correcting the deficiencies invites not only a cultural but a political divergence based upon distinctly ethnic grounds.

There is a further question that must be asked especially in relation to Tajikistan, for in Central Asia it is almost unique in the extent of its predominantly rural character. Perhaps we are not sensitive enough to the possibility that there may be a Tajik attitude that looks upon the rural existence as an ideal way of life. Contemporary poets like Gulrukhsor write about the attractions of country life at the present time and admire its traditional values of family, religion, and respect for the land. It is therefore quite natural for a rural people such as the Tajiks to resist mobilization for industrial (Russian) purposes that threaten an entrenched existence. If we are correct about this Tajik attitude, how long does this rural society want to be manipulated by an outside group that in its own estimation represents the other end of the political-cultural spectrum? At present, the Tajiks precisely fit the pattern of a society that rejects urbanization and thus opens the nationality question for reevaluation by frustrating the process of amalgamation that draws people together from diverse ethnic groups. This precludes mixing in the modern sense of the word.

6

RECENT ASSIMILATION TRENDS
IN SOVIET CENTRAL ASIA
Ronald Wixman

There has been a major change in the ethnic situation in Soviet Central Asia since the time of the 1917 revolution. This change is a direct result of various assimilation processes stemming from both prerevolutionary and postrevolutionary developments. The Soviet authorities have attempted to direct the development of the various ethnic groups either by actively supporting their preservation as distinct groups or by supporting their assimilation by other ethnic groups. Changes in the ethnic situation have a significant effect on the over-all nationality question. This leads one to consider the problems: (1) What are the major assimilation patterns that have occurred in Soviet Central Asia in recent times? and (2) Do these patterns follow or oppose the official Soviet policy?

In order to answer these questions, use has been made of ethno-linguistic data from the 1926, 1959, and 1970 Soviet censuses.[1] Pravda Vostoka, Komsomolets Kirgizii, and Kazakhstanskaia Pravda for the period September 1, 1971, to February 29, 1972, have also been surveyed for the purpose of finding references to assimilation in Central Asia, or problems in the teaching of Russian or native languages in Central Asian schools. Such references would be useful in determining attitudes toward the existing situation in terms of assimilation and bilingualism.

Two different types of assimilation must be considered: actual changes in ethnic affiliation (change in nationality) and linguistic assimilation. In studying assimilation by analyzing the census, "in which nationality is defined by the individual's response to a question as to his nationality, affiliation changes in nationality (i.e., the fact that a new national self-identification adherence has arisen) may be considered the final stage of assimilation. Changes in the second ethnic determinant—language (linguistic assimilation)—are less significant under these conditions."[2] While the loss of the native language does not signify complete assimilation, it does reflect a strong influence by another ethnic group, and is a good measure of "foreign" impact.

Pre-1917 Central Asia was an area in which the idea of "nationality," in the Western sense, had not yet developed. The consciousness of the people did not lie in a nationality (ethnic) spirit, as is so common in the "Western world," but rather in religious, tribal, clan, or locational (for example, Bukharan or Khivan) affiliations. "Before the October 1917 revolution, with some very rare exceptions, the idea of belonging to a particular nation, to an Uzbek, Turkmen, or even Tatar nation, simply did not exist in the consciousness either of the Muslim intelligentsia or of the public."[3]

The Soviet regime attempted to break down the social divisions that splintered the Central Asians into numerous small units and alter the ethnic situation by creating Western-style nationalities. Paradoxically, the tribal, clan, and location affiliations that the authorities were attempting to destroy were the same institutions that had aided them in their conquest of Central Asia. The lack of a strong ethnic self-identification, stemming from these numerous divisions, weakened the position of the indigenous population in terms of its resistance to the Russian conquest.

In effect extending that era of fragmentation, Soviet leaders attempted to create and maintain five distinct, well-defined nationalities (Kazakhs, Kirgiz, Tajiks, Turkmens, and Uzbeks) that would satisfy Stalin's definition of a nation, "a historically evolved, stable community of language, territory, economic life, and psychological make-up (national consciousness) manifested in a community of culture."[4] These five were to be able to maintain their own identities, and to develop nationally to an extent great enough to prevent the ethnic merging that had previously been taking place between the Uzbeks and Tajiks and the Kazakhs and Kirgiz. To attain this goal of partition the political boundaries of Central Asia were redrawn along ethnic lines, thereby creating ethnic nationality territories, and education was established in the native languages.

With exceptions, all ethnic minorities were to be assimilated by these five established nationalities. The Uyghurs, Dungans, and Beluchis were preserved to further Soviet international political aims, and the Karakalpaks to attain internal political goals.

Considering the facts—that the Karakalpak and Kazakh languages are so similar that czarist philologists considered them as one language; that the Karakalpak literary language was created during the Soviet era; that, linguistically and culturally, there were no major factors that would warrant the establishment of a separate Karakalpak nationality; and that the Karakalpaks (at least in the early 1960s) were provided education in their own language as far as intermediate levels, while many numerically larger ethnic groups, such as the Karbardians, Chechens, Avars, and Ossetians, were provided education in their languages only as far as the fourth or fifth grades—it is apparent that the Karakalpak nationality is receiving a great deal of official support. This was to prevent their being assimilated by either the Uzbeks or Kazakhs. Blocking the assimilation of the Karakalpaks, who numbered only 146,000 in 1926, cannot be considered an attempt to divide or weaken either the Kazakhs or Uzbeks, who in the same year numbered approximately 4,000,000 each. It is of great significance, however, that the Karakalpak Autonomous Soviet Socialist Republic, which now makes up one third of the area of Uzbekistan, was originally created as part of Kazakhstan and was later transferred. It is therefore possible that the Karakalpaks and the Karakalpak ASSR have served as political tools to continue friction between the Kazakhs and Uzbeks.

The Uyghurs and Dungans, both of whom have significant populations of kinsmen in northwestern China, possess schools and cultural establishments in which their languages are used. "Considering their small numerical strength the two national minorities enjoy the use of a comparatively large number of cultural institutions."[5] A literary language was also created for the Beluchi, who in 1926 numbered only 9,974 in the entire Soviet Union.

No separate cultural establishments were created for those ethnic groups appearing in the 1926 census that were to be assimilated: the Pamir ethnic groups (Vakhan, Ishkashim, Yazgul, Shugnan, Rushan, Bartang, Khuf, and Bajui); Yagnobs; the Kuramas, Kipchaks, and Farghana Turki (Uzbek tribes that maintained a separate consciousness); Central Asian Arabs; Taranchis and Kashgars, (subdivisions of the Uyghurs); and the Kurds of Turkmenistan.

The Pamir people "no longer appear as distinct ethnographic groups, inasmuch as all called themselves Tajiks by nationality,"[6] and the Yagnobs had decreased in population from over 1,800 to only 600 as a result of the same process. In terms of language, however, the number of speakers of the Pamir languages had increased between 1939 and 1959 and the number of Yagnob speakers remained the same,[7] indicating that linguistic assimilation had not yet been completed. The Kuramas, Kipchaks, and Farghana Turki and the Taranchis and Kashgars had for the most part been consolidated into the Uzbek and Uyghur nationalities.

The decline in population from 108,600 to 95,200 among the Uyghurs indicated that while the Uyghurs were consolidating into one nationality they were also being assimilated by other people (mainly the Uzbeks and, to a lesser extent, the Kazakhs). Decreases in population were also recorded among the Central Asian Arabs, the Kurds of Turkmenistan, and the Beluchis. At the same time the Karakalpaks

TABLE 6.1

Central Asian Minority Groups and Their Assimilators

Ethnic Group	Assimilators
Pamir groups	Tajik
Yagnob	Tajik
Kurama, Kipchak and Farghana Turki	Uzbek
Central Asian Arab	Uzbek, Tajik
Kurd	Turkmen
Beluchi	Turkmen, Tajik
Taranchi and Kashgar	Uyghur

Sources: Narody Srednei Azii i Kazakhstana (Moscow: Izdatel' stvo Akademii Nauk SSSR, 1962), Vol. I, pp. 13, 94-95, and 658; Ibid., Vol. II, pp. 489, 631, and 649.

registered an increase in population far below that which would have been expected.

The 1959 Census revealed that among the Central Asian ethnic minorities a great deal of assimilation had taken place. Some of the numerically small ethnic and tribal groups had to varying degrees been consolidated into larger nationalities. Others experienced declines in population, or population increases far below the expected level considering the high rate of natural increase of the Central Asians.

The Uzbeks, Tajiks, Kazakhs, Turkmens, and Kirgiz showed no signs of being ethnically assimilated; their levels of linguistic assimilation also remained very low. The most heavily assimilated linguistically of these five were the Tajiks, among whom only 1.8 percent of their total Central Asian population did not consider Tajik their native language. The high rate of linguistic assimilation among the Karakalpaks, Uyghurs, Arabs, Beluchis, and Kurds of Turkmenistan is obscured by the ethnic assimilation previously mentioned, and this leads in some cases to a possible misinterpretation. For example, the percentages of Karakalpaks and Uyghurs in the USSR in 1926 and 1959, considering Karakalpak and Uyghur their native languages increased from 87.5 to 95 percent and from 79.5 to 85 percent respectively. A comparison of linguistic figures gives the erroneous impression that these people were assimilated to a lesser extent in 1959 than they were in 1926.

Ethnic developments evidenced by the 1959 census are of particular interest when viewed in the light of Soviet policy. In their attempt

TABLE 6.2

Population of Central Asian Minority Groups 1926 and 1959,
in the USSR

Ethnic Group (s)	1926	1959
Pamir*	—	—
Yagnob	1,829	600
Kurama	50,079	—
Kipchak	33,502	100
Farghana Turki	537	4,000
Kashgar**	13,010	—
Taranchi**	53,010	—
Uyghur**	42,550	95,208
Arab	28,978	7,987
Dungan	14,600	21,928
Karakalpak	146,317	172,556
Beluchi	9,974	7,842
Kurd***	2,308	2,263

*Pamir ethnic groups were not listed in the 1926 census. Their
1939 population totalled 38,000.

**In 1959 all were considered Uyghurs. The total 1926 population
was 108,570.

***Only in Turkmenistan.

Sources: V. K. Gardanov, B. O. Dolgikh, and T. A. Zhdanko,
"Osnovnye napravleniia etnicheskikh protsessov u narodov SSSR,"
Sovetskaia etnografiia, No. 4 (1961), p. 13; Vsesoiuznaia perepis'
naseleniia 1926 goda, Turkmenskaia sovetskaia sotsialisticheskaia
respublika, Vol. XVI (Moscow: Izdanie Tsentral'nogo Statisticheskogo
Upravleniia SSSR, 1929), p. 7; Ibid, Soiuz sovetskikh sotsialisticheskikh
respublik, Vol. XVII (1929), pp. 12 and 14; Itogi vsesoiuznoi perepisi
naseleniia 1959 goda, SSSR (svodnyi tom), (Moscow: Gosstatizdat,
Tsentral'noe Statisticheskoe Upravlenie SSSR, 1962), pp. 186 and
188; Ibid, Turkmenskaia SSR (1963), p. 128.

TABLE 6.3

Population of Selected Ethnic Groups Within the Borders
of Central Asia in 1959, by Native Language
(in percent)

Ethnic Group	Population	Own	Russian	Other
Uzbek	5,973,147	98.5	0.4	1.1
Kazakh	3,232,403	98.8	0.8	0.4
Tajik[1]	1,385,835	98.2	0.5	1.3
Ukrainian	1,034,965	56.5	43.4	0.1
Turkmen[2]*	985,643	99.0	0.5	0.4
Kirgiz[3]*	962,001	98.8	0.2	0.9
Tatar	779,840	88.0	8.2	3.8
Korean	220,378	78.8	21.1	0.1
Karakalpak[4]*	170,822	95.2	0.2	4.7
Uyghur[5]	92,974	85.4	1.9	12.7
Dungan[6]	21,068	95.8	1.3	2.9
Kurd[7]	13,155	89.0	2.3	8.7
Beluchi[8]	7,626	96.1	0.8	3.1
Arab[9]	7,987	34.1	1.8	64.1

[1]Excluding Turkmenistan.
[2]Excluding Kazakhstan and Kirgizia.
[3]Excluding Turkmenistan.
[4]Including only Uzbekistan and Turkmenistan.
[5]Excluding Turkmenistan and Tajikistan.
[6]Including only Kazakhstan and Kirgizia.
[7]Excluding Uzbekistan and Tajikistan.
[8]Turkmenistan only.
[9]Total Arab population in the USSR. It is assumed that virtually
all were located in Central Asia. No Arabs were listed by individual
republic.

*Figures do not total 100 percent due to rounding.

Sources: Itogi vsesoiuznoi perepisi naseleniia 1959 goda,
Kazakhskaia SSR (Moscow: Gosstatizdat, Tsentral'noe Statisticheskoe
Upravlenie SSSR, 1962), p. 162; Ibid., Uzbekskaia SSR, p. 138; Ibid.,
SSSR (Svodnyi Tom), p. 188; Ibid., Kirgizskaia SSR (1963), p. 128;
Ibid., Tadzhikskaia SSR, (1963), p. 116; Ibid., Turkmenskaia SSR
(1963), p. 128.

to have the Pamir ethnic groups, the Yagnobs, Kuramas, Kipchaks, Farghana Turki, Taranchis, Kashgars, Arabs, and the Kurds of Turkmenistan assimilated by larger nationalities, the Soviets had relatively great success; this, however, represented a continuation of processes that had started prior to the 1917 revolution. In their attempt to stop the assimilation of the Karakalpaks, Uyghurs, and Beluchis Soviet authorities were far less successful. Most significant of all was the fact that each of the five major Central Asian ethnic nationalities had maintained its individuality, which represented a change from the prerevolutionary situation.

Among all the Central Asians the levels of linguistic assimilation by Russians were insignificant. In fact, the amount of linguistic assimilation accomplished by other Central Asians was greater than that of Russification among all Central Asians except the Kazakhs and Turkmens.

The non-indigenous people in Central Asia (Ukrainians, Tatars, and Koreans), on the other hand, exhibited significantly higher levels of linguistic assimilation into Russian than into Central Asian languages. Linguistically one of the most extensively assimilated ethnic groups in Central Asia was the Ukrainian. Only 56.5 percent of the Ukrainians in Central Asia in 1959 considered Ukrainian their native language. One cannot measure the degree of ethnic assimilation of the Ukrainians because there was a large influx of Ukrainians to Central Asia between 1926 and 1959, which obscures all comparisons. The Ukrainians, however, generally display a high degree of ethnic assimilation outside the Ukraine.

The Koreans also exhibited a significant degree of linguistic assimilation by the Russians (see Table 6.3). The Tatars, however, while being moderately assimilated linguistically, were not subject to one single influence as were the Ukrainians and Koreans. Some 8.2 percent of the Central Asian Tatars considered Russian their native language, and 3.8 percent specified other languages. Among the Central Asian Tatars the languages other than Tatar and Russian most often used as native languages were Uzbek and, to a lesser extent, Kazakh.

One can examine the relative "foreign" influences acting upon each of the six titular nationalities outside their own republics by removing their individual home territories from consideration in the Central Asian totals. Table 6.4 indicates the population for each of these six nationalities outside their own republics—within the borders of Central Asia, however—by native language.

In all cases of these ethnic groups, outside their own national territories, both the percentage of Russian speakers and those of other languages increased; however, while Russian influence increased only slightly, other influences increased significantly among most of these

TABLE 6.4

Titular Central Asian Nationalities in Central Asia Outside
Their Own Republics, by Native Language in 1959
(in percent)

Nationality	Population	Own	Russian	Other
Uzbek	934,874	97.9	0.8	1.3
Kazakh	1,115,968	97.4	1.5	1.1
Tajik	334,671	94.9	0.6	4.5
Turkmen	61,919	92.8	0.7	6.5
Kirgiz	125,170	92.5	0.3	7.1
Karakalpak	14,823	53.8	0.7	45.5

Sources: Itogi Vsesoiuznoi perepisi naseleniia 1959 goda,
Kazakhskaia SSR (Moscow: Gosstatizdat, Tsentral'noe Statisticheskoe
Upravlenie SSSR, 1962), p. 162; Ibid., Uzbekskaia SSR, p. 138; Ibid.,
Kirgizskaia SSR (1963), p. 128; Ibid., Tadzhikskaia SSR (1963),
p. 116; Turkmenskaia SSR (1963), p. 128.

people. The greatest difference was recorded among the Karakalpaks,
where 0.7 percent considered Russian and 45.5 percent other languages
to be native. Although on the Central Asian level the Russian influence
was greater than "other" influences among the Turkmens, outside the
Turkmen republic the "other" influences were stronger than that of
the Russian.

Outside their own republics the only Central Asians who acted
as major assimilators were the Uzbeks and Tajiks. The Uzbeks
exerted a major influence in Tajikistan, where more Central Asians,
excluding Tajiks, of course, considered Uzbek their native language
than Tajik, and in Osh Oblast (Kirgizia), where the Uzbek influence
was greater than that of the Kirgiz (in spite of the fact that the Kirgiz
population was double that of the Uzbeks). The Uzbeks were also
significant assimilators in Kazakhstan (among the Uyghurs, Dungans,
and, to a lesser extent, other Central Asians). The Tajiks, who appear
to be the principal linguistic assimilators of the Uzbeks in Uzbekistan,
also exerted an influence on the Central Asian Arabs and the Beluchis.

The Uzbeks are also the most dominant of the titular nationalities in their own republics. In Uzbekistan, excluding Uzbeks, there
were over 73,800 speakers of Uzbek as a native language, which was
far ahead of the republic in second place (Kazakhstan), where fewer
than 12,500 persons, excluding Kazakhs, considered the language of
that territory their native language. Among the Central Asian nationalities the Uzbeks are clearly the most significant assimilators.

The 1959 census also revealed a major urban/rural difference in assimilation trends. In urban areas the Russian influence was much stronger than that of the Central Asians, whereas the reverse was true in rural areas. In four of the five Central Asian Union republics (all but Uzbekistan) the Russians outnumbered the titular groups in urban areas. This urban dominance was particularly acute in the capital cities. This Russian dominance is reflected in the linguistic Russification patterns among the titular nationalities in the urban areas and the capital cities of each nationality's own republic. Linguistic Russification reached a significantly higher level in the capital cities.

Preliminary data from the 1970 census indicate some very significant ethnic developments, including a tremendous increase in population among the Central Asians (see Table 6.6). The only nationality that seems out of phase with the others is the Karakalpak. Considering the fact that the majority of Karakalpaks are rural people, and that they reside among the Uzbeks, Kazakhs, and Turkmens, their population increase should have been approximately 50 percent between 1959 and 1970. Apparently, despite favored treatment by the government, they are still subject to strong assimilation pressure.

Among three of the five major Central Asian nationalities (Uzbeks, Tajiks, and Kirgiz) there was an increase after 1959 in the percentage speaking their own languages (see Table 6.7).

TABLE 6.5

Percent of Russian Speakers Among Titular Ethnic Groups in Their Own Republics in Urban Areas and Capital Cities (1959)

Ethnic Group	Percent of Speakers of Russian	
	Urban	Capital City
Uzbek	1.4	1.7
Kazakh	1.8	6.0
Tajik	1.7	4.4
Turkmen	1.9	3.2
Kirgiz	1.2	2.7

Sources: Itogi vsesoiuznoi perepisi naseleniia 1959 goda, Kazakhskaia SSR (Moscow: Gosstatizdat, Tsentral'noe Statisticheskoe Upravlenie SSSR, 1962), pp. 164 and 172; Ibid., Uzbekskaia SSR, pp. 149 and 146; Ibid., Kirgizskaia SSR, pp. 130 and 132; Ibid., Tadzhikskaia SSR (1963), pp. 118 and 122; Ibid., Turkmenskaia SSR (1963), pp. 130 and 134.

TABLE 6.6

Increase in Population Between 1959 and 1970 of Titular
Nationalities (in percent)

Nationalities	Percent
Tajik	53
Uzbek	53
Turkmen	52
Kirgiz	50
Kazakh	46
Karakalpak	36

Source: "Naselenie nashei strany. Soobshchenie tsentral'nogo statisticheskogo Upravlenia pri Sovete Ministrov SSSR o vozrastnoi strukture, urovne obrazovaniia, natsional'nom sostave, iazykakh i istochnikakh sredstv sushchestvovaniia SSSR po dannym vsesoiuznoi perepisi naseleniia na 15 ianvaria 1970 goda," Pravda, April 17, 1971, pp. 2 and 3.

Undoubtedly their rates of natural increases were greater than the rate of their linguistic assimilation. The increases in the percentage of Karakalpak-speaking Karakalpaks, on the other hand, paradoxically reflects the ethnic assimilation of many of the Karakalpaks, who considered other languages to be native.

One cannot measure assimilation of the Dungans or Uyghurs with any degree of accuracy over this time period, because there was a major immigration of Dungans and Uyghurs from China. It is evident, at any rate, from the census that they are subject to strong linguistic assimilation pressure. It is significant that the Beluchi population in Turkmenistan increased from 7,600 to 12,000 (approximate),[8] which indicates that the Beluchis were no longer being assimilated by other nationalities. This was a major reversal of the trend from the previous period.

The 1970 census also revealed some startling information about the knowledge of the Russian language on the part of the Central Asians (see Table 6.8). Except among the Kazakhs, Uyghurs, and Dungans (inhabitants of Kazakhstan) the knowledge of the Russian language remains quite limited. The figure for the Karakalpaks, in fact, was the lowest for any ethnic group in the Soviet Union. This suggests that attempts at spreading Russian, not only as a native language but also as a second language, have not met with much success outside of

TABLE 6.7

Percentage of Ethnic Groups Considering the Language of
Their Nationality as Native Language in
1959 and 1970 in the USSR

Ethnic Group	Population (in thousands)		Percentage Speaking Own Language	
	1959	1970	1959	1970
Uzbek	6015	9195	98.4	98.6
Kazakh	3622	5299	98.4	98.0
Tajik	1397	2136	98.1	98.5
Turkmen	1002	1525	98.9	98.9
Kirgiz	969	1452	98.7	98.8
Karakalpak	173	236	95.0	96.6
Uyghur	95	173	85.0	88.5
Dungan	22	39	95.1	94.3

Source: "Naselenie nashei strany. Soobshchenie tsentral'nogo statisticheskogo Upravlenia pri Sovete Ministrov SSSR o vozrastnoi strukture, urovne obrazovaniia, natsional'nom sostave, iazykakhi i istochnikakh sredstv sushchesvovaniia SSSR po dannym vsesoiuznoi perepisi naseleniia na 15 ianvaria 1970 goda," Pravda, April 17, 1971, pp. 2 and 3.

Kazakhstan. In the Dushanbe press there was even a report about the lack of knowledge of and the poor teaching of the Russian language in Tajikistan. The major complaint was that good universities require the knowledge of Russian, which the Tajik students lack. No such complaints or even remarks concerning the teaching of language in Central Asian schools appeared in the Russian-language Central Asian press surveyed.

The low levels of linguistic Russification among the Central Asians, even in the capitals of the republics, which in general exhibit the highest levels of linguistic Russification, and the fact that only in Kazakhstan is the knowledge of Russian as a second language at all widespread, indicate that the Russians as a ethnic group in general have communicated very little with most Central Asians. It must also be kept in mind that Central Asia is an area that, for religious and commercial purposes, has had a long history of bi- and trilingualism, and that nonindigenous languages have long been spoken; therefore, the recent repetition of the bilingual pattern seen in the spread of Russian

TABLE 6.8

Among Those Considering the Language of Their Own Ethnic
Group as Native, the Percent With a Good Command of the
Russian Language in 1970

Ethnic Group	Percent
Uzbek	14.5
Kazakh	41.8
Tajik	15.4
Turkmen	15.4
Kirgiz	19.1
Karakalpak	10.4
Uyghur	35.6
Dungan	48.0

Source: "Naselenie nashei strany. Soobshchenie tsentral'nogo
statisticheskogo Upravlenia pri Sovete Ministrov SSSR o vozrastnoi
strukture, urovne obrazovaniia, natsional'nom sostave, iazykakh i
istochnikakh sredstv sushchesvovaniia SSSR po dannym vsesoiuznoi
perepisi naseleniia na 15 ianvaria 1970 goda," Pravda, April 17, 1971,
pp. 2 and 3.

as a second language does not have quite the significance that one might
otherwise attach to it. Even if total linguistic Russification were to
take place, as in the examples of the United States and other immigrant
nations or of Ireland, whose natives were linguistically assimilated by
a foreign people, there is no reason to believe that the present ethnic
awareness of the Central Asians vs. Russians would cease to exist.
    The 1970 census also makes it apparent that among the major
nationalities of Central Asia a great ethnic stabilization has occurred.
A stabilization is also taking place among the Karakalpaks, Beluchis,
and Uyghurs, and the Dungans do not appear to be in danger of being
assimilated in the near future. All other minorities have been or are
in the process of being assimilated. Ethnic Russification has been
minimal, and the major influences on the Central Asians come
primarily from other Central Asians. Thus in Central Asia assimilation of the Central Asians has clearly followed religious lines. This
means that there has been no appreciable amount of ethnic assimilation between the Muslims and non-Muslims.
    Both the stabilization of the major ethnic nationalities in place
of pre-1917 multiethnic formations and the assimilation of some of

the minority groups have radically altered the ethnic situation in Central Asia. This ethnic stabilization, accompanied by a very high rate of natural increase, has had a major effect on the nationality question in Central Asia by carrying with it the potential of making the Central Asians more confident and less acquiescent in their dealings with outsiders. Self-assured Central Asians are in a better position to make greater demands upon the central government in both economic and social spheres; at the same time they can be less acquiescent to the demands made upon them by the central authorities.

WHO SHALL BE EDUCATED:
SELECTION AND INTEGRATION
IN SOVIET CENTRAL ASIA
M. Mobin Shorish

Prior to the Russian revolution of 1917 there were no "modern" higher educational establishments in Central Asia. It was only in the late 1920s and early 1930s that some of these institutions came into being.

At this time (1930s) no clear definitions of the functions and the descriptions of structures differentiating the many so-called higher educational establishments were given. For example, there were few major differences between the pedagogical tekhnikums, which were to train teachers for the elementary schools, and the pedagogical institutes, which had the function of creating teachers for the secondary schools. Some tekhnikums had better qualified teachers and even higher grades than some of the institutes. It seems as if the name "institute" or "tekhnikum" was affixed to teacher-training establishments without reflecting either the actual function or the structure of these organizations. Both organizations were poorly equipped, and the level of instruction in both often was the same. Still, those who graduated from the institutes did teach the upper grades while the tekhnikum graduates instructed the pupils in the lower grades. A clear demarcation of the structures and the curricula of the two did not occur until many years later. Nevertheless, it was not until the end of the 1930s that the local graduates from the higher educational establishments in Central Asia joined the labor force; their number was very small in comparison to their European counterparts who had their higher educational training in places outside Central Asia and were competing with local graduates for the available jobs inside it. As Table 7.1 indicates, in higher education as in other levels Central Asians fell behind Russians; and the Tajiks, in turn, not only lagged behind all of the major nationalities in Central Asia but in fact

TABLE 7.1

Selectivity Index of Russians, Tajiks, Uzbeks, and Turkmens
in Higher Educational Establishments of the Soviet Union
for the Years 1928, 1930, and 1933

Nationality	Distribution in the USSR's 1926 Population (in percent) (A)	Distribution of Higher Education Students (in percent) (B)	Selectivity Index (B/A) (C)
Russians	52.9		
1928		56.1	106.0
1930		53.2	100.5
1933		56.0	105.8
Uzbeks	2.7		
1928		0.3	11.1
1930		0.4	14.8
1933		0.9	33.3
Tajiks	0.7		
1928		0.05	7.1
1930		0.1	14.2
1933		0.1	14.2
Turkmens	0.5		
1928		0.05	10.0
1930		0.1	20.0
1933		0.1	20.0

Source: Constructed from data in Sotsialisteskoe stroitel'stvo
SSSR: Statisticheskii ezhegodnik (Moscow: Tsentral'noe Upravlenie
Narodnoe-Khoziaistvennogo Ucheta Gosplana SSSR, 1934), p. 411.

had a selectivity index* that was the lowest among eighteen major nationalities in the USSR.** The Tajiks' position had improved considerably by 1959, when the indexes of national representation (selectivity indexes) for the above-named nationalities in the higher educational establishments were as follows: Russians 113, Uzbeks 76, Tajiks 71, and Turkmens 80.[1]

Table 7.2 gives selectivity indexes for the local populations of Central Asia—that segment of the population that does not have European background and has an Islamic tradition in its past history—and the most numerous Slavs (Russians and Ukrainians) for the academic year 1963-64 by dividing the proportion of students in higher educational establishments by the proportion of their nationality in the 1959 population. This method was chosen because of the lack of congruity between the breakdown for age cohorts in the census and those who "normally" attend different levels of education.

The ratios reported in Table 7.2 are somewhat inflated due to the fact that a lower population base existed in 1959. This is especially true for the local people, who have had higher birth rates than the outsiders and predominantly European population of the area. Nevertheless, this table shows a considerable improvement in the indexes of all nationalities listed relative to their proportions in the higher educational establishments during the first Five-Year Plan. Generally speaking, all of the Central Asian nationalities have advanced greatly, judged by their proportions who have acquired a higher education, relative to many Asian and even some European countries. However, as Table 7.2 demonstrates, the Slavs have kept their leading position in their proportion in higher educational establishments, whereas the Central Asians are still below their theoretical level of unity.

---

*This is an index of selection often used to compare and contrast, usually in education, pupils' positions in a system relative to social class and/or ethnic background. It can be used to give an index of representation of an ethnic group (or social class) according to the particular age cohort represented in an educational institution such as higher education. It is a ratio derived by dividing the proportion of an age cohort of an ethnic group represented in the higher educational establishment, for example, by its proportion in the combined populations of all ethnic groups in a country.

**Kirgiz people were not treated separately from the Kazakhs at this time by Soviet statisticians. Consequently they are not included in the longitudinal comparison of nationalities in this study. In fact, there are few differences between their index and those for other Central Asians, especially Uzbeks and Kazakhs.

TABLE 7.2

Indexes of Selection in Higher Education of Tajik SSR,
Uzbek SSR, Turkmen SSR, and Central Asia by Nationality,
1963-64 Academic Year

Ethnic Group	Tajik SSR	Uzbek SSR	Turkmen SSR	Central Asia
Uzbek	82.6	81.0	40.0	87.7
Tajik	84.4	56.4	—	67.0
Russian	178.0	185.0	141.0	160.3
Kazakh	—	109.7	35.5	94.4
Ukrainian	238.5	191.0	177.0	130.0
Kirgiz	38.4	66.3	—	85.5
Turkmen	—	115.7	103.0	78.8
Others	128.0	106.2	76.5	181.6

Sources: S. P. Tolstov, et al., Narody sredeni Azii i
Kazakhstana, Vol. I, 11 (Moscow: Izdatel'stvo Akademii Nauk SSSR,
1962); Narodnoe khoziaistvo srednei Azii v 1963 g. (Tashkent:
Izdatel'stvo "Uzbekistan," 1964), pp. 7, 324.

Curiously, the Tajiks have remained at the bottom in Central Asia
except in their own republic, where they are above the Uzbeks and
the Kirgiz.

At the same time, the situation in Tajikistan is fairly representative of other Central Asian republics. In general, the Tajiks and
Uzbeks have increased their proportions in Tajik SSR higher educational establishments over the period 1950 to 1960. Their selectivity
index remained still less than unity. Tajiks and Uzbeks, who constituted 76 percent of the Tajik SSR's population in 1959, had selectivity
indexes of 72.2 (1950), 80.3 (1955), and 83.6 (1962).[2] Only Turkmens
seem to have acquired an index higher than unity in their republic,
probably at the expense of other local people. However, this, as we
shall see, is temporary.

Indexes of selection of the local women in Central Asia fall far
below their European sisters and their male counterparts in the
Central Asian higher educational establishments. Again, the situation
in the Tajik SSR is representative of the other republics in Central
Asia.

The female population in the higher educational establishments
of Tajikistan fell below its already underrepresented proportion in

the higher educational establishments during 1950-62. Their proportion to the total student body in higher education fell from an all-
time high of 35.2 percent (selectivity index 70.4 percent) in 1950-51
to 29 percent (selectivity index 58 percent) in the 1962-63 academic
year.[3] The reasons for the lower participation of women in the educational establishments in Central Asia, and especially Tajikistan,
are many. Most of the factors contributing to the relatively small
proportion of women in the educational establishments of Tajikistan
and Central Asia stem from the local customs and traditions having
their roots in antiquity and/or official Islam. This broad and complicated topic has been dealt with elsewhere.[4] The relatively low
participation of the local women in higher education has probably
pushed down the indexes of the entire local population at this level.

       Table 7.3 shows the selectivity indexes of major Central Asian
ethnic groups in the USSR's higher educational establishments (those

TABLE 7.3

Selectivity Indexes of Selected Nationalities in the USSR
Higher Educational Establishments, and Higher Education
Enrollment per 10,000 Population, 1959 and 1970

Ethnic Group	Selectivity Index		Higher Education Enrollment/ 10,000 Population	
	1959	1970	1959	1970
Russian	113	112	72.0	211.0
Ukrainian	78	na	49.6	152.0
Uzbek	76	84.2	48.2	160.0
Kazakh	88	96.0	54.7	185.0
Kirgiz	80	83.3	58.0	168.0
Tajik	71	68.1	47.0	127.0
Turkmen	80	63.5	57.0	148.0

Sources: For 1959, see Nicholas Dewitt, Education and Professional Employment in the USSR (Washington, D.C.: National Science
Foundation, 1961), p. 359; for 1970, see Narodnoe khoziaistvo SSSR v
1969 g. Statisticheskii ezhegodnik. (Moscow: Izdatel'stvo "Statistika,"
1970), p. 690, and "Dar borai strukturai sinnu sol, darajai ma "lumot,
hayati milli, zabon va manbai daromadi aholii SSSR muvofiqi
baruykhatgirii umumiittifoqii aholi to 15 ianvari soli 1970," Tojikistoni
Soveti, April 18, 1971, pp. 3-4; Roman Szporiuk, "The Nations of the
USSR in 1970," Survey, XVII, 4 (Aug., 1971), 94; "Census Data: Age,
Education, Nationality," Current Digest of the Soviet Press, XXIII, 16
(May 18, 1971), 14-18.

situated within and outside Central Asia) in 1959 and 1970. These two years are chosen primarily because the last two Union-wide censuses were taken in 1959 and 1970, which would probably give much more accurate population figures than for any of the intervening years. The growth in the selectivity indexes of these people is not great except for Uzbeks, whose index increased from 76 to 84.2 percent. Even this is not impressive, considering (a) the general development of Uzbekistan, (b) that most Uzbeks have been literate during the past thirty years, and (c) that half of them had acquired some level of secondary or higher education by 1970. The Kirgiz during the same period gained by about 3 percentage points while the Tajiks lost three points. The biggest losers seem to be the Turkmens, who suffered about a seventeen-point decline in their index of representation. The decline of the Tajik and Turkmen indexes is very surprising.

The differential net growth in the population of these people explains some of the decline apparent in their indexes; from 1959 to 1970 the Tajik population grew by 5.5 percent annually, and for the other three nationalities net growth in population averaged about 5.3 percent annually.*[5] Nevertheless, as can be seen from the figures cited, differences in the net growth rates of the four ethnic groups do not explain the differences in their selectivity indexes. Part of the decline in the indexes of Tajiks and Turkmens could possibly be explained by the probable decrease in their representation in the higher educational establishments outside their republics. In the case of the Tajiks, for which data are available, it can be a possibility. In 1965 Tajik students enrolled in Tajikistan's higher educational establishments had a selectivity index of 81.6 percent. This, in turn, is a relatively low index when compared with other major ethnic groups within Tajikistan, who in 1965 had the following indexes: Uzbeks, 87.4 percent; Russians, 180.2 percent; Ukrainians, 264 percent; others, 123 percent.**[6]

The indexes for these USSR minorities presented in Table 7.3 are probably higher than those in almost any country that has large minorities, including the U.S., Canada, or Western Europe. Table 7.4

---

*All of these growth rates do not take into account migration into and out of these republics. Growth rates are treated in the Union-wide census as if generated by net birth rates within each republic.

**The indexes were constructed by combining percentages of each of these nationalities in Tajikistan's population of 1959 and 1970 and then dividing them by two, 1965 being about midpoint in the decade 1959-70.

TABLE 7.4

Selectivity Indexes in Higher Education (Undergraduate) of
Major Ethnic Groups (1968-69 Academic Year)
in the United States

Ethnic Group	Proportion in Population, 1969 (A)	Proportion in Higher Education, 1968 (B)	Selectivity Index (B/A)
Whites	82.5	90.5	110.0
Blacks	11.1	6.0	54.0
American Indians	0.4	0.6	150.0
Orientals (includes Filipinos and others in addition to those having Japanese and Chinese background)	1.0	1.0	100.0
Population of Spanish origin (includes Puerto Ricans, Cubans, Mexicans, Latin Americans, etc.)	5.0	1.9	38.0
All "nonwhites"	17.5	9.5	54.3

Sources: 1970 Census of Population. General Population
Characteristics. United States Summary, PC (1)-B1 (Washington,
D.C.: U.S. Government Printing Office, 1972), p. 262; Current
Population Reports. Population Characteristics, Series P-20, No.
213 (Washington, D.C.: U.S. Government Printing Office, February
1971), pp. 2-4; Undergraduate Enrollment by Ethnic Group in Feder-
ally Funded Institutions of Higher Education (Washington, D.C.: Dept.
of HEW, Office for Civil Rights, Fall 1968), p. 171.

shows selectivity indexes of major ethnic groups in the United States
higher educational establishments for the academic year 1968-69.
Probably there are no major ethnic groups in the USSR with indexes
as low as those reported here for the blacks and "population of
Spanish origin." No attempt was made to do a longitudinal study of
these U.S. minorities. It is possible that the gain acquired by the
American minorities is proportionately lower than that acquired by
the minorities in the Soviet Union during the period under study.

Although more Central Asians are seemingly enrolled in the higher educational establishments of the USSR, they are probably much more unevenly distributed among available fields of instruction than their American counterparts. Most Central Asian students admitted to higher educational establishments seem to frequent the faculties of social sciences and humanities much more than the technical fields. In Tajikistan students in the field of education alone constituted more than 82 percent and 70 percent of those graduating from higher educational establishments of the republic in 1955 and 1965 (Table 7.5).

Probably the requirement of fluency in the Russian language for admission to many of the faculties in the higher educational establishments of Central Asia has kept a great many local boys and girls from attending the faculties that concentrate on technical and natural sciences. This may in turn have somewhat affected their selectivity indexes in higher education by narrowing their options for various career futures.

Also, familiarity with material in terms of students' cultural and traditional backgrounds has influenced flocking of local students into the social sciences and humanities. This in turn contributed to the Central Asians' filling technical and managerial posts less and less in the Soviet occupational structure. As a result it has led to an oversupply of local people trained in social sciences and humanities. The problem of unemployment has apparently become alarming enough in the Tajik SSR to cause a republic level council to be formed (May 1970) to find jobs for these and other young people.[7] The problem of unemployment among the Central Asian people is discussed in more detail in the following pages.

Taking into account the ratio of students enrolled in higher educational establishments of the Central Asian republics per 10,000 of their population (Table 7.3), these republics have surpassed in their level of educational development almost any nation in the world. In 1966 the enrollment (full- and part-time) ratios in higher educational establishments per 10,000 people for selected countries were as follows: France 100, West Germany 73, Sweden 99, United Kingdom 81, Turkey 30, U.S. 282.[8]

A comparison with countries neighboring Soviet Central Asia is of special interest, since Afghanistan founded a university in Kabul about twenty years before the one established in Tajikistan in 1948. The Afghan ratio of enrolled students in higher educational establishments of the country per 10,000 population ranged from a very low figure of 0.9 in 1958 to a low of 3.2 in 1968 (Table 7.6).

Table 7.7 shows the educational attainment of each of the Central Asian republics and the whole USSR for 1939, 1959, and 1970. There has been a narrowing of the educational differential that existed

TABLE 7.5

Graduates of Tajik Higher Educational Establishments According to
Field of Specialization for Selected Years

Field of Specialization	1940		1950		1955		1960		1965	
All graduates	280	100.0%	855	100.0%	1,624	100.0%	2,360	100.0%	3,173	100.0%
Engineering-industrial*	—	—	—	—	—	—	—	—	289	9.1
Agriculture	27	9.6	60	7.0	138	8.5	376	16.0	424	13.4
Medical and health	—	—	184	21.5	142	8.7	231	9.8	246	7.8
Education (universities, pedagogical and teachers institutes)	253	90.4	611	71.5	1,344	82.8	1,753	74.2	2,214	69.7

*Includes also construction, transportation, communications, and trade.

Source: Narodnoe khoziaistvo tadzhikskoi SSR v 1965 g. (Dushanbe: Izdatel'stvo "Statistika," 1966), pp. 232–233, and Narodnoe khoziaistvo tadzhikskoi SSR v 1959 g. (Dushanbe: Izdatel'stvo "Statistika," 1960), p. 244.

TABLE 7.6

Afghanistan: Population, Enrollment in Higher Education, and Higher Education Enrollment per 10,000 Population

Year	Population (millions)	Students Enrolled in Higher Education	Higher Education Enrollment per 10,000 Population
1958	13.3	1,300	0.9
1959	13.6	1,500	1.0
1961	14.0	2,000	1.4
1965	15.1	3,400	2.2
1967	15.8	4,300	2.7
1968	16.1	5,200	3.2

Source: Statistical Yearbook for Asia and the Far East (Bangkok: United Nations, 1969), p. 11.

TABLE 7.7

Educational Levels of the USSR and the Central Asian Populations (Local and Outsiders Combined) Who Were Ten Years and Older in the Labor Force (1939, 1959, and 1970)

Administrative Units	Number in the Population (Ten Years and Older) Having Some Level of Secondary or Higher Education per 10,000 Population			Number in the Labor Force Having Some Level of Secondary or Higher Education per 10,000 of the Labor Force		
	1939	1959	1970	1939	1959	1970
USSR	1,080	3,610	4,830	1,230	4,330	6,530
Uzbek SSR	550	3,520	4,560	610	4,470	6,610
Kirgiz SSR	460	3,420	4,520	560	4,290	6,430
Tajik SSR	400	3,520	4,200	450	4,070	6,020
Turkmen SSR	650	3,820	4,750	780	4,970	6,820

Sources: "Dar borai strukturai sinnu sol, darajai ma''lumot, hayati milli, zabon va manbai daromadi aholii SSSR muvofiqi baruykhatgirii umumiittifoqii aholi to 15 ianvari soli 1970," Tojikistoni Soveti, April 18, 1971, pp. 3-4; "Aholii respublikai mo: Akhboroti Upravleniiai Markazii Statistikii Nazdi Soveti Vazironi RSS Tojikiston dar borai strukturai sinnu sol, darajai ma''lumot, hayati milli, zabon va manbai daromadi aholii RSS Tojikiston muvofiqu baruykhatgirii umumiittifoqii aholii to 15 ianvari soli 1970," Tojikistoni Soveti, May 6, 1971, pp. 1 and 3.

in 1939 between the Central Asian republics and the USSR, presumably
as an effect of Soviet efforts to equalize educational levels. By 1959,
a period of only twenty years, Turkmenistan exceeded the average
for the USSR (for populations ten years and older) having some level
of secondary or higher education. (This is not a satisfactory classification as used by the Soviets. Essentially, it lumps together all
those who have had eight years or more of education.) The other
three republics seem to be not too far behind Turkmenistan. The
figures for the labor force of these republics compare even more
favorably with the USSR average for the same year. Then, Turkmenistan and Uzbekistan exceeded the USSR average while Kirgizistan
was not too far behind. This may not have reflected the level of
educational attainment of the local Central Asians who were in the
labor force. In fact, it may well have been due to the inflow of relatively well-educated outside workers who came into Central Asia
attracted by the better climate and availability of work. If the labor
force operating the Nurak Hydroelectric Plant and Dushanbe Textile
Mill can be considered representative of Tajikistan's overall industrial
labor force (which presumably requires a higher level of education
than those engaged in some primary industries), then the local people
(Tajiks and Uzbeks) have not fared well in gaining employment in
these industries. In 1964 they constituted about 30 and 25 percent
of the labor force in the Nurak Hydroelectric Plant and Dushanbe
Textile Mills, respectively, whereas workers having their origins
west of the Urals constituted 66.2 percent of the workers in
Nurak and 68.8 percent of the labor force in the Dushanbe Textile
Mill.[9]

Nevertheless, by 1970 more than half of the labor force in the
USSR and Central Asia had achieved some level of secondary or
higher education. Only the Tajik and Kirgiz SSRs have a labor force
still below the USSR average in their educational achievement. There
is little doubt that any one of these republics possesses a sufficient
quantity of developed human capital (judged by schooling alone, although other components of human capital such as health are also
well developed) to reduce the need for immigration from the remainder
of the Soviet Union. This reduction seems to be already in progress.
Of the net increase of about 9.8 million people in Central Asia between
1959 and 1970, about 1.2 million came from outside of these five
republics.[10] This accounts for about 12 percent of the total net growth
in the population of the area. As a result, the Russian and other
European populations declined in 1970 from their proportion in the
1959 population of these republics. The Russian share decreased
from 13.5 percent in 1959 to 12.5 percent in 1970 in the population
of the Uzbek SSR. Figures for other republics are similar: Kazakh
SSR, from 43.2 percent to 42.8 percent; Tajik SSR, from 13.3 percent

to 11.9 percent; Kirgiz SSR, from 30.2 percent to 29.2 percent; Turkmen SSR, from 17.3 percent to 14.5 percent. In general, the Kazakhs, Uzbeks, Turkmens, Kirgiz, and Tajiks have augmented their proportions in the population of their republics by percentage points that ranged from a low of 2.6 for the Kazakhs to a high of 4.7 for the Turkmens during the decade 1959-70.[11]

Nevertheless, the immigration of Europeans into Central Asia, which greatly contributed to its economic development, has now become a problem adversely affecting the local people, in their acquisition of places not only in the higher educational establishments but also in the labor force. The following will further explain this question and the unemployment problem of the indigenous Central Asian people:

1. The inflow of relatively skilled immigrants and/or "floating" non-Central Asian workers is motivated by the existence of better-paying jobs, relatively better climate, availability of potential husbands, or all three, among others,

Many local men who are unable or unwilling to pay the "bride price" and undergo the traditional and customary parts of the marriage, marry European girls (see Appendix to this chapter). For them there is no bride price to be paid, and in addition some of these girls left the Ural towns in search of husbands and jobs (in that order) to begin with.[12]

As a result of their having better training in the Russian language and technical skills, the newcomers can effectively compete with local men and women for the available positions in the economy, especially in the urban centers. This inflow, in turn, has pushed out of the labor market many local people whose quality of formal education or on-the-job training is not on a par with that of European immigrants. As a result, the surplus of trained local men and women is forced to remain in the rural areas and occupy traditional roles.

2. A relatively high birth rate among the local people (which might be able, in the long run, to keep the European immigrants from becoming the major "ethnic group" in Central Asia) has increased the pressure on the available occupations in the rural areas and decreased the average physical productivity per man on the farm. Increased mechanization in the countryside as a result of the directives of the September 1965 plenum of the Communist Party of the Soviet Union has compounded this problem further.

3. The entrance into the labor force of the post-World War II children, which has already shown its effect on many areas of occupation, especially farming, is causing a general shift of the supply curve to the right, particularly among women and juveniles. This problem has been aggravated further by a hesitancy on the part of the managers of farms and factories alike to hire juveniles (ages sixteen-eighteen) regardless of ethnicity because there are too many restrictive laws regarding their employment and treatment.

4. Reluctance on the part of the local population to emigrate from their homelands to other parts of the Soviet Union results, in general, in proportionately many more local people than immigrants being unemployed, underemployed, and occupants of traditional roles in the rural areas. The large urban centers of the republics, where almost all immigrants reside, have become so Europeanized that living in them represents almost a totally new experience for a Central Asian farmer. Rural-urban differences exist, as in all countries, but the economic difference is a less crucial deterrent to rural-urban migration than is the cultural gap, which seems to be the most important factor apart from the scarcity of jobs in the cities.

Probably as a response to these four problems and the lower selectivity indexes of the local people in higher education, a new educational policy has been adopted by the Tajik SSR (and possibly other Central Asian republics), which may have an immediate effect in remedying the situation. According to this decision any qualified Tajik or Uzbek student can follow any area of specialization in higher educational establishments of the republic without being fluent or even being acquainted with the Russian language.[13]

This recent development, in combination with a reduction in the rate of inflow of the immigrants into the area, the establishment of quotas for the local population in the occupational structures of the economy, better allocation of the existing labor force of Central Asia by means of material incentives, adequate housing, and better and more realistic wage schedules, and the extension and expansion of the educational (academic and vocational as well as on-the-job training) opportunities for the local population, will not only increase the selectivity indexes of the local people in higher education but will also reduce existing problems in the labor markets of the republics.

Such an institutional arrangement would reinforce further the cultural interpenetration of the Europeans and the local people in process in Central Asia. It is posited here that the European and the local cultures will continue to flourish side by side for many years to come. The situation is analogous to that of Poland when it was partitioned and ruled by Germany, Russia, and Austria for more than a century without losing its "Polishness."

APPENDIX

The following is an abridged version of an article written in response to a person who inquired about the high cost of marriage in a letter to the Tajik cultural newspaper Maorif va madaniyat. The newspaper asked the well-known Tajik writer Jalol Ikromi, a long-time campaigner for the emancipation of women, to answer it.*

"The High Cost of Marriage"

In Central Asia parents are the most important obstacles in the path of the emancipation of women. Parents, many of whom can be Party members and some of whom have even fought for women's freedom, are preventing progress toward the full equality of women with men. This is due to the greediness of parents who ask exorbitant amounts of money for their daughter when she is ready for marriage. As a result, many men cannot afford to get married. For example, fathers want their daughters to be very comfortable in their married lives; as a result, the "price" goes higher and higher as time passes. They ask for ten to twenty velvet dresses, two golden earrings (leaf type), two kholak (from khol, the beauty mark) earrings, five gold rings, one diamond ring, two bracelets, one gold watch with jewel movement, three strings of pearls. All of these (with the exception of the dresses, of which the bride wears only one) should be on the bride on her wedding night. At the wedding the bridegroom is asked to provide at least four sheep, one cow, five goats, and forty chickens. [He should also provide] two sacks of rice, five sacks of flour, two khum (a tanned sheep or goat skin in which, in that part of the world, are stored liquids such as water, milk, butter, and, in some places, wine) of cooking oil to be consumed on the wedding night. Also [he is expected] to give the numerous relatives of the bride [especially] gifts of all sorts so that the news of the groom's generosity reaches all corners in the cities and villages.

There are several stages (in the form of huge feasts) prior to the actual wedding. The most important of these feasts are three: the musafidoni (literally, for the white-haired ones, elders), the dukhtaroni (literally, for the girls), and the most important one of all, which is called tui kalon (the big wedding). These expenditures cannot be borne by many people. Consequently, many young men are forced to remain single.

---

*Jalol Ikromi, "Dar fikri imruzu fardo: Navisanda va hayot," Maorif va madaniyat, June 20, 1968, p. 3.

LEADERSHIP AND
NATIONALITY:
A COMPARISON OF
UZBEKISTAN AND KIRGIZIA
John Hanselman

The course of nationality relations within the Kirgiz and Uzbek Soviet Socialist Republics is and will be affected by the success (or lack of success) the indigenous Central Asians experience in their attempts to follow careers within the leadership of their republics. In 1970 Central Asians made up approximately 2 of the 3 million people living in the Kirgiz SSR and 10 of the 12 million in the Uzbek SSR. It seems probable that a low degree of access to leadership positions for these Central Asians would lead to the growth of discontent, both for economic and political reasons, among the Central Asians qualified for such positions. This dissatisfaction could easily focus upon the non-Central Asians, or "outsiders," who hold executive positions desired by indigenes. The object of this analysis, therefore, is to learn the degree to which the Central Asian nationalities are integrated into the political and economic hierarchies of their part of the Soviet Union in order to determine from these findings how the nationality question in Central Asia, seen as a set of relationships among Russians, indigenous, and nonindigenous nationalities, may be affected by such patterns of integration.

Many theorists have dealt with the problem of such integration as it relates to the development of a unified political community claiming the loyalty of its citizens. Given the limited data available from the Soviet Union, the theories on integration that are of greatest relevance to the study of Soviet Central Asia are those proposing that one of the crucial prerequisites for the creation of a viable integrated state is a multinational political leadership sharing common values and participating equally in the government of the state.[1] This type of analysis—one that focuses on the staffing of government positions and on attitudes—can be carried out through a survey of the local press, for it is possible to discover in these publications both an indication of local attitudes and the identity of incumbents in republic offices. For a long-term understanding of the relationships among the elements of nationality, leadership, and integration it would be necessary to conduct a study over time to determine trends in their development. By dealing with a single contemporary period, 1971, this study is intended to show the current situation in Kirgizia and Uzbekistan and to assess its implications for the nationality question.

Integration, as it relates to the Central Asian nationalities, can best be discussed in terms of the existing territorial political units. It is in these administrative units that the indigenous people can be expected to have the most ready access to leadership, and it is here that the lack of such access would be most visible. Leadership positions in the economy of these republics range from the local level of kolkhoz chairman or factory director on up to republic minister. Within the republic Party and state administration there are three main levels: the lowest is represented by the raion or district level, the oblast or province constitutes the middle level, with the republic being the highest. The staffing of this network of jobs provides the outline from which the framework for the first part of this study is patterned.

Data used in the following analysis were gathered from materials appearing in 1971 in the local Russian-language newspapers: Sovetskaia Kirgiziia published in Kirgizia and Pravda Vostoka published in Uzbekistan. Of particular interest was information concerning the delegates to two republic bodies: the highest legislative body of each republic, the Supreme Soviet, elected in July 1971, and the Central Committee of each republic's Communist Party, chosen in early 1971.[2] These two political bodies serve well as units of analysis because they constitute comparable structures in each republic and the local press provides adequate information about them. Also, delegates to each can be said to represent a sample of the positions considered important by the political leaders of the republics. The Central Committees are made up of the Party members deemed important enough to warrant membership, either because of their position within the Party or state structure or because of their expertise in areas of government (with the addition of some representatives of the factory and agricultural workers within the Party membership). The Supreme Soviets of the republics play a limited operational role within the government; their primary function is to confer greater legitimacy upon the state by providing the basis for the claim that the leaders rule in the name of the people. A position within the hierarchy of government councils, the raion, gorod (city), oblast, and republic soviets, is the only one to which men in authoritative positions are formally and directly elected by the population—

the republic Supreme Soviet is the highest of these bodies. Election to the Supreme Soviet symbolizes the status of an executive's job within the state structure, for it has been found advisable to legitimize this position by having its incumbent elected in the system of soviets. Therefore, the positions represented by the membership of the Central Committees and Supreme Soviets seem to provide a sample of the leadership in Uzbekistan and Kirgizia of sufficient breadth and depth to allow for a comparison of the nationality aspect of that leadership between the two republics.

In analyzing the data regarding members of these two political bodies, the Turkic or Muslim forms of some names provided the basis for the determination of nationality. In a large majority of cases both the first and last names were available, making such ethnic identification a reliable means of distinguishing between Central Asians and non-Central Asians.* Since this study is concerned with the integration of Central Asians as a whole into Soviet society and institutions, the sample for each republic will not be divided into each individual nationality. It is important to note, however, that there are substantial numbers of various Central Asian ethnic groups in both Kirgizia and Uzbekistan: non-Uzbek Central Asian nationalities made up approximately 12 percent of the population in the Uzbek SSR in 1970, while non-Kirgiz Central Asians constituted approximately 14 percent of the population of Kirgizia.[3] Again employing personal names as a guide, it is possible to determine the ethnic identity of Russian, Ukrainian, and other members, but for the present purpose it is sufficient to place all such "outsider" groups under the heading "non-Central Asian."

A profile of the two current Supreme Soviets may be outlined as follows: both were elected on June 13, 1971, with the election results appearing in the June 17 editions of the Russian-language republic newspapers; 458 delegates were elected to the Uzbek Supreme Soviet and 337 to the Kirgiz. When the delegates' names have been divided according to nationality, it is evident that Central Asians and non-Central Asians sit in the republic Supreme Soviets in roughly the same proportion as their percentage of the total population would warrant. Non-Central Asians comprise approximately one-third of the Kirgiz SSR population and 31.4 percent of the Supreme Soviet; in

---

*Within this paper Tatars are included in the category "Central Asian" even though they are actually an "outsider" group, for it was not possible to distinguish them from the indigenous people systematically on the basis of name analysis. However, the Tatar population in Central Asia is not large enough to affect the findings significantly.

Uzbekistan the figures are approximately 14 percent of the population and 19 percent of the delegates. Also, in both Supreme Soviets the percentage of delegates from manual occupations is the same: approximately 45 percent of the members are factory workers, laborers, or farmers—both sovkhozniks and kolkhozniks (see Table 8.1). Among representatives drawn from that labor force, Central Asians remain proportionately underrepresented in both republics, with outsiders comprising 40 percent of the work force. The difference between the figures for farmers elected to the Kirgiz and Uzbek Supreme Soviets seems particularly important. In the Uzbek Supreme Soviet outsiders make up less than 1 percent of the farmers (actually, the figure is 1 out of 127), whereas in the Kirgiz case non-Central Asians constitute 18 percent of the farmers elected as delegates to the Supreme Soviet.

Even more relevant to this inquiry are the numbers of elected delegates who hold positions of executive power within the two republics. Executive positions embrace those jobs, either elective or appointive, that involve some decision-making powers and the supervision of the work of others. This category includes executives on or above the level of factory director and kolkhoz chairman. Using such criteria for defining Central Asian employment levels, 55 percent of the delegates to the Kirgiz and Uzbek Supreme Soviets can be considered to function as executives. Within this percentage, non-Central Asians overrepresent their category throughout both republics: in Uzbekistan more than 23 percent are outsiders, but in Kirgizia the figure runs above 38 percent. This ethnic underrepresentation of Central Asians in executive positions appears most pronounced in the factory management of both republics. Only 16 percent of the factory managers in the Kirgiz sample turn out to be Central Asians, while Central Asian managers make up 56 percent of the Uzbek sample.

Paralleling the great incidence of outsiders found among the farmers in Kirgizia, a significant number of non-Central Asians may be seen both on the raion level of administration and, below that, in charge of collective or state farms. Outsiders make up one-third of the kolkhoz and sovkhoz chairmen in the Kirgiz Supreme Soviet. One-half of the outsiders involved in administration on the oblast level or below serve on local, raion committees. A similar distribution of non-Central Asians cannot be found in the Uzbek sample, for there is only one non-Central Asian sovkhoz chairman and only one outsider in the Party or state administration below the oblast level. There is a striking contrast, then, in the location of outsiders in the two republics. In Kirgizia a marked non-Central Asian presence is noticeable in local positions, whereas in Uzbekistan outsiders appear to be concentrated on the oblast level or above.

TABLE 8.1

Distribution of Delegates to the 1971 Uzbek and Kirgiz Supreme Soviets by Occupation

	Executive Occupations			Manual Occupations				
	Republic Level Party and State	Oblast, City and Raion Party and State	Factory Managers	Sovkhoz and Kolkhoz Chairmen	Farmers	Factory Workers	Other*	Total
Kirgiz Supreme Soviet delegates:								
Central Asians	30	44	2	18	94	23	20	231
non-Central Asians	25	16	10	8	20	15	12	106
Total								337
Uzbek Supreme Soviet delegates:								
Central Asians	55	72	11	33	126	46	24	367
non-Central Asians	16	24	8	1	1	31	10	91
Total								458

*Included in "other" are such occupations as artists, writers, dancers, and soldiers.

Sources: "Spisok deputatov verkhovnogo soveta kirgizskoi SSR," Sovetskaia Kirgiziia, June 17, 1971, pp. 3-4; "Uspekha vam, izbranniki naroda!" Pravda Vostoka, June 17, 1971, pp. 3-4.

Non-Central Asians are represented out of proportion to their numbers in both the Party and state apparatus among executives sitting in the two republics' Supreme Soviets. However, within the Uzbek SSR sample, outsiders tend to be concentrated in Party work, although in Kirgizia they are more apt to be found in the state administration.

This pattern in the non-Central Asian presence throughout the Party and state bureaucracy of Uzbekistan and Kirgizia reveals itself more clearly when the membership of the republics' Party Central Committees is scrutinized. Central Committee membership may be related to positions of real power within the republics more closely than are seats in the Supreme Soviets. This is because the Central Committees hold a position at the center of the Party decision-making apparatus. The Supreme Soviet is primarily a formal structure that merely approves legislation referred to it, but the Central Committee of the Communist Party forms a pool of advisers who can be consulted on policy formation. The Central Committee serves as a medium through which the party leadership can exchange information with experts in various fields and can draw upon its members for criticism concerning proposed policies. Presumably for the purpose of this information exchange, the Central Committee co-opts technicians and others into itself because of their expert knowledge or because they occupy a vital position within the state or economic hierarchies, and not as a result of their political standing. The distinction to be made in the Party Central Committee membership, then, should come between those members who are recruited into the Central Committee because of their Party positions and those who are co-opted because of their important place outside of the Party structure. The number of Central Asians in each category becomes the significant factor, for this reflects the degree to which the indigenous people of Central Asia take part in the control of both the party and state administration of the area.[4]

The two Central Committees now under consideration were chosen at Party congresses held in Kirgizia and Uzbekistan in March 1971, prior to the 24th Congress of the Communist Party of the Soviet Union. The Uzbek Central Committee has 162 members and the Kirgiz 115. When the membership of these committees is divided according to nationality, the data show that non-Central Asians constitute a proportionately large section of both. However, among those identified by the position they hold within the republics, a clear contrast appears between the membership of the Uzbek and Kirgiz Central Committees. In the Uzbek sample 75 percent of the non-Central Asians hold Party positions. The remaining 25 percent of outsiders, those co-opted into the Central Committee, constitute only 11 percent of the total number co-opted; Central Asians comprise

89 percent of those brought into the Central Committee from posts other than political ones. In contrast, outsiders in the Kirgiz Central Committee show up prominently in both types of membership (40 percent of each), with an almost even distribution between them. From these figures it seems that Central Asians in Uzbekistan may play a significantly larger role in the state administration than they do in Kirgizia's bureaucracy. Even though non-Central Asians constitute a comparatively small number in state and economic posts, such outsiders stand very high in positions of control within the Party. Non-Central Asians supply the Second Secretary of the Central Committee of the Communist Party of Uzbekistan, the Second Secretaries in at least ten of the eleven oblast Party committees in Uzbekistan, and the deputy chairmen of the oblast soviet executive committees in at least seven of the eleven oblasts. This corresponds to the findings in a recent study of Tajikistan in the 1940s and 50s where non-Central Asians were found to occupy "control" positions within the republic.[5]

Other factors involved in the integration of Central Asian people into the political and economic system of the Soviet Union as a whole include education and levels of skills possessed by the population. From the figures given above dealing with the labor and management involved in factories, it is evident that non-Central Asians are significantly overrepresented in those enterprises. Such findings corroborate a recent Soviet study dealing with urbanization and ethnographic processes.[6] The same study maintains that in areas such as Central Asia, which were underdeveloped when the Russian revolution of 1917 took palce, the need for new administrative personnel and labor created by the industrialization process led to the immigration of Russians, Ukrainians, and other non-Central Asians to fill these openings. The lack of indigenous personnel qualified for positions within an industrializing system brought "outsiders" in to fulfill the system's requirements. As a result, the current distribution of positions within the economy between Central Asians and non-Central Asians may be seen as the outcome of a natural process rather than of a discriminatory policy on the part of outsiders.

Figures are available for 1963 showing the distribution, by nationality, of specialists who have acquired special secondary or higher education and who are employed in the economy. When these data are analyzed, it becomes evident that non-Central Asians comprise a dominant portion of these technicians. In this area of training, outsiders constitute almost 60 percent of the total number of specialists in Kirgizia and almost 40 percent in Uzbekistan. This disproportionately large share of outsiders found among the specialists in Central Asia is also reflected in the ethnic composition of the student body attending higher educational institutions during the academic year

1963-64. Non-Central Asians supplied almost half of all such students in Kirgizia and provided approximately one-fourth of those in Uzbekistan.[7] This substantial proportion of outsiders in Central Asian higher education suggests the probability that non-Central Asians have continued since 1964 to be dominant in positions of executive authority within the economy. These two sets of figures tend to support the claims of Soviet authorities that insufficient numbers of Central Asians in Kirgizia and Uzbekistan have yet to attain education and skills to administer their own economies.

Besides levels of education and skill, other factors pertinent to the integration of Central Asians into the political and economic hierarchy of the Soviet Union include cultural values and standards associated with industrial mass society. If Central Asia continues to industrialize, the successful integration of the indigenous population into technically advanced society will be contingent upon the adaptation of traditional value structures to conform with the needs of contemporary organization and society. When an individual is faced with a job involving incompatible or conflicting standards, his ability to utilize his capabilities within the industrial system is hindered.[8]

Manifestations of such cultural problems involving values and standards incompatible with modern industrial society or continued integration receive attention in both the Kirgiz and Uzbek press.[9] In both republics the need to raise the political consciousness of Party as well as non-Party people in order to eliminate needless bureaucratization and to raise productivity levels is frequently discussed in print. Such writings stress the necessity to improve the level of efficiency and rationality in the productive and administrative systems through an increased awareness and understanding by their personnel of societal needs and conditions. This type of public debate also appears in the central press of the Soviet Union, reflecting a problem facing the Soviet Union as a whole, including Central Asia.

Two types of related discussion that appear in the Kirgiz press rarely emerge in Uzbek publications. These debates deal with aspects of cultural standards that affect the Kirgiz SSR's political and social systems. The first has to do with the persistence of traditional culture within Kirgizia, in forms that hinder the modernization of the republic. Turdakun U. Usubaliev, the First Secretary of the Kirgiz Communist Party, stated in his report to the Kirgiz Party Congress in March 1971 that the Party and educational structures in Kirgizia must "overcome such vestiges of the past as harmful customs and morals, tendencies toward private ownership, feudal and bey-type [traditional] attitudes toward women, drunkenness, hooliganism, religious prejudices and superstition."[10] The Party should strive, he felt, to increase labor discipline, decreasing absenteeism and improving the fulfillment of the economic plan on schedule through an exchange of values between the local traditional culture and the more advanced Soviet culture. In the Party Secretary's view only those parts of traditional culture that are congruent with the needs of contemporary society should be maintained.

The second aspect of cultural standards important to modernization and political integration has to do with relations between ethnic groups. The need for friendship and cooperation between nationalities or between them and outsiders receives much more public attention in Kirgizia than in Uzbekistan. Uzbek SSR references tend to repeat formulaic praise for Leninist nationality policy and brotherly cooperation among the people of the Soviet Union. In sharp contrast, the Kirgiz press emphasizes the need for friendship between ethnic groups. In his report to the Party Congress Kirgiz First Secretary Usubaliev repeatedly spoke of the Party's obligation to strengthen the "friendship of peoples" by stressing contemporary aspects of that friendship rather than by references to historical or pre-Soviet eras.[11] Similar emphasis upon the development of cooperation on the basis of contemporary events appears in discussions about bringing up "internationalists" (citizens without ethnic prejudices) in Kirgiz newspapers.[12] Such reports discuss the themes to be used in promoting internationalism among the ethnic groups located in Kirgizia. The basic premise underlying these themes is that common ideological and historical ties have linked the nationalities, as well as the Russians and the nationalities, from the time of the October 1917 revolution to the present. The openness of such discussions in the Kirgiz press conveys an idea that there is some degree of friction between the nationalities and the outsiders that can be lessened through the development of a common culture and value system. However, this is not meant to indicate that such problems do not emerge on the pages of the Uzbek press, but merely to draw attention to the fact that reports about such problems seem more prevalent in the Kirgiz newspapers.

Finally, the evidence has shown that in both Kirgizia and Uzbekistan Central Asians lack representation among leadership positions in numbers equal to their percentage of the population. Yet Central Asians within Uzbekistan appear to be more equitably represented in executive positions than those in Kirgizia. This more favorable position of Central Asians in Uzbekistan is also reflected in educational and cultural fields. Hence, it would seem as though the Central Asians in Uzbekistan had achieved a higher degree of integration into the political and economic systems of their republic than those who live in the Kirgiz SSR.

If Central Asian managers and trained personnel successfully enter into top posts in their republics, this could strengthen a movement or tendency on the part of the indigenous people toward a merger with the dominant political and cultural systems. However, outsiders still hold a large number of major posts in both Uzbekistan and Kirgizia. This non-Central Asian presence could undermine the political integration already achieved in Central Asia, especially in Uzbekistan, for the Central Asians in Uzbekistan are perhaps even more aware of the positions they do not fill. This supposition is related to the theory that discontent can result from the frustration of rising expectations. As Central Asians become more educated, and adapt themselves to industrial society, they could reasonably expect greater career opportunities in the state and economic hierarchy of their republics. Once it became evident that these positions were not available thanks to the existence of non-Central Asian incumbents, ethnic friction could result. This type of ethnic conflict appears most likely in Uzbekistan, where outsiders retain controlling positions in the party and a large number of economic enterprises and hierarchies.

The state of ethnic relations in Kirgizia is modified by the presence of non-Central Asians on all levels of Kirgiz life, from the kolkhoz to the ministry. Whereas outsiders appear in Uzbekistan in industrial and urban executive positions, in Kirgizia non-Central Asians are prominent in the rural as well as urban population. The presence of this non-Central Asian population in rural areas, which are traditionally conservative in any country, could create the ethnic friction that is implicit in recent discussions in the Kirgiz press.

From the materials surveyed it does not appear as though there is cooperation or integration taking place between the leadership of the Kirgiz and Uzbek republics. In each case, the focus of the executive's career remains within a single republic. This narrow focus renders unlikely executive support of or belief in the creation or maintenance of regional integration. Whereas scholars or humanists in the two republics might be concerned with a more general Central Asian unity, the executive's career is centered in the various bureaucracies of the Soviet system, which are organized on a republic basis. This difference could give rise to tension within the intelligentsia of the Central Asian nationalities between technicians and humanists. Unless interregional bureaucracies and consequent lateral mobility emerge, it seems unlikely that a Central Asian unity will emerge among executives, unless it be a unity forged through the presence of a common adversary, the outsiders. Just as there does not appear to be a movement toward a merger of Central Asian nationalities into a single group, so there does not seem to be overt hostility or exclusiveness among them. Although executives may not have mobility across republic borders, the pre-Soviet patterns of ethnic distribution persist with Central Asians of all nationalities living and working in both the Kirgiz and Uzbek republics.

TAJIK AND UZBEK
NATIONALITY IDENTITY:
THE NON-LITERARY ARTS
Eden Naby

Development of nationality arts has played a vital part in the whole nationality question of the Soviet Union, because distinctive aspects of culture, reflected in language, literature, literary heritage, music, painting, dress, local customs, and the like, form one of the components of a "nation" (nationality) as defined in the Soviet Union. Stalin's early definition of "nation" and that of T. Burmistrova in Theory of the Socialist Nation (1970), while they differ in some respects, both emphasize "community of culture" and "nationality culture."[1] Therefore, in order to assure the separateness of recogni ethnic nationalities, particularly on the Union Republic and Autonomou Republic levels, effort has been exerted toward developing distinct Soviet nationality arts.

In differentiating groups along ethnic nationality lines in Central Asia, Soviet policy has relied heavily on creating, emphasizing, or enlarging those cultural differences that existed historically. Langua provides the basic cultural division among Central Asians, and while it remains the cornerstone of "nationality" identity, particularly between Tajiks and Uzbeks, attempts have been set under way to channel the nonliterary arts—music, dance, painting, sculpture, film, and theater—into "nationality" slots as well.

Despite the significance attached to the issue of creating culturally distinct nationalities, considerable evidence points to the fact that the present state of development of "nationality" arts affects to a low degree the ethnic consciousness of Central Asian Tajiks and Uzbeks. This low degree of impact implies a number of questions with respect to identity of these two groups as distinct nationalities, as "modern" Soviets, as Central Asians, and in terms of their relations with the Russians. This examination of evidence concerning cultural identity through the nonliterary arts is directed along the following lines: (1) participation of the indigenous people in the arts, both as performers and as audience, (2) impact of the large population of outsiders, especially Russians, concentrated in urban centers, (3) incentives and pressures for development in a prescribed direction, (4) alternatives to the official "nationality" arts.

Sources employed for this inquiry include four Tajik and Uzbek periodical publications: Maorif va madaniyat (Dushanbe), 1971 (156 issues); Sadoi sharq (Dushanbe), 1970, 1971 (24 issues); Ozbekistan mädäniyäti (Tashkent), 1971 (104 issues); Shärq yulduzi (Tashkent), 1970, 1971 (24 issues). References to the additional sources used may be found in the notes.

Several Unionwide, Tajik Republic, and Uzbek Republic activities occurring during 1971 made this an ideal year in which to study developments in the arts. First, on the Unionwide level, the Twenty-Fourth Communist Party Congress met in April. Following this political event the artists' and performers' unions met in each republic to acquaint members with Party guidelines and review accomplishments of the five previous years. Second, preparations for celebrating anniversaries of the Soviet Union, Soviet army, and Lenin's birth called for special exhibits, festivals, and shows in theaters and movie houses. In addition, in the Tajik and the Uzbek Republics celebrations commemorating the 650th anniversary of the birth of Hafiz and the fiftieth anniversary of the Soviet-Afghan friendship treaty and the Kazakh Literature and Art Festival (dekada) (in Uzbekistan only) led to wide coverage of cultural affairs in the press.

In Central Asia as well as in the remaining Middle East the arts, under the patronage of kings, khans, or wealthy landowners, traditionally drew talent from the surrounding countryside to the main cities. In the geographical area of present-day Tajikistan and Uzbekistan in recent history the main cultural centers were Bukhara, Khiva, Kokand, Samarkand, and Tashkent. Eventually these cities evolved a mixed ethnic cultural appearance, because they attracted artists and other people of Tajik, Uzbek, Turkmen, and Kazakh origins. Therefore, for Tajiks and Uzbeks particularly, the urban areas constituted focal points for an artistic heritage held in common within Central Asia and in common with Turkic and Iranian people of the Middle East and the Caucasus. Today many of the traditional urban centers are diminished in importance and the new cities contain more outsiders than Central Asians. This factor influences the development of art in Tajikistan and Uzbekistan considerably.

Russians, from the czarist through the Soviet periods, have based their attitudes toward Central Asian arts on the official axiom that "Western" (Russian) arts are cultured, "elevated," and better than Eastern arts, which by comparison are implicitly considered inferior. This attitude, echoed by some indigenous Central Asians, has led to vigorous promotion of pure or adapted Western arts in the Central Asian republics. In an attempt to remove both the slur on their cultural heritage and to confirm the bases for their present traditional "nationality" arts Tajiks and Uzbeks often reach back to Arab, Iranian, and Central Asian scholars and artists for support. Central Asian musicologists and art critics frequently point to al-Farabi, (d. 950) Ibn Sina (d. 1037), and Behzad (d. 1505), among others, as examples of outstanding contributors to classical "Uzbek" and "Tajik" arts.[2] Thus in present-day Tajikistan and Uzbekistan "Western" arts, strongly supported for decades by official policy for each nationality, and traditional "nationality" arts, officially tolerated particularly in the last decade,[3] exist concurrently.

All visual and performing arts in the Soviet Union, like the literary arts, are organized into unions (Taj. ittifoq, Uz. soyuz) or, as in the case of theater, into societies (Uz. & Taj. jamʿiyat). These organizations function on two, at times three, levels: Unionwide, Union Republic, and district levels. Though a Central Asian heads each of the unions in Tajikistan and Uzbekistan, in cases where information about other officials was available the second person in command turned out to be an outsider.[4] Membership in a union assures artists of better employment opportunities, and so in Tajikistan and Uzbekistan unions include most artists, whether Central Asians or outsiders. Unions mount exhibitions, commission compositions, organize contests, award prizes, conduct regional Republic or Union-wide meetings, and generally sponsor the arts, leading them according to the guidelines set by the Party. Emphasis remains on the Western arts, but the Painters' Union in Uzbekistan includes traditional Central Asian craftsmen such as potters. In fact, potters like Safar Sohibov from the village of Chorkuhi, Isfara region (Tajikistan), have had bowls and jugs displayed in many exhibits, including the 1967 Montreal Exposition. Sohibov is a member of the Unionwide Painters' Union, a distinction rarely achieved by Central Asian artists.[5]

The government administrative apparatus for the arts, the Ministry of Culture, conducts the policies of theaters directly, since theater societies are loosely associated groups whose members, such as painters, writers, and musicians, also belong to one or the other of the art unions. The Ministry of Culture also appoints all directors of theaters, concert halls, opera companies, and museums. However, the area of film, both artistic and documentary, falls within the jurisdiction of the Cinematography Committee, which is responsible directly to the Republic Council of Ministers. Film, the only Western art form without a traditional Central Asian counterpart, would appear to operate under the most tightly controlled conditions of any of the arts. Central Asian film production, in its conceptual stages especially, is often initiated in Moscow.[6]

Film, being the only art form alien to Central Asia and one often pointed to by Soviets as an indication of the advanced state of the arts in Central Asia and in Uzbekistan particularly, merits examination in some detail. The steps involved in filmmaking entail first of all the presentation of a proposed scenario, written in Russian, to the local and then to the Moscow Cinematographers' Committees. At the local level the Central Asian republics' committees include more outsiders than do their counterparts in Armenia and Georgia, for example. The Party is represented on the committees at all levels. If a scenario is recommended by the republic committees to the Moscow Cinematographers' Committee, it must receive the backing of an editor on that committee assigned to a Union republic, or, as in the case of Central Asia, to the region as a whole. Should a scenario pass this rigorous series of inspections it is recommended to the republic studios, such as Uzbekfil'm or Tajikfil'm, for production. Because films shot in Central Asia often employ Russian-speaking outsiders, resident and nonresident, as well as Central Asian persons, film tracks record a mix partly in Russian and partly in a Central Asian language such as Tajik or Uzbek. Only after the final screening of the completed film by the Moscow Committee are film studios allowed to dub such films wholly into local Central Asian languages. Some films do not pass the final inspection. This may have been the case with Semurgh (The Phoenix), shot in Uzbekistan during 1971.[7] Scenario writers and directors, at times assigned by Moscow, may, like actors, often be outsiders also. As a result, indigenous Central Asians, trained for five years at the Moscow Institute of Cinematography or in Leningrad, find themselves competing in their own republics for the limited number of jobs with outsiders who, because of contacts with the Moscow Cinematographers' Committee, may receive the choice assignments.[8]

Following the process described above, during 1971 six "artistic" feature films were made in Uzbekistan and three in Tajikistan. The total number for the Soviet Union comes to about 120 films per year. Seventy-five films produced outside Uzbekistan were dubbed by the Tashkent studio, sixty-five into Uzbek and ten into Karakalpak. Altogether, about 90 to 95 percent of the films distributed in Tajikistan and Uzbekistan were not produced locally. Russian films are screened first in Russian, to be followed some months later by the local-language versions.

Plans for film production in 1972 by Tajikfil'm illustrate accurately both the range of subjects inspiring films and the degree to which local Central Asians participate in the film industry. Of the four feature films planned, one, Ahmadi Donish, based on the life of a nineteenth-century Central Asian writer, diplomat, and scholar, is being jointly produced by Tajikfil'm and Lenfil'm (Leningrad) with a cast of Russian and indigenous Central Asian actors. A second film, Asrori qabila (Secrets of the Tribe), written by N.G. Yakutskii, deals with Yakuts "building socialism," and employs talent from Tajikistan, the RSFSR, the Ukraine, and Latvia.[9] Among the five films planned in 1972 for Uzbekfil'm at least three will be either produced by outsiders or written by them.[10] Thus in both republics only a portion of films produced are even nominally controlled by Central Asians. Furthermore, these films represent but a fraction of the number of films to be distributed in the republics.

In terms of fostering or reinforcing nationality identity, either Tajik, Uzbek, or Central Asian, the development of "national Tajik" or "national Uzbek" film industry apparently has little effect. The small size of the industry and the domination by Moscow Committees of content and participation assures films a minimal place in the cultural lives of Central Asians. The effect of a "nationality" film is further diminished by the influx of outside films. Though the effect of "nationality" films may be minimal, the precise effect of all films, documentary and artistic, on the local population remains uncertain. In order to reap the most benefit from the medium of film, showings are accompanied by lectures and comments by the audience or Party propagandists, construction of new movie theaters is accelerated, and administrators devise other means of insuring participation by both rural and urban audiences in film showings. Party and state are hastening to raise Tajikistan from last place in the Union with respect to public film attendance and to elevate Uzbekistan from seventh place.[11]

The other nonliterary art forms, music, dance, theater, painting, and sculpture, exist on two distinct levels: Western classical genres (ballet, symphony, and the like), often solely associated with Russians and termed "professional" arts, and traditional Central Asian genres. With the exception of occasional references to classical Eastern music (maqām and shash maqām) in connection with reviews of cultural history or musicological works, there is little evidence of the performance of classical Eastern music. Traditional Central Asian music, consisting mainly of adaptations of local folk tunes and some Russian melodies, constitutes the popular music in Tajikistan and Uzbekistan. Likewise, in painting, rather than miniature paintings large mosaics and frescos using the style of miniature painting or their subjects form traditional painting today. Ganj, carving in wet plaster, may be considered an Eastern equivalent of sculpture. In the area of theater Central Asians now regard musical comedy as peculiar to their culture.[12]

Participants in traditional Central Asian forms of the arts appear to include indigenous persons exclusively. Audiences and participants for these arts may be found throughout the two republics in cities, towns, and villages. Music and dance ensembles, probably the most representative expression of adapted traditional arts, when appearing in cities like Tashkent or Dushanbe play at small theaters rather than at the ballet and opera halls. However, when they travel outside Tajikistan and Uzbekistan to the rest of the Soviet Union, Eastern Europe, or Afghanistan, their performances are extolled and they form a source of pride for their countrymen. For example, when "Lola," one of the first Tajik music and dance ensembles to be organized (1965), made its initial visit outside the Soviet Union to Afghanistan, its success in Kabul was widely discussed in Dushanbe. One observer said, "The dances brought to the stage by [Gaffar] Valamatzoda [the choreographer] come from the ancient and present life of our people." [13] Similarly, when the "Lazgi" ensemble (an Uzbek group from Khwarazm Oblast) traveled to Turkmenistan, Azerbaijan, and Georgia, the following was quoted in Tashkent from the Turkmen press: "The 'Lazgi' dances are reminiscent of minia- tures" and from the Azeri press: "The dances from 'ancient Khwarazm' resemble our Azeri dances." [14]

Ensemble repertoires apparently include a number of modified traditional songs as well as modern pieces such as waltzes foreign to traditional Central Asian art. Musical comedy songs probably comprise at least some of the repertoires. One of the foremost indigenous composers of Western classical music, Ibrahim Hamraev, a teacher at the Tashkent Conservatory, "does not remain ignorant of Uzbek classical and folk music," but writes music for popular songs and classical poems. [15]

In spite of the popularity of music and dance ensembles and the obvious pride which the indigenous Tajiks and Uzbeks take in their performances, indications are that training facilities for traditional music are neglected. An Uzbek philologist complains about the mutilated lyrics of popular songs. He claims that in remote regions like Kokand as well as on Uzbek television singers remain ignorant of the meaning and exact words of classical ghazals. They substitute their own words for the original, thus making the poem incom- prehensible or offensive. He says, "This is a disgrace to the Uzbek people's nationality culture." [16] Another Uzbek, a composer, accuses musicians of handicapping musical comedies with poor playing. [17] A university teacher from Dushanbe criticizes a Tajik-language music program for mutilating lyrics out of sheer ignorance and for the inconsistent quality of the program. His suggested cure calls for standardizing folk songs and recording folk melodies. [18]

Both the constructive criticism offered and the praise of traditional art forms express a lively interest and identity of Central Asians with their own arts, even in modified or adapted forms. Some of the most obvious departures from the past in the traditional arts lie in the deliberate changes wrought upon Eastern musical instruments,[19] the singing of ghazals to new tunes, the use of Soviet subjects such as the October 1917 Revolution, Lenin, and the native land as themes of songs and plays, and, perhaps most important, the appearance of women on stage as singers, dancers, and actresses. These modifications, however, have been made in arts basically sharing a common background in Tajikistan and Uzbekistan. Therefore, in spite of the attempt of Soviet authorities to split traditional arts into "Uzbek" and "Tajik," with respect to elements other than language the visual and performing arts remain in fact very similar in the two republics. Both Tajik and Uzbek musicians use essentially the same musical instruments and the same kinds of costume with the obligatory four-cornered skull hats; they produce the same styles of pottery, varied from village to village perhaps but not from republic to republic; and they employ similar themes and styles in frescos, mosaics, and paintings. Furthermore, exchange of performers occurs often between republics, particularly the exchange of dance and music ensembles and theater troupes. The "Shadlik" ensemble of Uzbekistan traveled to towns and even villages in Tajikistan performing Russian as well as Uzbek, Tajik, Azeri, and other nationality songs of the Soviet Union.[20] The Lohuti Tajik Drama Theater of Dushanbe, in addition to its travels within Tajikistan in 1971, also visited Uzun and Dehnavi in Uzbekistan.[21] There are many other examples of a special exchange relationship between Tajikistan and Uzbekistan. No doubt the presence of 457,000 Tajiks in Uzbekistan (about 3 percent of the population) and 666,000 Uzbeks in Tajikistan (about 23 percent of the population) encourages such exchange.[22] In his statement summarizing cultural accomplishments of the Five-Year Plan from 1965-70 the minister of culture of Tajikistan commended past cultural exchange between the two republics and called for continuation of the exchange policy.[23]

In sharp contrast to the popularity of traditional arts, Western arts like ballet, opera, figure sculpture, symphonic music, and chorus appear to attract mainly urban audiences, and even then in small numbers. In Dushanbe the star ballerina of the Sadriddin Ayni Opera and Ballet Theater complained in a recent interview that in Moscow she danced before eight or nine thousand people, but in Dushanbe "eight or ten years ago we performed Guli javon (The Young Flower) for twenty or thirty people." She goes on to explain that now a theater that holds 700 persons can expect to fill only about half the seats. She attributes the lack of interest in ballet to a lack of understanding of that art by the Dushanbe population. In fact, for her the benefit in belonging to the state opera and ballet theater of Dushanbe lies in the fact that such a company is requested to perform in cities of the Soviet Union and foreign countries.[24] From Uzbekistan a critic replies to charges brought by local persons against opera performances. The writer chooses to answer two questions which he says are often asked: (1) Why does the Uzbek theater undertake such complicated works as Verdi's Il Trovatore and can they cope with them? (2) Is a fifteenth-century opera relevant? Emphatically affirmative answers are offered to both questions.25

The role of outsiders in the Western "nationality" arts ranges from virtual domination (in film) to very little participation (in theater). Russians maintain Russian-language theaters in both the capitals of the two republics and in some smaller towns. In opera, ballet, and film outsiders not only receive credit and gratitude for creating the first "Tajik" or "Uzbek" nationality product, but works by outsiders even today, within and without the two republics, can and do officially "represent" Tajik or Uzbek art. Among many examples illustrating this practice is one offered in a recent issue of Soviet Literature (published in French, English, Spanish). A painting by the Slavic artist Yuri Taldykin called "Cacti," representing "Uzbek painting," was the sole Central Asian painting to be reproduced in the journal.26

In an effort to attract more participants and audiences from among Central Asians who live in Tajikistan and Uzbekistan, and in order to render Western arts more acceptable as "nationality" arts, several steps have been initiated by the authorities. Generally they involve training young Central Asians in Western music, dance, and painting or sculpture both at home and in the Russian SFSR; expansion of film distribution into rural areas, thereby introducing many Soviet ideas into otherwise remote regions; constructing schools and culture houses, theaters, and movie houses in rural areas; bidding urban performers, singers, painters, actors, and theater troupes to travel among and assist rural cultural groups; and offering prizes of considerable value to persons creating new plays and musical scores that adhere to prescribed themes.27

But perhaps the most important concession to local preference continues to be the adaptation of Middle Eastern and Central Asian themes to Western music, dance, painting. Some examples include the themes of Layli and Majnun, the star-crossed lovers frequently found in Middle Eastern literature, used for the first "Tajik" ballet (composed by an Armenian from Russia) and an "Uzbek" opera; Farhad and Shirin, a pair of Iranian lovers, providing the theme of another "Uzbek" opera; "Tänavär," a folk tune on which a recent Uzbek ballet was based; Yariltash, a Central Asian folk hero used in an Uzbek opera; Ali Shir Nawaiy, the fifteenth-century Chaghatay poet and scholar and subject of an Uzbek symphony, and the like. In painting, subjects employed frequently by both Central Asians and outsiders include Lenin in the company of Central Asians, legendary figures like Farhad, Central Asian landscapes and cotton workers, and Central Asian heroes of the Soviet state.

The comments from Central Asians about performances, as well as policy statements delivered by union leaders and the ministers of culture in Tajikistan and Uzbekistan, confirm the fact that Western "nationality" arts have yet regularly to attract substantial audiences there in spite of the adaptations of themes and other steps taken. Given the limited participation on the part of Central Asians inhabiting Tajikistan and Uzbekistan in the Western "nationality" arts so vigorously espoused by authorities, one can conclude that notwithstanding official encouragement Western arts do not affect to a great extent, foster, or enforce nationality identity in these republics. In fact, their status serves mainly to pinpoint the separateness of the bulk of rural and urban Tajiks and Uzbeks from outsiders and from those few urban Central Asians who disdain traditional arts and boast of the advanced state of the "elevated" arts in their republics.[28]

On the other hand, the officially tolerated traditional "nationality" arts, though popular, do not advance an individual ethnic nationality identity specifically within the Tajik or Uzbek republics, but rather confirm the basic common cultural tastes uniting Uzbeks and Tajiks with each other, and also point to the still active cultural attachments among people of Islamic, Central Asian, and other Middle Eastern backgrounds.[29]

Certain events occurring in connection with development of the arts in Central Asia as a whole indicate how both positive and negative tendencies operate to further a sense of unity among Central Asians in the cultural sphere. Since 1970 representatives from different Central Asian Republics, in recognition of their "shortcomings" with regard to the development of Western "nationality" music, have agreed to meet annually to discuss musical theory. In 1971 musicologists and music teachers met in Dushanbe. Not surprisingly, the experts attending these sessions, even when coming from Central Asian republics, tend to be non-Central Asian outsiders.[30] In 1971 the Painters' Union of the Soviet Union met in Tashkent to plan the exhibition of painting entitled "Central Asia and Kazakhstan" to open in Moscow in April 1972.[31] Both these meetings addressed themselves to development of Western arts in the entire Central Asian region, and as the ethnic composition of the group of persons attending them suggests, served as a means of allowing Moscow to dictate development and furnish criticism. Such events, by singling out Central Asia as a region and by pointing to deficiencies felt to be common to the region, reinforce a unique Central Asian cultural identity separate from the rest of the USSR. Further confirmation of internal Central Asian cultural ties occurs in the policy statements of official cultural leaders in Tajikistan and Uzbekistan who defend musical comedy, a genre often censured by authorities for frivolity, but very popular in both republics. One reporter called musical comedy an intermediate step serving to acquaint local persons with opera,[32] and a second called musical comedy a feature of Central Asian culture as unique as the languages spoken. In this connection the minister of culture of Tajikistan called for more cooperation among Central Asian republics not only in economic matters, already attempted, but also in cultural affairs.[33]

Perhaps the late painter Mirzorahmat Olimjon, a person respected for his efforts on behalf of the Soviet government and esteemed as a Tajik painter, serves best as a final example illustrating the development of the nonliterary arts in Uzbekistan and Tajikistan. Olimjon, "the pride of the Tajiks," in his lifetime trained at least one student who plans to carry on the work of the master. Olimjon's paintings, highly reminiscent of Middle Eastern carpet designs and ganj sculpture, utilize delicate arabesques, floral designs, and symmetrical patterns. These would delight the most traditional Central Asian taste. Superimposed upon this very traditional background are pictures of Lenin, red stars, and Tajik inscriptions in Cyrillic letters.[34] Through the blending of these disparate elements Olimjon combines a Western medium (large canvas painting) with traditional motifs, and renders the composition acceptable to Soviet authorities by his representations of Soviet subjects. Though acclaimed as Tajik paintings, in fact these works could easily have been accomplishments of a Central Asian in Uzbekistan who might have substituted Uzbek Cyrillic inscriptions for the Tajik.

Thus the development of the nonliterary arts in Uzbekistan and Tajikistan, guided by Party policy concentrating, on the one hand, on promoting Western (Russian) art forms and, on the other, on creating within each Central Asian republic separate Western "nationality" arts, has met with limited success so far. The future development of the arts, insofar as they may be affected by policies emanating from Moscow, must be studied in connection with guidelines set forth at the Twenty-Fourth Party Congress and disseminated within the republics by union leaders and the Ministry of Culture. Prominent among the guidelines provided for the arts is idealization of "Soviet" man, a modern industrial citizen of the Soviet Union.

Such an ideal has been projected as the subject of paintings and plays, specifically, as well as other forms of art. Khushvakht Khushvakhtov, head of the Tajik Painters' Union, in stating goals for the next five years, urges use of workers as subjects and emphasizes the need to represent the economic progress of the country.[35] Rahim Ahmedov, Khushvakhtov's counterpart in Uzbekistan, points to the necessity for using contemporary subjects and depicting industrial scenes.[36] In a similar vein, criticism leveled at the Tajik theater includes complaints about the tendency of the Lohuti (Tajik-language) Theater to stage a small number of contemporary plays (50 percent) in comparison with the Mayakovsky (Russian-language) Theater in Dushanbe (75 percent) and with Unionwide theater production (70 percent). Contemporary subjects suggested for the Tajik theater include hydroelectric dam workers of Norak, food canners of Kani Badam, weavers of Dushanbe and Leninabad factories, and miners of Shurab. Only after dealing with these preferred topics are artists encouraged to shift to other subjects, which are, in order of preference (1) proper behavior, (2) Communist workers generally, (3) history, (4) revolutionary history. These topics, according to M. Nazarov, the Tajik Minister of Culture, will serve to "strengthen the people's feelings of nationality (millati) and friendship among the Soviet people."[37]

Emphasis on contemporary industrial subjects would create an atmosphere contrary to that which fosters nationality differences in terms of culture because, by nature, industrial life remains fairly universal and the life of factory workers varies little from area to area. By providing an order of preference for subject matter in the arts, and by stressing subjects little related to "nationality," the authorities are inhibiting use of legendary Middle Eastern and folk figures, traditional life styles, and Central Asian country scenes that have been a mainstay of Central Asian if not "nationality" arts. If successful, this effort to channel subjects in the direction of the "Soviet" man would lead to minimizing of cultural distinctions that have contributed toward substantive nonterritorial boundaries among Union and Autonomous Republics. Therefore, not only would distinctions in terms of nonliterary arts between Tajiks and Uzbeks or Central Asians in general become less discernible but also distinctions among all Soviet people would be de-emphasized. Should such a policy continue over an appreciable period of time, its significance for the "nationality" question would indeed be great.

INTERDISCIPLINARY
GROUP III

THE SEARCH FOR A HERITAGE
AND THE NATIONALITY QUESTION
IN CENTRAL ASIA
Anna Procyk

A reawakened interest in the past and a genuine concern for the restoration and preservation of a specific heritage has marked the cultural life of each of the numerous nationalities comprising the Soviet Union during the 1960s. This inquiry seeks to examine the salient features of this search for the past in Central Asia and discuss some implications that this phenomenon may have for the nationality question in the region. The legacy of close internal religious, linguistic, and cultural kinship of the Central Asian nationalities suggests that if this trend continues it may reinforce or at least resuscitate the awareness of cultural kinship of the indigenous population of that region.[1]

The quest for heritage is not a new phenomenon on the Soviet scene. In Central Asia, as in other regions of the USSR, it emerged and achieved wide popularity in the mid-1920s, when leading nationalist writers selected great poets of the past as a base for their modern literature. This "heritage school" of writers achieved high prominence among the Uzbek literary men who chose classical Chaghatay poets, such as Ali Shir Nawaiy, Zahiriddin Muhammed Babur, Ahmad Yassaviy, Mashrab, and Fuzuliy, as their literary background.[2] The idea of cultural union between the Uzbeks and all Turkic people who regarded Chaghatay literature as their cultural heritage was thus revived precisely at a time when Central Asia was carved into separate ethnic republics.

It is not surprising, therefore, that these nationalist poets became the targets of incisive criticism in the late 1920s, were constrained in their work and activities in the early 1930s, and that most disappeared during the bloody purges of the late 1930s.

The great cultural achievements of the past, however, were not consigned to oblivion even after the eclipse of the nationalist writers, but the utilization of classical poets at the end of the 1930s became extremely cautious and selective, closely supervised by Party authorities and always accompanied with Marxist interpretations and justifications.

In the late 1940s and early 1950s the cultural heritage of the nationalities was placed under such severe restrictions that one could have predicted its virtual extinction. In Central Asia even the widely popular folk epics such as Kolandy Batur, the Korkut Ata, and the Alpamysh were mercilessly criticized for "idealization of the feudal past" and "religious fanaticism," and one by one they disappeared from the literary heritage of the people.[3]

The post-Stalin leadership exhibited more leniency toward the nationalities, and it is exactly to this period—the second half of the 1950s—that one can trace the roots of the present quest for the past. During the Khrushchev period (1957-64) two trends clearly came to the fore: while on the one hand the regime's nationality policy was openly geared toward assimilation and eventual merging of all nationalities, the Party First Secretary's sensational de-Stalinization campaign contributed to weakening feelings of fear, isolation, and political inefficacy and emboldened the intelligentsia of each nationality to exhume its latent national identity and to re-examine the official attitude toward its past.

In contrast to the fate of some other nationalities,[4] the post-Khrushchev period has been relatively advantageous to the growth of assurance among the Central Asians, primarily in view of the strategically sensitive position they occupy both with respect to China and with respect to the Muslim countries of the Middle East, whose sympathy the Soviet leadership is endeavoring to win. In addition to the Sino-Soviet conflict and the increasing importance the Middle Eastern countries attained in international politics, the 1960s have also witnessed a rapid growth of a well-educated local intelligentsia and considerable improvement in the standard of living in Central Asia. The present generation of writers, scholars, artists, and teachers is, in modern terms, better educated and less timid and therefore equipped with the necessary intellectual tools and personal courage for a thorough and meaningful examination and re-evaluation of the past.

This fascination with the past is Unionwide and can be easily discerned among the more advanced nationalities of the Soviet Union. But neither in the Transcaucasus republics nor in the Ukraine, where one would expect a similar resurgence of an interest in the glories of the past, has the stress on heritage and traditions been as great as in Central Asia. A survey of the recent local press gives the impression at times that the Soviet leadership is not only acquiescing in the eagerness with which the Central Asians set about to explore

the past but is actually encouraging the indigenous nationalities individually to rediscover their roots so that they may be in a position to
establish their present national republics on firmer foundations.

Concurrently with the search for the cultural heritage, the 1960s
were marked by strenuous efforts on the part of the local intelligentsia
to restore the purity of national traditions. A number of conferences
on non-Russian languages were held in the five Union republics of
Central Asia. Typical of these was a conference about "language
culture" in Tashkent in 1969, the objective of which, according to one
participant, was to correct the erroneous policies of the past that
caused local words to be systematically replaced by Russian terms.[5]

The restoration of the purity of local languages was, of course,
not exclusively the concern of linguists and educators. Private
individuals, too, exerted efforts to arrest the steady incursion of
Russian words into the local languages and to correct the careless
attitude toward the official medium of the republic by local authorities.
A student of the Alma Ata High Party School, T. Tilegenov, for example,
wrote an indignant protest to the principal Kazakh-language newspaper,
Sotsialistik Kazakhstan, criticizing the poor spelling and the ludicrous
literal translations from the Russian painted on the signs of the
capital of the Kazakh republic. Tilegenov was especially annoyed at
the use of Russian words when appropriate Kazakh terms were
available. He called upon the store managers, Party leaders, and
civic organizations in Alma Ata to correct the situation, concluding
with the remark: "To write signs without errors is a proper way of
enriching our culture."[6]

Numerous articles in which the words "culture" and "heritage"
figured prominently in the recent Uzbek press have dealt with the
2,500th anniversary of Samarkand. Books about the history of the city
have been written, ancient architectural structures have been restored,
and new buildings have been hastily brought to completion for this
festive event. In 1967 a well-known Soviet historian and authority
concerning the ancient city published a study that has been described
as the first attempt to trace the history of Samarkand from the
earliest times up to 1917. Four years later the same author wrote a
more popular version of the city's history. It has received an ex-
cellent review in the Tashkent Russian-language literary journal,
Zvezda Vostoka. The book is especially praised for "debunking with
authoritative finality" the theory of some Western historians who
assert that the cradle of world civilization included only the region
adjacent to the Mediterranean Sea, and who "slander the past of the
Central Asian people by arguing that in ancient times they were allegedly passive and incapable of any historical creativity, that they
did not have their unique culture, and that their culture was allegedly
an imitation of ancient Iranian and Arab cultures." With great

professional skill the historian elucidates the fact that the "Uzbek Tajik, and other people of Central Asia . . . throughout the centuries created their rich independent culture and exerted an important influence on the entire history of the world."[7]

Although the book has been designed for the general reader, and a section in it is devoted to the end of the nineteenth and the beginning of the twentieth centuries, in the reviewer's opinion the volume does not elucidate sufficiently the new way of life and the new traditions that have emerged since the 1917 revolution. Considering the chief purpose of the work—to present a popular history of Samarkand—as well as the fact that the book is already a second study by the same author dealing primarily with the prerevolutionary period of the city, such neglect could have been considered a serious short-coming. But the reviewer mentions it only in passing and seems to be immensely impressed with the great mastery and erudition with which the author describes the splendor of Samarkand, and even quotes Mikhail Ivanovich Kalinin, who during a visit to the city forty years earlier had noted that culture already existed in Samarkand when "the European countries were still practically barbarian."

The numerous articles that appeared in the local press devoted to the subject of Samarkand's jubilee are filled with lavish praise for the awe-inspiring architectural masterpieces of the fifteenth and sixteenth centuries. Over and over again it is stressed that visitors to the city find it difficult to comprehend that such structures as those that stand on the city's main square, the Registan, were built centuries ago.

Just as in other parts of the Soviet Union, societies for the preservation of cultural landmarks have existed in the Central Asian republics since 1966. The chief task of these semivoluntary organizations, formed in each republic separately, has been to compile a list of all historical monuments, to uncover new ones, and to disseminate information about the past among the people. Membership in these societies consists predominantly of teachers, museum workers, local historians, and especially the youth. Important Party and government personalities too are actively engaged in promoting the idea of safeguarding cultural treasures in each republic.[8]

According to the most recent reports the work of these societies is being greatly intensified. Architectural congresses have been held, contests between oblasts with respect to the implementation and popularization of the work of the societies have been announced, and at a recent plenum of the society in Tashkent the dissemination of ideas concerning the significance and importance of historical monuments among the public in the countryside was urged.[9]

The founding and the intensification of the work of these societies for the preservation of historical landmarks is only a culmination of what has been a decade of genuine interest in the past, expressed through literary works, art, music, dance, and history. Several recent compositions, especially one literary study and two historical novels, deserve special mention. The first, written by a young Kazakh scholar, Mukhtar Magauin, is a study of twelve Kazakh akyns and zhyrau.[10] With few exceptions the folk poets examined in the book have been unknown so far not only to the public in general but also to the specialists in the field. A reviewer seems to be inordinately pleased that "a young literary scholar with deep love and devotion gathered together widely scattered and diverse information" about the folk poets, and grateful for the fact that "the author filled new pages in Kazakh literature; he deepened it by three centuries."[11]

A recent Kazakh novel deals with the past indirectly only; nevertheless it does add to the discussion.[12] One of its principal heroes, Batyrov, is an archeologist whose great dream in life is to discover Otrar, the city-state first to be overrun by the armies of Chingiz Khan, because to him Otrar represents one of the most heroic and glorious pages in Kazakh history. This chronology is especially interesting because eminent Russian and non-Soviet historians place the formation of a separate Kazakh group in the mid-fifteenth century or a few decades earlier. Before that, they say, the Uzbeks and Kazakhs formed one nomadic group.[13] The archeologists's attitude toward the past, as well as that of his friends, is contrasted to that of an elderly Kazakh who has a deep respect for the past but understands it as something sacred, to be admired and revered but not examined or investigated. To touch the relics of the past, in his understanding, would be a sacrilege. The silent ruins speak to the elderly Kazakh of the eternal spirit of his forefathers—to him they are the symbols of his motherland, and he himself considers it his duty to be the guardian of the sacred relics.

To the young hero, too, the ruins represent sacred temples, but temples with walls enclosing living testimonies of the glorious past of his people, of the people's spiritual and material culture. To know the past, in the understanding of the hero, means to comprehend the present. The tragic lessons of history forewarn the succeeding generations of mistakes. Therefore the past must be examined and explored. At the end, the old Kazakh recognizes his "mistaken" attitude toward national treasures and, together with Batyrov and the latter's youthful colleagues, rejoices at the success of the expedition.

What is interesting for us in this story is that even the pragmatic Kazakh archeologist, Batyrov, and his assistants idealize and revere the past. They explore history not only to learn a lesson but also to discover the hidden spiritual and material wealth of their people. The novel can be interpreted as an encouragement to carry on the work that is being promoted by the societies for the preservation of historical monuments. The juxtaposition of the old mystical attitude toward history and national heritage to the new "enlightened" and "progressive" view of the past can be understood as a justification for the present preoccupation with and idealization of the past.

The second historical novel has received favorable mention in the Uzbek cultural newspaper, Ozbekistan mädäniyäti, though it deals exclusively with the past, while the emphasis of literary criticism, especially in Central Asia, focuses upon contemporary themes. The novel concerns the life of one of the greatest nineteenth-century Karakalpak poets, Ajiniyoz. It is highly praised for its style and language as well as for the fact that it "calls the present-day youth to learn about the past of the Karakalpak people, their history, and the wealth of their language, and to view these with love."[14]

Closely related to this insistence on the traditional themes is the aura of profound esteem that envelops regard for the poets of the distant past in Central Asia. A most vivid description of how poetry and traditions permeate every strand of life in Tajikistan was recorded by a young Ukrainian Soviet poet during his recent visit to Tajikistan. His impressions were published in the Ukrainian literary journal Vitchyzna.[15] He was astonished and seemingly delighted to see how everyone, including the shepherds in the fields, spoke of ancient Tajik literature, and how schoolchildren's faces brightened at the mention of the beloved poet Firdausi (ca. 940-1020), who, like most old "Tajik" writers, is claimed as a national poet by Persia as well. It is reported that a journalist from the capital of Tajikistan, Dushanbe, gave a lecture to a group of elderly village Tajiks about new excavations and restorations in Penjikent. Only after reciting several verses of Firdausi—at the specific request of one of his listeners—was he able to gain the confidence of his audience. "Thank you, son," said an elderly Tajik, "it is nice that you know this, too [the Shahname, a poem by Firdausi], and not only about the excavations, in which we are also interested. The Shahname, too, is a history of your people."[16]

In one of the largest kolkhozes in Tajikistan, named in honor of Shatalov, who was reportedly killed by the Basmachis (anti-Russian partisans) in the region in 1931, there stands a statue of that Soviet hero along with a colorful picture of the Tajik-Persian thirteenth-century poet Hafiz. To the astonished visitor the chairman of the kolkhoz explained: "Memory should be deep—700 years deep, 2,000 years deep. Otherwise the people will perish. Let the kolkhoz workers know everything about Hafiz and about Shatalov. One defended our lives, the other our word and our spirit." The chairman of the kolkhoz acknowledged with pride that he could recite hundreds of verses by the ancient Tajik poets Omar Khayyam, Hafiz, and Rudaki. This has earned him great respect among the people because, as he explained, in Tajikistan it is not sufficient for a kolkhoz chairman to be an expert in cotton and cattle-breeding. He must know the past of his people as well.[17]

What does this search for the past, this stress on the national uniqueness in art and literature signify? Most certainly it does not appear to be a passing phenomenon. Recent developments, such as the intensification of the work of societies for the preservation of historical and cultural landmarks, the publication of scholarly and popular works regarding the glories and cultural achievements of the pre-Communist past, the organization of conferences on historical themes, and the plethora of articles written for popular consumption dealing with the heritage of ancient times, indicate that the movement for the rediscovery of the past is just gaining momentum. Only recently it was reported with great joy that the Uzbek scholar, Abduvahid Shakirov, had discovered forty-six previously unknown verses by Muqimiy, a nineteenth-century Chaghatay-Uzbek poet.[18] During the past several months Central Asians have been repeatedly reminded of the life and works of the great Khwarazmian astronomer, mathematician, historian, and pharmacologist, Biruni (973-1051), whose 1,000th birthday anniversary is to be celebrated in September 1973. Sometimes as many as three front-page articles devoted to Biruni appear in a single issue of <u>Ozbekistan mädäniyäti</u>.[19]

These incessant reminders regarding the ancient roots of the Central Asians most certainly strengthen the pride of the indigenous population in the region. Prompting of this sort makes the idea of the Russians as leaders in art and civilization more than awkward, and indeed in the local-language press today specific references to the "elder brother" are extremely rare.

Whether the continuing examination and re-evaluation of the past is also reinforcing the national consciousness and feeling of solidarity of the titular ethnic nationalities in the region is a question more difficult to answer. Some Western scholars argue that the recent growing search for the past is bound to lead toward drawing together the local nationalities, in view of their common "Arabo-Irano-Turkic traditional culture, for the simple reason that there is no such thing as a purely Uzbek tradition, no purely Karakalpak culture, and that when a Karakalpak or an Uzbek intellectual tries to discover his origins he discovers a past common to many Turkic or rather to all Muslim people in the territory of the Soviet Union."[20]

Certain signs of a rapprochement among the Central Asian nationalities do appear in recent years. An annual conference dedicated to the 530th birthday anniversary of the great Chaghatay-Uzbek poet Ali Shir Nawaiy drew an impressive number of scholars, predominantly from the Central Asian republics and from Azerbaijan, who gathered in Tashkent to discuss Nawaiy's contribution to their respective branches of literature.[21] A recent article in the Turkmen literary journal opened with the remark that the "Uzbeks and Turkmens are kinsmen by blood, and friends and brothers from ancient times." It stressed over and over again that the two nationalities are not only culturally and economically very similar but are closely tied together through their history and common literary heritage.[22] A Kirgiz poet, Baydilda Sarnogoev, dedicated a poem to the Uzbek people, which began with a firm assertion of the brotherhood and kinship between the two ethnic nationalities: "Greetings to you, my Uzbek, our thoughts and reveries are one, you are the closest kin, the right hand of a Kirgiz, and Tashkent is the capital of Central Asia."[23]

Especially telling has been a joint conference of the Social Studies section in the Academy of Sciences of the USSR and the Institute of Marxism-Leninism of the Central Committee of the Communist Party, held in Tashkent at the end of March 1972.[24] Representatives of the five academies of science in Central Asia reported on the scholarly achievements in the field of social sciences in their respective republics and presented the tasks they have set before themselves for the near future. Interestingly, the conference became a forum of complaints, at which dissatisfaction was voiced with the low status of the study of the cultures and languages of the Eastern countries in Central Asia, as well as the lack of cooperation and coordination among the literary scholars and philologists of the five republics. Even the representatives of the Uzbek and Tajik Academies of Science, where the study of the Eastern cultures is most highly developed, noted that in their republics too treatment of the ancient history of the East and the mutual ties of the Eastern people is far from being adequate. It was strongly urged that closer attention be paid to the study of Arabic and Turkic languages in Central Asia.

In Kazakhstan it was said, serious study of Eastern languages and culture have not as yet begun. The vice president of the Kazakh Academy of Science sadly admitted "that many questions of Kazakh history, culture, and literature have not yet been elucidated, primarily because of the lack of well-trained specialists who know how to read old manuscripts and rare books written in different Eastern languages."

The second question raised at the conference, namely the joint preparation of the history of literature of the peoples of Central Asia, received a thorough examination. While the achievements regarding the recent history of Turkmen, Tajik, and Karakalpak literature were highly praised, it was pointed out that the time has come "to unify these literatures into an integral whole, to trace their common principles, to penetrate the depths of the sources of their literary ties." Furthermore, it was stated that the literary scholars of Central Asia have been confronted with a series of theoretical questions, such as, for example, the relationship of the early monuments of written literature to the present Turkic people or the question of the relationship between branches of the written and oral literature, that could be resolved through a concerted effort only. "There are many other related questions," it was reiterated again and again, "that require a common effort not only of literary scholars but also of historians, ethnographers, archeologists, and linguists." The speakers emphasized especially the need for a concerted effort in the study of the folklore of Central Asia because" . . . such epics as Korogly, Alpamysh, Koblandy, and Layli and Majnun are found among the people of Central Asia, . . . the Caucasus, the Volga, and the Altay. We need scholarly works dealing with their emergence and dissemination, the process through which they have became subject to various changes."

It seems likely that such assertions of kinship, brotherhood, and similarities, as well as the urgent call for a concerted effort among the Central Asians in their scholarly endeavor, go beyond the mere idea of "the friendship of peoples." One may discern in these statements elements of self-assertiveness and spontaneity strongly reminiscent of the atmosphere prevailing among the Central Asian writers up to the mid-1920s. Today's intellectuals seem to be eager to correct the anomalies in the field of scholarly endeavor that have resulted from the arbitrary decisions of the authorities. They are seemingly indifferent that they too may be accused of propagating ideas akin to Pan-Turkism or Pan-Islamism, charges that abruptly ended many a career in the previous decades.

The recent resurgence of Islam in Soviet Central Asia—another facet of the search for the past—is also an important factor favoring the drawing together of the indigenous nationalities. Indicating the omnipresence of Islam throughout Central Asian society was a recent statement in a local Communist journal complaining that many members had left the Party because they had lost their materialistic world outlook.[25]

The common Muslim-Irano-Arabic cultural heritage notwithstanding, it should be remembered that the formal existence of the Central Asian ethnic nationality republics for almost half a century must have left an imprint on the Central Asian community that goes beyond the development of different literary languages. It is possible that the present titular nationalities are developing in the direction of individual state formations on the European model. At least, there is evidence of this trend in the local press as well.

While professing mutual friendship and brotherhood, representatives of each nationality always emphasize the achievements of their own ethnic group. After summarizing the proceedings of the 530th anniversary conference of Nawaiy scholars, the Uzbek correspondent noted with pride that the conference indicated the profound interest

of scholars in the immortal works of the genius of the "Uzbek" people,
Ali Shir Nawaiy.[26]

During an interview a secretary of an obkom committee in
Tajikistan made the following remark to a visitor:

> We love this land, love it very much because it is ours.
> The Mongols, the Chinese, the Turks, and the Arabs have
> been here, and what have they accomplished? Nothing.
> Who learned to love them? No one. In addition to
> everything else, this is so because nobody except the
> Tajiks has planted a single tree here.[27]

In the office of a raikom secretary, a historian by profession,
a visitor noticed two maps: one of the world and one of Tajikistan.
Referring to this and to other similar observations, he said:

> The Tajiks are seeing themselves more and more dis-
> tinctly against the panorama of the Soviet Union, the
> panorama of contemporary Asia, the panorama of world
> culture. They are proud. Is it not on this consciousness
> that national dignity is being built in . . . people who have
> found their place in history?[28]

In an obvious allusion to the overt intrusion of an alien culture,
the visitor, appalled to see two paintings by Russian artists which
though of high artistic value were utterly out of place in a Tajik
restaurant where the atmosphere was purely local character, makes
the following observation:

> The Tajiks, when confronted with something vulgar or
> something esthetically unacceptable, with an astonishing
> adroitness turn away from it. . . . Never have I noticed
> that a Tajik would assimilate something that is not worthy
> of his upbringing and of the culture of his people. . . .
> Traveling through Tajikistan, I became convinced that a
> thousand years of tradition builds a foundation in every
> soul, and the mere awareness that in your culture there
> was an Omar Khayyam, and artists creating unsurpassed
> ornaments, provides a guarantee against a fascination
> with "Bears" [name of one of the paintings in the
> restaurant].[29]

It is difficult to predict on the basis of evidence at hand in
exactly which direction the Central Asian nationalities will develop:
whether they will converge as a result of the rediscovery of a common

cultural heritage, or whether they will, while recognizing their
cultural and over-all ethnic affinity, safeguard their ancient as well
as their recently acquired national peculiarities.

But no matter in which direction the evolution of the Central
Asian nationalities proceeds, one thing appears definite: the recent
widespread interest in the past among the Central Asians is bound
to contribute toward divergence between them and the outsiders. At
least, it will hinder the process of assimilation between Central
Asians and Russians. In other words, while the indigenous nationalities,
from the cultural point of view, are drawing together, from the point
of view of identification they as a group are diverging from the
Russians and from other Soviet nationalities. Thus, the recent
turning to the past can be considered as a destabilizing factor if the
nationality question in Central Asia as a whole is taken into
consideration.

In view of the Sino-Soviet conflict one could assume that the
Soviet leadership would continue to tolerate the eagerness with which
the Central Asians seize upon the opportunity to explore their past.
This is more likely because the Chinese have made a special effort
to appeal to the Central Asians, branding the Soviet leadership as the
new czars, as vile enemies of all nationalities of the Soviet Union.[30]
The Soviets, in turn, have been charging the Chinese with conducting
policies of forced assimilation, and a Turkmen-language newspaper
in Central Asia recently accused the Chinese of relocating people of
the Chinese Republic's nationalities in their home territories and thus
depriving them of their right to self-determination.[31] Obviously,
such charges and countercharges give food for thought to the Central
Asians, whose land has been flooded with outsiders, especially with
the dominant group. The Soviet leadership will no doubt use special
care not to antagonize the Central Asians by abruptly curbing their
spontaneous and passionate drive to rediscover the past. Thus, all
evidence both of local and international character seems to indicate
that the nationality question will play an increasingly important
role in Central Asia in the near future.

11

ETHNIC GROUPS OF THE BUKHARAN STATE CA. 1920 AND THE QUESTION OF NATIONALITY

Ian M. Matley

In attempting an assessment of the degree to which a feeling of Bukharan national identity may have developed among the inhabitants of the state of Bukhara by the time of its absorption into the Soviet Union there are several general factors that must be considered. First, many countries of the Middle East and Central Asia contain a variety of ethnic groups, a situation that in some cases has led to a lack of cultural and linguistic unity, inhibiting the development of European-style "national" identity. This disunity may, on the other hand, have been partially offset by the existence of religious unity in the Muslim states. Second, in some countries the existence of a sedentary agricultural population along with a nomadic pastoral population has led on many occasions to conflict and even warfare between the two groups. Third, even the lack of any conflict between ethnic or social groups may not lead automatically to feelings of national unity in a particular state. Scattered populations, often living in groups isolated in mountain valleys or separated by stretches of desert, at a time before the development of modern transportation and mass communications, had little feeling of identification with an area larger than their own immediate region.

An accurate assessment of the size and location of the major ethnic groups forming the population of the Bukharan state around 1920 is made difficult by two main factors. The first is the lack of any reliable population data for the region before the Soviet census of 1926, and the second is the change in boundaries that took place with the formation of the Soviet republics there in 1924. These boundary changes, which resulted in the division of Bukharan territory among the Uzbek, Tajik, and Turkmen republics, make it virtually impossible to use the 1926 census material to arrive at any accurate estimates of the population of the area once encompassed by the boundaries of the state of Bukhara.

134

One of the problems associated with the utilization of published data concerning the composition of the population of Bukhara before 1924 is the lack of accurate estimates for the total population of the state. No census was ever taken by the Bukharan authorities, and we must rely on the estimates of Russian observers. A figure of 2.5 to 3 million is quoted by several sources as the most probable population of the state during the first decade of the twentieth century.[1] However, even if these estimates are accepted we must face the problem of the great losses of population that took place in southern Central Asia during the famine of 1919 when at least a million people died.[2] A solution to the problem may seem at first sight to lie in the use of the data published at the time of the delimitation of the ethnic groups of Central Asia and the formation of the Soviet republics in 1923-24, but these figures are unreliable and not based on any census-taking.[3]

It is possible, however, to arrive at an approximate figure for the total population of Bukhara in the early 1920s by comparing estimates of the ethnic and economic composition of the population made by various authorities, and from these derive a total. An official Soviet estimate of 1.53 million in 1924 is quoted by an American historian who states that a Soviet scholar claimed a population loss of at least 25 percent during the period 1917-22. Although the American scholar thinks that this loss is exaggerated, it is nevertheless possible that deaths in the 1919 famine and the period of the basmachi troubles totaled some quarter to half a million. The evidence suggests that the total population of the Bukharan state around 1920 was approximately 2 million.[4]

The same problems attend any attempts to arrive at an accurate assessment of the numbers of persons belonging to the various ethnic groups inhabiting the Bukharan state. Information assembled on the eve of drawing the boundaries for the new Soviet republics was not based upon any census material, but was derived from the crude estimates already mentioned. However, it is possible to estimate the numbers of the various ethnic groups by a selective use of data published between 1900 and 1924, comparing them, when possible, with data from the 1926 census.

A Soviet scholar, in his recent work about the formation of the Uzbek socialist nation, has published a table providing figures for the ethnic population of the Bukhara Soviet Socialist Republic in late 1924. This table lists Uzbeks 975,569; Tajiks 802,632; Turkmens 174,135; and Kazakhs 7,000.[5] The population of Central Asian origin thus totaled 1,959,335. Unfortunately, the reliability of these figures is also open to question. Elsewhere, the same author states that 3,757,309 Uzbeks were living on the territory of the Turkistan ASSR, the Bukhara SSR, and Khwarazm SSR combined, in the

MAP 11.1

The Ethnic Composition of the Population
of Bukhara ca. 1920

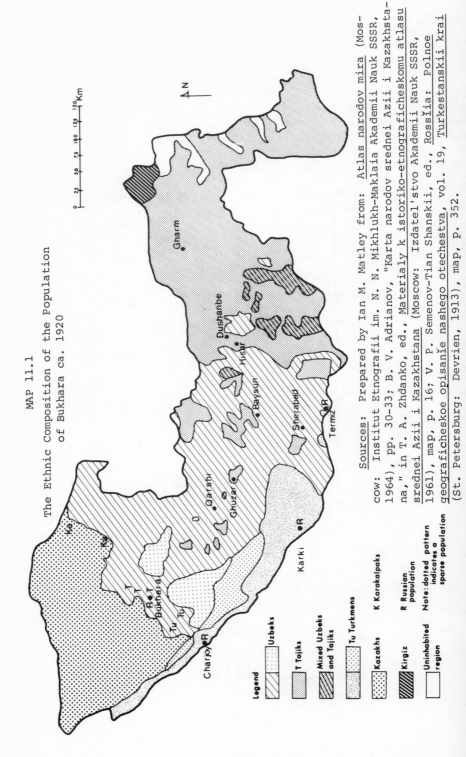

Legend

Uzbeks	K Karakalpaks
T Tajiks	
Mixed Uzbeks and Tajiks	Kazakhs
Tu Turkmens	Kirgiz
R Russian population	Uninhabited region

Note: dotted pattern indicates a sparse population

Sources: Prepared by Ian M. Matley from: Atlas narodov mira (Moscow: Institut Etnografii im. N. N. Mikhlukh-Maklaia Akademii Nauk SSSR,
1964), pp. 30-33; B. V. Adrianov, "Karta narodov srednei Azii i Kazakhstana," in T. A. Zhdanko, ed., Materialy k istoriko-etnograficheskomu atlasu
srednei Azii i Kazakhstana (Moscow: Izdatel'stvo Akademii Nauk SSSR,
1961), map, p. 16; V. P. Semenov-Tian Shanskii, ed., Rossiia: Polnoe
geograficheskoe opisanie nashego otechestva, vol. 19, Turkestanskii krai
(St. Petersburg: Devrien, 1913), map, p. 352.

proportions of 66.5 percent, 22.3 percent, and 11.3 percent respectively.[6] This means that the Uzbek population of the Bukhara SSR was some 834,000, or 41,000 less than the figure he gave, above, for the same data. He also states that Uzbeks made up 50.1 percent of the total population of the Bukhara SSR.[7] If he means by this the population of Central Asian origin mentioned above he is consistent, but because this figure omits the population of Russians and other non-Central Asians, it is misleading. A 1924 Soviet report gives a figure of 47.1 percent for the proportion of Uzbeks in the total population of the Bukhara republic, which seems more reasonable, making a recent Western figure of 50 to 60 percent seem slightly too high.[8]

The use of the more accurate statistics of the 1926 census would not necessarily resolve the problem even if we could convert them to apply to the territory of the Bukhara state. As late as the time of the census there was still doubt in the minds of many Central Asians about who was an Uzbek. Many thought of themselves tribally, as Qipchaqs, Naymans, and the like. There was also some confusion over the identification of Uzbeks and Tajiks due to the large number of bilingual persons among them and considerable intermarriage between the two groups.[9]

The Tajik population of 802,632 in the Bukhara SSR cited from the 1961 Soviet work seems high. In the 1964 History of the Tajik People it is stated that 52.3 percent of Soviet Central Asia's Tajiks lived in the Bukhara republic in 1924.[10] The Tajik population of the entire USSR given in the 1926 census totaled 979,000. In this case the number of Tajiks in the Bukhara republic would be around 512,000, or some 290,000 less than the 802,632. The figure for the Tajiks suggests that they formed about 41 percent of the Central Asian population of the Bukhara republic. Some sources offer a figure of 40 percent while another gives a low figure for Tajiks of 30 percent of the total population.[11] The problems of identification of Tajiks and verifying the accuracy of census data of course complicate the issue.

The 1961 Soviet source cited gives a figure of 174,135 for Turkmens living in the Bukhara republic. They formed only a small percentage of the total Turkmen population of Central Asia, which totaled 764,000, according to the 1926 census. The figure from the 1961 source suggests that they formed about 8.9 percent of the Central Asian population of the Bukhara republic, while in 1924 a figure of 8.5 percent was given and in 1968, 5 to 10 percent of the total population.[12] Other sources state that 27 percent of all Turkmens lived in the Bukhara republic in 1924 and they formed 10.6 percent of the population of the republic.[13] Applying these percentages to the total Turkmen population recorded in the 1926 census gives a Turkmen population of the Bukhara republic of some 206,000 and also suggests a total population of the republic of some 212 million. However, it should again be remembered that some Turkmens, especially in the Charjoy region, thought of themselves as Uzbeks and that the 1926 figure may thus be low.[14]

The remainder of the Central Asian population of the Bukhara state consisted mainly of Kazakhs, who, according to the 1961 source, totaled 7,000 in 1924. Whether this figure is accurate or not is difficult to say, but it is certain that the number of Kazakhs was extremely small. There was also a handful of Kirgiz, but they are rarely mentioned in accounts of the ethnic composition of the population. In 1926, 11,500 Kirgiz were counted in the Pamir region of Tajikistan.[15] Only the western part of this region belonged to the Bukhara state; therefore, the numbers of Bukharan Kirgiz must have been considerably smaller than this figure.

In Bukhara lived small numbers of persons of non-Central Asian origin, the Russians being the most important group. The 1897 census of Russia showed some 12,000 Russians in the emirate, but this total increased fairly rapidly during the following couple of decades. By 1911 the Russian population was estimated at some 30,000.[16] The 1924 source reports Russians in 1924 to have constituted 1.5 percent of the total population, which seems reasonable.[17] These Russians were located mainly in Yangi (Novaya) Bukhara, Charjoy, Karki, and Termiz.

Other ethnic groups included the Jews, Arabs, Hindus, and Persians, about whom little accurate information is available. In 1926 there were 18,200 Jews in the Uzbek SSR, of which some 3,300 lived in the city of Bukhara.[18] Also, some 2,000 Persians (Farsis) and 300 Arabs lived in the city of Bukhara about the same time.[19]

Besides the problems, already cited, with the statistical information available from the prerevolutionary period, and the famine losses, there are also difficulties associated with the quite wide variation among estimates made by different Russian observers. They had no accurate statistics or reliable information with which to work. For example, one Russian author, who discussed the ethnic composition of Bukhara state in some detail in 1913, estimated a Tajik proportion of some 20 percent only and quoted an estimate of "not more than 350-400,000."[20] He pointed out that no accurate information was available, and consequently ran into trouble with his estimates of the Uzbek population, which he placed as high as 900,000- 1 million or 36-40 percent of the total population, adding to this a population of 700,000 Sarts or 27-28 percent of the population.[21]

The Russian observer thought that this figure for Sarts ran too high and suggested that most of them were in fact Uzbeks. Without entering here into the question of identifying the Sarts, there is no doubt that he was right but had overestimated the size of the Uzbek compared to the Tajik population.

In order to understand the ethnic situation in the Bukhara state fully, we must also examine the distribution of the population. The physical features of the country had the effect of limiting the areas suitable for settlement. The eastern half of the country is mountainous, with the height and ruggedness of the terrain increasing as one moves eastward until the 20,000-foot peaks of the Pamirs are reached. In the west the mountains end and the dry plains change to desert as one approaches the western border. Settlement in the eastern half was thus limited to valleys in the mountains, such as the upper Surkhan Darya, Kafirnihan, Vakhsh, Qizilsu, and Yakhsu valleys. In the west population density was greater and a rural and urban population was supported by irrigated agriculture, using the water of the lower Surkhan Darya, the Qashqa Darya, and the Zarafshan. Water from the last two rivers supported the largest urban centers of the country, Bukhara and Qarshi, as well as a moderately dense rural population in the Qarshi plains, lying between the two rivers. The Amu Darya also supported several settlements, such as Charjoy, Karki, and Termiz, as well as a rural population settled along its banks.

This concentration of the settled population in relatively small and widely separated areas of the country led to several results. First, communications between communities separated by mountain ranges or desert were difficult, resulting in fragmentation and a lack of unity. This situation helped to isolate and preserve the existence of numerous tribes of Uzbeks and Tajiks, who in many cases had no feeling of belonging to a larger ethnic community.[22] Second, a great difference in way of life developed between the settled urban and rural population of the irrigated lands and the nomadic and seminomadic people of the plains and deserts and of the mountain region of the east.

The division of the population into settled agriculturalists and urban dwellers on one hand and nomadic or seminomadic livestock herders on the other is a major feature of Central Asian and Middle Eastern societies and has in many cases caused deeper divisions in these traditional societies than have ethnic differences. In the case of the Bukhara state we encounter the inevitable problem of a lack of accurate information on this subject. In 1903 it was estimated that 65 percent of the population was settled, 20 percent nomadic, and 15 percent seminomadic.[23] In 1911 another Russian estimated Bukhara's urban population at 300,000, other settled population at 500,000, seminomadic population at 1,700,000, and nomadic population at 500,000.[24] These figures, expressed as percentages, are completely at variance with those just previously cited, because they suggest that only 26.7 percent of the population was settled, whereas 56.5 percent was seminomadic and 16.7 percent nomadic. An assessment of the truth is further complicated by the fact that, as a 1961 work points out, data collected at the time of the delimitation of the Central Asian ethnic nationalities in 1924 shows that there were practically no groups in the Uzbek and Tajik regions of the Bukhara state, with the exception of some Kazakhs, leading a purely nomadic way of life. There was a small number of seminomadic tribes, mainly Qonghirats (Kungrats), in the regions of Tangikharam, Baysun, and Sherabad (central Bukhara), numbering 67,500.[25] The same work puts this seminomadic population at 4 percent of the rural population of the Bukhara state.[26] Whatever conditions may have been at an earlier period, it is indeed probable that by the early 1920s a large part of the nomadic and seminomadic population had become sedentary.

Various factors in the composition of the population and the nature of the country that would lead to division having been identified, an assessment of their relative importance is called for. Although one might expect the division of the population along ethnic lines to be a major factor in any explanation for a lack of national unity, this was probably not the case to any great extent in Bukhara if we are talking in terms of confrontations between the major groups, especially the Uzbeks and the Tajiks. The Uzbeks were clearly the dominant group politically and economically as well as being the most numerous single group. The next largest ethnic group, the Tajiks, stood apart from the Uzbeks and the other Turkic-speaking groups because of their Iranian language and to a certain extent because of the adherence of many of them to the Ismaili sect of Shiism.[27] An American scholar thinks that the presence of the Tajiks probably constituted the "major ethnic and linguistic obstacle to harmony" in the region.[28] In the central and western parts of the country many Tajiks and Uzbeks were bilingual, and intermarriage between Tajiks and Uzbeks had helped to soften the lines of ethnic demarcation. In the eastern mountains the population was composed of small groups such as the Yagnobs, Shugnans, Bartangs, and Rushans, often referred to as the Pamir people, who spoke their own languages as well as Tajik, and thus introduced an element of diversity into the Tajik culture region itself.[29] However, there is no reason to assume that a serious state of confrontation existed between the two major ethnic groups in the country. In fact both groups shared the common bond of Islam, which united them against the Russian threat.

In the case of the Turkmens we have already seen that some in fact considered themselves to be Uzbeks. Their numbers were small and there is no evidence that they had any serious quarrels

with the other Turkic-speaking groups in the country. Kazakhs and
the Kirgiz were too small in numbers to play any significant role.
There seems in fact to have been a tendency toward assimilation,
not only of some members from the smaller Turkic-speaking groups,
but also of some Tajiks, by the dominant Uzbeks. However, because
many of the Uzbeks did not identify themselves as a united group,
but by their tribe, city, or village, such assimilation does not necessarily suggest a trend toward the development of a major group
identity, let alone a "national" one. In fact, the clue to an understanding of the ethnic situation in Bukhara state in the early 1920s
is to be found in the existence of an identification on the part of the
population with their family, tribe, locality, or region rather than
with a larger linguistic or cultural group.

This tendency toward identification with a locality was encouraged if not partially caused by the uneven distribution of the
population and its tendency toward clustering along the banks of rivers
and in the valleys of the eastern mountains. This situation led to the
relative isolation of many centers of population and the development
of a feeling of regional or local identity. Most members of the sedentary rural population identified themselves with the oasis or district in which they lived, while the urban dwellers linked themselves
with their city or town. In some countries the urban population,
especially the inhabitants of the capital city, have led the movement toward the formation of a national identity. In Bukhara most
urban dwellers (Sarts) had lost their tribal connections. However,
the urban component of the Bukhara state comprised probably no
higher than 15 percent of the total population by the early 1920s.
The population of the city of Bukhara was only some 47,000 at the
time of the 1926 census.[30]

The nomadic and seminomadic groups had developed little
sense of location, and allegiance in their case was given to the tribe
or family. Most of the Kazakhs and Kirgiz, many Turkmens, and
some Uzbeks and Tajiks belonged to these groups, most of whom
were clearly giving up their traditional mobile way of life by the
1920s and becoming farmers. However, many of these people still
retained strong tribal feelings. This was true, for example, of
many Turkmens, who often settled as tribal units.[31] Although the
traditional strife between the sedentary and the nomadic populations
can be ruled out as a major divisive force in the Bukhara state
in the 1920s, the legacy of this division was apparent in the survival
of tribal allegiances.

All indications suggest that a combination of ethnic, social,
and geographical factors militated against the formation of an over-
all national identity among the people of the state of Bukhara. In
this, Bukhara was not unique. Other Central Asian and Middle Eastern

countries have encountered the same conditions and faced the same problems on their road to statehood and have met with varying degrees of success or failure in overcoming them. The process of nation-forming never reached a stage in the independent Bukharan state that would enable us to predict what level of national identity might ultimately have been achieved among all the inhabitants of the Bukharan state.

12

**FARSI,
THE VATAN,
AND THE MILLAT
IN BUKHARA**
William L. Hanaway, Jr.

This study will pose an answer to the questions: "Was there
a sense of nationality awareness among Bukharans in the period 1909
to 1925, and if so, what was its nature?" The evidence will be supplied mainly by the literary output from Bukhara, by Bukharans, or
directed to Bukharans in the Iranian language used there, during this
period. Two major publications stand at either end of this period,
and may be considered its boundary markers. In 1909 Abdalrauf
Fitrat published his Munāzara (The Debate),[1] and in August 1924
there commenced the publication of the newspaper Avāz-i Tājīk,
described by Sadriddin Ayniy ('Ainī) as the first newspaper [in the
Tajik language] published by the Communist Party after the October
Revolution.[2] The arguments presented will be based largely on the
statements and feelings, overt and covert, expressed by the Bukharan
intellectuals in their literary prose and poetry. When intellectuals
of this era wrote with a social or reformist purpose, they often used
classical Persian literary forms such as the munāzara (debate,
disputation) or the qasīda (lengthy, formal court poem), and they
strove for certain literary effects, the better to convey their message.
Thus, the dividing line between what is literary and what is not is
sometimes difficult to draw, but in general is sufficiently clear.

The Iranians of Bukhara, although part of the larger Iranian
cultural area, had by 1920 been cut off from direct contact with
Persia proper for about 400 years. The barriers were both ethnic-
political and religious. The ethnic-political barrier comprised a
body of Turkic-speaking peoples occupying the territory between
Bukhara and the Oxus River. The religious barrier was created
by the foundation of the Safavid state in 1501, when Shiism became
the state religion of Persia. This development alienated the Sunni
Muslims in areas outside of Safavid political control, some of whom

were the Turkic people to the north of the Oxus. Thus, there was a strong internal division within the Iranian cultural area that separated the Bukharan Iranians from those south of the Oxus but did not shatter the cultural unity of the area.

One element of this divided cultural area that remained constant until the third decade of the twentieth century was the written language used by the Persians of Iran and by the Iranians of Bukhara. As late as the early 1920s the literary Iranian language of Bukhara showed only the slightest morphological and syntactic differences from that of Iran. The spoken languages of the two areas varied widely from each other, and during this period there were numerous Iranian dialects spoken in Bukhara, most of them mutually intelligible but showing strong morphological, lexical, and syntactic differences.

The way a people refer to their language can be an indication of how they view themselves culturally. For example, one hears "American" for the kind of English spoken in the United States, or Darī for the Persian spoken in present-day Afghanistan. This question is especially interesting in the case of those writing in the Iranian language of Bukhara in the pre-1925 years. Fitrat's Munāzara (1909) provides us with numerous examples. This is a work of fundamental importance, which presents the Jadīd position with regard to education and the schools, the religious classes, and the administration of Bukhara. The focus of the Munāzara and its companion piece, the Bayānat-i sayyāh-i Hindī (Tales of a Hindu Traveler), published in 1912, is Bukhara, its people, and the parlous state into which they had fallen.

In an angry exchange between the two characters of the Munāzara, Fitrat has the Bukharan schoolteacher say to the European, "I don't think you know Persian (Fārsī)," to which the European replies, "Either I don't understand Persian properly, or you speak it wrongly!"[3] Thus we see that in 1909 this Bukharan referred to the language he was speaking as Fārsī, Persian. That this use of the word Fārsī applied not because Fitrat was using a literary form in a literary language seems confirmed by the author's statement in his introduction. There, he says that he heard this story recently and decided that since it dealt so well with the sources of Bukhara's internal dissension, he would cast it in the colloquial spoken language of the Bukharans, so that his compatriots would understand his message.[4] Naturally what he wrote was not the same as the spoken language of the Bukharans, but he did make an effort at it, and a phrase like "I don't think you know Persian" has the ring of authenticity.

In any case, it was not only the spoken language that was called Fārsī, Persian. The newspaper Bukhārā-i sharīf edited by Mīrzā Jalāl Yūsuf-Zāda, which ran from March 1912 to January 1913, states in the lead article of the second issue, "We feel that we should write first of all in as simple a Persian as possible (Rūznāma-i mā har che mumken bāshad be zabān-i pārsī-i sāda neveshta mīshavad).5 In a later issue of 1912, while discussing religion in the lead article, the editors translate certain technical religious and philosophical terms from Arabic to Persian: "The translation of ᶜilm in Persian is 'knowing,' and the translation of ᶜirfān and maᶜrifat is 'recognizing'." (Tarjuma-i ᶜilm be fārsī dānestan va tarjuma-i ᶜirfān va maᶜrifat shenākhtan ast).6 There are other examples of Bukharans calling their language Fārsī (Persian), but these will suffice. There are no other names used by them for their language until late 1924.

During this period the same writers who referred to their Iranian language as Fārsī referred to Bukhara as their vatan, "the homeland, place where one comes from or to which one belongs." The inhabitants were referred to as the millat, "the people, nation." The tone is again set by Fitrat in the Introduction to his Munāzara, where he addresses the people of Bukhara. The opening line is: "My dear compatriots, the noble people of Bukhara" (Hamvatanān-i 'azīzam, millat-i najība-i Bukhārā). Later in the same sentence he says that it is "the mistaken actions and corruption of some traitors to the people (millat) that have engulfed our sacred homeland (vatan)."7

There are numerous references to both the vatan, Bukhara, and its millat throughout this work, and their meaning is clear, since Fitrat repeatedly states that he is addressing the Bukharans about their own problems. At the end of the Munāzara, after the European has convinced the Bukharan schoolteacher that modern education is the only road to salvation for the Bukharans, the teacher says, "you are a wise man and truly you have put your finger on all the weaknesses of our homeland (vatan) and our people (millat)."8

In a small collection of poems entitled Sayha (The Shout), published in 1911, Fitrat continues to express these sentiments. One poem begins: "Oh my dear mother, O land of Bukhara / My pride is with you, and my trust is with you."9 In another poem in the same collection he says, addressing the morning breeze:

> Begin to blow about my homeland (vatan) in the morning
>   Oh, did I say homeland (vatan), rather the place where
>   I prostrate my body and soul
> Both my safe place of rest, my honor and glory
>   And my ka'ba, my qibla, and my garden.10

In a poem entitled "Tāziāna-i tà'dīb" (The Chastising Lash), published in Behbudiy's journal Ayinä in 1914, Fitrat speaks of both the millat and the qowm of Bukhara:

First take account of the state of your own people (millat)
Then blame fortune and destiny. . . .
Some have taken the path of divisiveness
And have opened a thousand wounds in the pure heart of
    the homeland (vatan)
To their base jealous cravings they have sacrificed
Fame and honor and glory, the land (molk), the people
    (qowm), and the religion.[11]

There is more of the same throughout the poem. But Fitrat
is not the only intellectual to use these terms. A writer named As'ad,
in an article in Ayinä in 1914, says that the ulema stand ready to
devour the pious endowments belonging to the people (millat).[12]
Moving ahead some years, we find Ahmad Jān Makhdūm Hamdī's
poem "Khitāb be fuqarā-i Bukhārā" (An Address to the Poor of
Bukhara), published in the journal Qutulush in 1920, saying: "Arise
dear friend and fight: / Deal with the oppressors of your people
(millat)." And he goes on to appeal to those who are true to their
homeland (vatan).[13] From this time on, the poetry takes on a clearly
revolutionary tone. There are calls to unite against the tyrants and
oppressors, to raise the flag of justice, to punish the evildoers, and
so on in the familiar revolutionary vein, but all directed toward the
millat or qowm of the vatan, Bukhara.
In this same year, 1920, Fitrat published a poem in four stanzas
in the same journal, which he entitled "Yek takhattur-i alīm" (A Pain-
ful Pace). In it he says, amidst a great deal of weeping over the sad
state of things in Bukhara: "The thought of my homeland (vatan) has
taken over my mind / Her poison has poured darkness into my drinking
cup."[14]
Ahmad Jān Makhdūm Hamdī wrote a nazīra parallel poem on
the last stanza of Fitrat's poem, which begins: "O my wounded,
grieving people (millat), / The object of our anxiety is your comfort."
It continues with a call for the blood of their tyrannical leaders.[15]
In the same spirit speaks a poem called "Bayān-i hāl" (Explanation
of How Things Are), by Mīrzā 'Abd al-Vāhid Munzim, published in
1920.
Nostalgia for the splendid medieval Bukhara of Fārābi, Ibn
Sīnā, Ulugh Beg, and others played a prominent role in the literature
of this period. Fitrat used this theme in his Munāzara as an effective
contrast with present conditions, which he claimed to be just the
opposite of what they used to be. In the same spirit, Munzim says:
"Bukhara was a fount of learning and justice at one time. / Now it is
obvious that it is a center of oppression and ignorance." Later he
says: "Come, let's shackle the necks of the enemy / And free this
helpless people (millat) from bonds of grief."[16] Throughout the poem

he feels himself at one with the millat of Bukhara. A further example appears in a poem of 1920 called "Be sharaf-i inqilāb-i Bukhārā" (In Honor of the Bukhara Revolution) of Mīrzā Mohsen 'Akkās, which begins: "Arise, youth of the homeland (vatan): Now it is our turn— it is the time to be faithful; / The pain in our hearts, the helpless population (millat), / has been cured—it has become our freedom."[17] The poem carries on in a fervently revolutionary manner.

The revolutionary poetry of this period usually took one of two forms. Ayniy's and Lāhūtī's poetry generally celebrated the revolution in the larger sense, and addressed all the oppressed workers of the world. This was the far horizon to which the poets looked, while in the foreground lay Bukhara. Here was Bukhara, and there was the world at large, and what lay between the two seems not to have inspired the poets in any way.

As a final example of how Bukharan intellectuals felt about Bukhara we will return to the year 1909, when Fitrat sets the tone for the next 15 years. In the Epilogue to the Munāzara, addressed to the amir of Bukhara, Fitrat says: "Bukhara is our sacred homeland (vatan), our loving mother, the place where we grew up, where we make our living; our beloved, whom we love as our own souls. Bukhara is ours, and we are Bukhara's."[18] Nothing is said to contradict this declaration until the political division of the nationalities in 1924.

The question must now be asked, what does all this mean? What does it add up to in terms of a sense of nationality awareness? The volume of literary evidence that can be brought to bear is not as abundant as one would wish. On the other hand, it is quite consistent in what it expresses. In addition, there are other factors, better known perhaps, that must be added to the preceding in order to make the mosaic complete.

Leading Bukharan intellectuals referred to Bukhara as their vatan, to their compatriots as the millat, and to the Iranian language they wrote as Fārsī. Most of the modern Bukharan intellectuals of the period were part of the Jadīd movement, which was active in urban centers within and outside Bukhara. Sometime before 1917 the Jadids of Bukhara began using the title Young Bukharans, which is a good example of the special kind of solidarity that existed in Bukhara.

The Jadids and Young Bukharans included speakers of both Turki and what the Bukharans called Fārsī. In fact, it appears from the literary evidence that most intellectuals of this period were bilingual. This can be said with certainty of Fitrat, Ayniy, and Behbudiy, and must have been true for the majority of the other Jadīds. Not only were the intellectuals bilingual, but some of the periodicals such as Ayinä and Qutulush were also bilingual. Literary

works were translated from one language to the other, Munāzara
being an example.[19] Because this was the case, it is very difficult
to divide the intellectuals into ethnic or linguistic groups, and in
fact this is an irrelevant distinction until 1924. From the fact that
many of them wrote and spoke both languages, and from the way they
use the terms vatan and millat for Bukhara and its inhabitants, for
which they considered themselves spokesmen, it is clear that they
felt their primary loyalty and identity to lie with Bukhara and its
people.

        Departing from our theme of key words for a moment, we
might mention some other factors operating in favor of Bukharan
solidarity. For example, Pan-Turkic and Pan-Islamic ideas were
still active during this period, and Fitrat for one was clearly sympathetic to Pan-Islamism. One of his most impassioned pleas in the
Munāzara, and one that echoes in many of his other writings, calls
for the unity of Islam against the Christian world. Pan-Islamic
influences can be seen to a greater or lesser extent in the statements
of other Bukharan intellectuals, while Pan-Turkic ideas are less
overt. Fitrat was accused of Pan-Turkism in 1928 in connection
with his views on the Latinization of the Arabic alphabet for the
Tājīk language,[20] but prior to this I am not aware of any Pan-Turkic
statements on his part issued in the Iranian language of Bukhara.
Thus an overt Pan-Islamism and a covert or indirect Pan-Turkism
were also influencing Bukharan intellectuals at this time.

        An additional factor that might be set against any tendency
toward pan-Turkism among Bukharans was their common literary
and artistic heritage, which was Iranian. The ethnic Iranians who
spoke the Iranian language in Bukhara during this period were in
a numerical minority, but exerted a disproportionate cultural influence, especially in the literature. The literary forms were those
of classical Persian for those writing in that language, and the same
may be said by and large for the Uzbeks. The weight of the classical
Persian literary tradition can be seen in Fitrat's poem "Tāziāna-i
ta' dib" mentioned above. One of his principal themes here asserts
that life requires effort and struggle, and that the Bukharans are
sunk in lethargy and bent on pursuing base and unworthy ends. He
then describes his compatriots' using a series of metaphors drawn
from classical Persian lyric poetry. "One," he says, "is a prisoner
of the tresses of fairy-faced beauties, drinking his cup to the memory
of the languid glance of his idol," and so on for three more lines.
Another example is found in Abu al-Qāsim Lāhūtī's poem written
in Dushanbe in 1925, entitled "Sarai-i tamaddun" (The Palace of
Civilization). Here he laments the current state of "Tajik" culture
by describing a ruined palace, where only shattered, dusty fragments
hint at its past splendor. In the palace he finds an old book, written

in the Persian script. "Ah," he sighs, "this building was Tajik civilization, which shed its light on the firmament." Lāhūti was well aware of the cultural bond between the newly-formed Tajikistan and Persia.[21] Those writing in what they called Fārsī were conscious of being a part of the larger Iranian culture area and of being heirs to its heritage. It was an Iranianized Islamic culture, which both major ethnic groups shared.

What cannot be ignored in this argument is the fact that we are using as evidence only the statements and sentiments of the intellectuals. They were by necessity an urban group, while the majority of the population, the millat of Bukhara, was rural. Therefore, one must be cautious not to assert the universality of the intellectuals' beliefs. Furthermore, in all the statements cast in literary form, it is almost impossible to distinguish the ideal from the actual. This is not to question the sincerity of the writers, but to point out that as advanced and revolutionary as they might sound in the poetry, for example, they were still products of a traditional society and were writing within a highly conventional literary tradition. One prominent aspect of this literary tradition is a tendency toward hyperbole. In the late 1920s the younger generation of intellectuals were often unable to accept the older-generation Jadīds as their equals in leading the revolution, not because of the older generation's stand on particular questions, but because the younger men believed that their older comrades were intellectually incapable of living and breathing the Bukharan revolution. They were products of the old culture and their espousal of the new culture could only be superficial. Maybe they were right. In any case, the weight of tradition lay heavily on the shoulders of the Fitrats and the Ayniys, and this must be considered when evaluating what they said.

The sum of these diverse elements might be characterized as a manifestation of urban 'asabiyya, as posited by Ibn Khaldūn. Ibn Khaldūn believed that it was blood and family ties that held tribal groups together and produced the group or social solidarity so characteristic of them. When, however, tribal members take up residence in a city, mix and intermarry with others not of their blood-group, and live in areas of mixed population, the force of the old blood and family ties abates, and a solidarity based on being a part of the urban population, all under a single ruler, takes its place. I suggest that with the necessary changes this line of thinking could be applied to the population of Bukhara before the division of the (ethnic) nationalities.

By "nationality awareness" it seems that we often have in mind the feeling of identity among individuals of a single ethnic, linguistic, culturally distinct group. Within this framework we cannot properly speak of nationality awareness in Bukhara at this

time. The bulk of the population comprised two ethnically and linguistically distinct groups, the majority group with a pastoral nomadic
background but having been strongly influenced some 400 years
earlier by the culture of the minority group, Iranian sedentary
agriculturalists. Thus the linguistic and ethnic bonds for such
"nationality awareness" were lacking.

These two groups had come together in urban centers, blending
their cultural identities, at least according to the literary evidence,
into a seemingly homogeneous, undifferentiated supraethnic urban
culture with a common religion, a common intellectual and social
outlook, under a single ruler. The appropriateness of Ibn Khaldūn's
theory perhaps may not be pushed very far, for it is not sufficient
to explain the whole complex situation of Bukhara. The concept of
'asabiyya, however, may be suggested in an attempt to point out the
differences between, on one hand, the very clear feeling of solidarity
among urban Bukharans in the face of what normally would be strongly
divisive forces and, on the other, what later came to be called "nationality awareness" or something similar.

A situation similar to that in Bukhara is probably not unique,
but in this case it is sufficiently different from that which followed
after 1924 that a different term might usefully be applied to it.
From the literary evidence, it seems quite clear that these Central
Asian intellectuals considered themselves Bukharans first. Their
distinctive identity was that of being Bukharan Muslims.

13

THE EXISTENCE OF
A BUKHARAN NATIONALITY
IN THE RECENT PAST
Timur Kocaoglu

It is important to examine the nationality question in the context of the Bukhara People's Conciliar Republic between 1920 and 1924. This state occupied a very significant place and held a particular meaning in Central Asia. In considering the idea of nationality prevailing in the Bukharan state, it would be useful to make clear that the European ethnic-linguistic concept of nationality, which was brought to Central Asia by czarist Russia, differed from the understanding of "nationality" known by the Central Asian people. First of all, although there were distinctions between the nomads and settled people of Central Asia, both groups were conscious of belonging to a unified Islamic community.[1]

After the czarist Russian conquest in the nineteenth century, the beginning of ethnic nationality consciousness, in the European understanding, appeared rather late and only among the Kazakhs of northern Central Asia and the Turkmens of the Transcaspian area, owing to the rather distinct homogeneity among each of these two ethnic groups.[2] During the czarist occupation of these areas, the tribes of the Kazakhs and Turkmens considered themselves either Kazakh or Turkmen as contrasted to Russian. The primary reason why both these Turkic groups called themselves by their ethnic names in the late nineteenth century is that they intended to distinguish themselves from the Russians, not other Central Asians. In the Khivan khanate and the Bukharan emirate there was a kind of Eastern nationality consciousness, but it differed from the Western or Russian understanding. Both Khiva and Bukhara were "multiethnic" states. (Because the Khivan khanate lies outside the scope of the research, this chapter discusses the nationality question only in the Bukharan state).

The Bukharan nationality concept was based on a view of the entire state. In this state there were many Turkic tribes, like the Manghit, Ming, or Qipchaq, found among ethnic groups such as the Karakalpak, Kazakh, Kirgiz, Turkmen, Uyghur, and Uzbek. In addition, Afghans, Arabs, Galchas, Indians, Iranians, Jews, Tajiks, and others, most of whom had been living together with the Turkic groups for centuries, made up the population in the same state. Various Central Asian authors have reported the size of these ethnic groups or their percentage in the total Bukharan population. These calculations seldom agree with one another, although they usually accept a figure of about 3 million to be the Bukharan total around 1920. Data from different local sources are compiled in Table 13.1. Three million may be a rather small number for the Bukharan population between 1920 and 1924. One of the estimates given for the Bukharan state in 1913-14 was 3.6 million.[3] If the 1917 census data (tahrir-i nufus hesabi) of the Bukharan Government for some of its eastern provinces (see Table 13.2) is examined, it can be estimated that the population of the Bukharan state came rather close to 4 million in 1917. Those eastern provinces comprise a land area of only 81,424 square kilometers out of the total (217,000 square kilometers) comprising the Bukharan state.

Close examination of the Tables suggests the possibility that government and local sources did not focus primarily on ethnic or racial differences within their population. Especially in Table 13.2 it appears clear that the government wanted to estimate only the distribution, not the exact location or the size of ethnic groups. Also, information about the ethnic groups of the Bukharan state is scanty in local sources. Because most of the people did not identify themselves primarily according to ethnic group, and also as a result of mixing and scattering, neither the government nor the intelligentsia could give data about ethnic groups in detail. (See Figure 11.1, "The Ethnic Composition of the Population of Bukhara, ca. 1920," which shows the considerable dispersion of ethnic groups throughout both the state and cities.) This fact is confirmed by local sources which are used in Table 13.1. According to them, Uzbeks were scattered from one end of the Bukharan state to the other; although Tajiks too, were found in every part of the state, the majority of them was located in Baljuvan, Bukhara, Darvaz, Gharm, Hisar, Kolab, Qarategin, Rushan, and Shughnan; Turkmens lived on both banks of the Amu Darya river, especially in Charjoy, Karki, and Sherabad; Ghalchas in the mountain range of Darvaz; Hezaras (Hezargan) were located on the banks of Qizil Su river; and Russians settled in Kagan (Yangi Bukhara), Karki, Termiz, and Yangi Charjoy (Divana Bagh).[4] A Central Asian publication from Tashkent in 1918 expresses the nationality view of the Bukharan state as follows: "At the present

TABLE 13.1

Population of the Bukharan State Between 1909 and 1924, According to Local Sources

Ethnic Groups	Fitrat (1909)	Bakir (1918)	Akhrari (1924)	Others[a]	
Uzbek	—	—	ca. 2,000,000	(1,413,000)	47.1%
Tajik	—	—	ca. 400,000	(1,185,000)	39.5%
Turkmen and other Bukharans	—	—	(568,500)	(402,000)	13.4%
Russian	—	30,000	32,500	—	
Total:	2,000,000	3,000,000	3,000,000	3,000,000	

[a] Özbekistan SSR tärikhi (Tashkent: Özbekistan SSR Fänlär Äkädemiyäsi Näshriyati, 1958), II, pp. 170, 237; Edward Allworth, Central Asian Publishing and Rise of Nationalism. An Essay and a List of Publications in the New York Public Library (New York: New York Public Library, 1965), pp. 20-21.

Sources: Fitrat-i Bukhārāyī, Munāzara (Istanbul: Matbaʿā-yi Islāmiya, Hikmat, H. 1327/1909), p. 4; Mukhtār Bakir, Turkistan tarikhi (Tashkent: n.p., 1918): trans. to Persian as Turkistan by Sayyid Rizā ʿAlizāda (Lahore: Nashriyāt-i Shīr Muhammad, 1927), pp. 296-300. Although Bakir identifies the ethnic groups of the Bukharan state as follows: "Afghans, Arabs, Galchas, Hezaras, Indians, Jews, Kirgiz, Lūlī or Chūgīs (Gypsies), Russians, Tajiks, Tatars, Turks, Turkmens, with the Uzbeks in great majority," he doesn't give a number or percentage for any except the Russians; Shakir Yaʿqub-Säʿid Akhrari, Bukhara jāghrafiyāsi (Old Bukhara: Bukhara Khālq Shuralar Jumhuriyātining Dävlät Näshriyati, August 1924), pp. 20-21. The numbers shown in parenthesis have been calculated from totals and proportions given in the sources.

TABLE 13.2

1917 Census Records of the Bukharan Government
for Some of Its Eastern Provinces

(Vilayat) Province	Square Kilometers	Population
Gharm	28,726.5	(349,078)
Kolab	11,342	(297,435)
Dushanbe	12,251.5a	(234,941)
Oratepa	5,617.5	(66,420)
Sari Asiya	a	63,040
Qorghan Tepa	9,416	58,250
Panjakent	8,720.5	44,352
Pamirb	5,350	22,130
TOTAL:	(81,424)	(1,135,646)

aDushanbe and Sari Asiya vilayats (provinces) together total
12,251.5 square kilometers. No separate figures are given for them.
bDaghliq Badakhshan.

Source: "Turkistanin nufus hesabi," Yeni Turkistan, Istanbul,
No. 7 (December 1927), p. 18. These estimates were taken from the
journal Tajikistan, Tashkent (1925). The numbers shown in
parentheses have been corrected for this Table.

time the inhabitants of Bukhara [state] consist of a combination of
people who resulted from an intermixture of various ethnic groups"
(Dar zamān-i hāzir ahālī-yi Bukhārā az khalq-i mukhtalitī ʿibarat
and ki az ikhtilāt-i qillathā-yi gūnāgūn hāsil shuda and).[5]
    Because to some extent religion, common culture, customs,
and economic community within the Bukharan state provided the
basis for the community of the Bukharan population, all these people
(except outsiders like the Russians) called themselves Bukharayi
or Bukharali (in English, "Bukharan"). Like other modern Bukharans,
the writer, thinker, and politician Abdalrauf Fitrat (1886-1947) signed
his name as a Bukharan. The signature "Fitrat-i Bukharayi" appears
on his work Munāzara (The Debate), published in Persian in Istanbul
(1909), and in the Persian-language poem Tāziyāna-yi taʾdib (The
Scourge of Warning), issued in Samarkand in 1914.[6] In the Russian
translation of Munāzara, published in Tashkent in 1911, Fitrat's
name was signed as Fitrat Bukharets, that is, Fitrat the Bukharan.[7]

Also, in his Persian-language Munāzara we see from the following passage that the nationality consciousness of Fitrat was based upon his awareness of the unitary Bukharan state: ". . . Bukhara is our holy homeland. Bukhara is our kind mother. Bukhara is the place where we grew up. . . . Bukhara belongs to us, we belong to Bukhara."[8] His cognition of the millat (nation) was based on the population of an entire dävlät (state) when he said: "My dear compatriots, noble nation of Bukhara. . . ."[9]

The European style of ethnic-linguistic nationality consciousness was alien to Central Asia because, according to former citizens of the Bukharan state, among the Bukharan people a nationality was defined simply as people "living in the same state, belonging to the same religion, and sharing the same cultural heritage."[10] The well-known poet, novelist, and historian Sadriddin Ayniy (1878-1954)—who first worked with the "Young Bukharan" group and after 1924 became known as a Tajik writer—said, about qualities held in common by the Iranian and Turkic people, "They both drank from the same river."[11] Ayniy's thought is shared by other authors. Ghafur Ghulam (1903-1966), a modern Uzbek writer, said, "We are children of one river, sons of one mother, daughters of one father!"[12]

Most of the Bukharan people knew both the Turki (Turkic) and Farsi (Persian) tongues. Like other Bukharan Jadid (Reformist) authors, Ayniy and Fitrat wrote in both languages. Before 1925 in the Bukharan state the words Turki and Farsi were used instead of "Uzbek" and "Tajik" to identify these languages. Farsi had been the state language of Bukhara until 1921, when Turki became the official tongue. It is very significant that Ayniy, in his works published before 1925, for instance the Persian-language History of the Manghit Emirs of Bukhara (1923), used especially the words Turki and Farsi for these languages, as follows: "These two letters in the Turki [emphasis added] language are appended at the end of Mirza Azim's History," and "The History of Molla Khāmuliy-i Samarkandiy, which was written in Farsi, has not been published yet."[13] Also, Ayniy, in Materials for the History of the Bukharan Revolution (1926), used the same words: "The newspaper Bukhara-i sharif [Noble Bukhara] was published in Farsi, and Turan in Turki."[14] After 1924 or 1925 he began to employ the terms "Uzbek" and "Tajik" in the Soviet manner.

Before 1925, the local press printed in northern Central Asia designated the respective languages or ethnic groups in newspaper names like Kazakh gaziti (Kazakh Newspaper), 1907, Kazakh, 1913-18, Kazakh sozu (The Kazakh Word), 1919.[15] But in the Bukharan state during the same period the names of newspapers call attention to the "multiethnic nationality"; for example, there was the Iranian-language Bukhara-i sharif (Noble Bukhara), published between March

11, 1912, and January 2, 1913; the Turkic-language Turan, July 14,
1912-January 2, 1913; Bukhara akhbari (Bukharan News), issued
before 1922; and Azad Bukhara (Free Bukhara), printed beginning
on September 9, 1922.[16]

The government of the Bukhara People's Conciliar Republic
worked to advance the spirit of Bukharan nationality. Its leaders
wanted to secure an independent Bukhara. The third paragraph of
the Bukharan Republic's constitution (1921) reads: "The Bukhara
People's Conciliar Republic is free and independent in its present-
day frontiers."[17] Also, the Young Bukharan movement and the
Bukhara People's Conciliar Republic's government were certainly
multiethnic in composition. Various members of the Bukharan government and administration came from different ethnic groups. For
instance, Faizullah Khoja (Prime Minister and Minister of Foreign
Affairs), Osman Khoja (first Minister of Finance, then President of
the Republic), and Abdulhamit Arif (Minister of War) came from
Uzbek ethnic origins; Mirza Abdulkadir Muhiddinoglu (first Minister
of Economy, then Justice) was from the Tajiks; Kari Yoldash (Minister
of Education) and Abdurrahim Yusufoglu (Minister of Justice) represented the Turkmen ethnic group.[18]

Although Soviet publications call the Bukharan Republic the
"Bukharan People's Soviet Republic," the Turkic/Persian word shora
is appropriate here instead of "soviet," because the Russian term
soviet was not used locally in this title until late 1924. From the
beginning the Republic was named "Bukhara Khälq Shoralar Jumhuriyäti" (Bukhara People's Conciliar Republic) by Bukharans. Most
or all of the Soviet books issued after 1924 give the name "Bukhara
Khälq Sovet Respublikasi" (Bukharan People's Soviet Republic),[19]
apparently substituting the last two words from Russian in order to
Sovietize the name and diminish the appearance of separateness or
independence of the Bukharan state. However, certain original
materials show the proper Bukharan form of the name. On the flag
and money of the Bukharan Republic were inscribed the Arabic letters
"Bä," "Khä," "Shin," and "Jim," which are the initials for "Bukhara
Khälq Shoralar Jumhuriyäti."* Also, in official papers and books
from the period, for instance in the volume Bukhara jäghrafiyäsi

---

*All these documents were displayed during the Conference on
the Nationality Question in Soviet Central Asia, April 7-8, 1972, in
the exhibit in the International Affairs Library, Columbia University.
The author wishes to thank Prof. Edward Allworth, Raci Cakiroz,
Yakub Elbek, Dr. Naim Oktem, and Nadir Ricaloglu for providing
several documents and publications used in research for this
article.

(Geography of Bukhara), published by the state press in August 1924,
"Bukhara Khälq Shoralar Jumhuriyäti" was registered.[20] The word
khälq (people) was sometimes omitted from the title, and the Republic
was called simply "Bukhara Shoralar Jumhuriyäti (Bukhara Conciliar
Republic), as Figure 13.1 demonstrates in the official seal of the
"Charjoy Faizullah Khoja Namuna Daru'l-Muallimi" (The Faizullah
Khoja Model Teacher's Institute in Charjoy). Moreover, the word
mustaqil (independent) was occasionally added to the Republic's name,
notably in Ayniy's Iranian-language "History of the Manghit Amirs
of Bukhara," published in 1923, where the country's name was
written "Mustaqil Bukhara Khälz Shoralar Jumhuriyäti" (The Independent Bukharan People's Conciliar Republic).[21] Although the word
shuralar (conciliar) is a translation of the Russian word "soviets,"
it is important to remember that the Russian word was not used
until 1924 in the Republic's name. At last, on September 19, 1924,
at the Fifth Bukhara-wide Congress (Bishinchi Butun-Bukhara
Qurultayi), "Bukhara Khälq Shuralar Jumhuriyäti" was replaced with
"Bukhara Sovet Sosyalistik Jumhuriyäti" (Bukhara Soviet Socialist
Republic).[22]
    This nationality question was specifically discussed recently in
my correspondence conducted with some emigrants from the Bukharan
state who had lived there until 1922 or 1923. They report that before

FIGURE 13.1

Seal of the Faizullah Khoja Teachers Institute
of Charjoy, Bukhara, 1923

        Stamped on school documents in the Bukharan Republic,
1923.

1924 neither illiterate nor literate Bukharan people expressed any
consciousness of belonging to a single ethnic nationality such as the
Tajik, Turkmen, or Uzbek groups known today.[23] This belief in
belonging to the Bukharan nationality continues up to the present,
outside of Central Asia, among the surviving emigrants from the
Bukharan state. In south Asian and Middle Eastern countries such
as Afghanistan, Arabia, India, Pakistan, Persia, and Turkey, Bukharan
emigrants still call themselves "Bukharan." In 1929 in Peshawar,
Central Asian emigrants established an organization called in Persian
"Anjuman-i Saᶜādat-i Bukhara va Turkistan" (Council for Benefit of
Bukhara and Turkistan). Similarly, another association in Delhi
named itself in Persian: "Anjuman-i Ittihādiya-yi Muhājirīn-i
Bukhara va Turkistan" (Council for the Union of Emigrants from
Bukhara and Turkistan).

Thus, it is possible to say that, until 1925, in the Bukharan state
there was a single Bukharan nationality and nation of an Eastern type,
and this is shown by the following arguments and evidence: (1) The
nationality consciousness of the Bukharan people, based upon the
Bukharan state, conveyed an idea of nationality different from the
European ethnic-linguistic concept; (2) Bukhara was a "miltiethnic"
state populated by several different large groups and many smaller
ones; (3) Although the Bukharan people mainly spoke both the
Turki and Farsi languages, along with some others, they did not
identify their nationality with their languages or ethnic groups; (4)
The first constitution of the Bukharan Republic based itself upon the
unity of the Bukharan nationality; (5) The composition of the leading
bodies in the Bukharan government was multiethnic; (6) In both the
state and cities of Bukhara ethnic groups were quite mixed and
scattered; (7) Not only political leaders but the Bukharan intelligentsia
often expressed in writing a consciousness of belonging to this
Bukharan nationality both before and after 1920, the year the Bukhara
People's Conciliar Republic was established.

If we assess the larger meaning of Bukharan nationality, it will
be seen that Soviet Russian policy in 1925 divided the Bukharan population into different major administrative units (particularly the Tajik,
Turkmen, and Uzbek) according to an ethnic-linguistic principle,
because the existence of the Bukharan nationality offered a great
threat to Soviet Russian nationality policy. If the multiethnic Bukharan
Republic and nationality had been allowed to remain, it might have
provided a conflicting principle and rallying point around which all
the Central Asian ethnic groups could have united and become one
supraethnic nationality and nation.[24]

14

NATIONAL CONSCIOUSNESS AND THE POLITICS OF THE BUKHARA PEOPLE'S CONCILIAR REPUBLIC

Seymour Becker

The khanate of Bukhara (1500-1920) was an agglomeration of towns, villages, rural districts, and nomadic and seminomadic tribes, held together loosely by economic ties but primarily by loyalty to a common dynasty enforced through political and military sanctions. Identity with the state was very weakly developed, since subordination to the amir of Bukhara, as opposed to the khan of Khiva, the khan of Kokand (until 1876), or the Russian governor-general of Turkistan (after 1867), was entirely a matter of the fortunes of war and politics and always subject to change. Kokand itself until the eighteenth century and for brief periods in the mid-nineteenth century had been part of Bukhara, as had Samarkand and the upper Zarafshan valley until the Russian conquest in 1868. Furthermore, the cohesiveness of this dynastic agglomeration was directly dependent on the energy and skill of the ruler of the moment and was continually threatened by the separatist tendencies of such provinces as Shahr-i Sabz, Hisar, and Kolab.[1] Bukhara's political boundaries thus simply reflected the relative strength of the amir vis-à-vis his rivals in any given period; that those boundaries should coincide with ethnic or linguistic frontiers was a thought not entertained by anyone before the development of national consciousness.

Although a sense of political community was not highly developed, a sense of religious community was. Except for small minorities of Jews and Hindus in the major towns, all of the amir's subjects were very conscious of belonging to Dar ul-Islam, the community of the faithful. This was a community, however, that included, in addition to Bukhara, the rest of Central Asia and many lands beyond, embracing a multitude of ethnic and linguistic groups. The intrusion of Russian infidels into Central Asia in the second half of the nineteenth century had further strengthened the religious consciousness of the indigenous population.

159

Within Bukhara, as within Central Asia in general, the primary
social division was that between nomads and the sedentary population.
Among the nomads the great tribal formations provided the framework for group consciousness, and a common way of life, regulated
by Islamic customary law (adat), set the nomads apart from their
sedentary neighbors and coreligionists. A supratribal ethnic consciousness may have been emerging by the beginning of the twentieth
century among the nomads south and west of the Amu Darya, based
on shared historical experiences and interests in dealing with their
sedentary neighbors and perhaps also on a common language (Turkmen)
more closely related to Azeri and Osmanli Turkish than to the other
Turkic languages of Central Asia. Among the nomads north and east
of the Amu Darya, bearers of common historical traditions and common tribal designations different from those of the Turkmens, the
existence of two major Turkic languages (Kazakh and Uzbek) and a
host of dialects seems to have been a factor of very little significance
in the formation of group identities.[2]

Linguistic differences played an even less important role among
the sedentary population. Distinguished from the nomads by its way
of life, which was regulated by Koranic law (Sharia), the sedentary
population was internally differentiated through its identification with
particular towns, villages, and districts. The fact that the khanate
of Bukhara was divided between speakers of Uzbek, a Turkic language,
and speakers of Tajik, an Iranian language, had virtually no influence
on the ways in which individuals conceived of themselves. Speakers
of both languages had lived for centuries geographically intermingled
and economically interdependent in western Bukhara and shared a
common religion, culture, and history. In the larger towns a good
part of the population was bilingual. The use of the terms Uzbek and
Tajik to establish primary group identity among the inhabitants of
Bukhara was an innovation introduced by the Russians in the mid-
1920s and caused no end of confusion. These terms had previously
been employed in Bukhara, but with no great precision, consistency,
or linguistic significance. While some of the indigenous Tajik-speaking
Sunnites of Bukhara city called themselves Tajiks, others reserved
that label for Shiite immigrants from Persia, whose own name for
themselves was Irani or Farsi. The Farsi in turn called all native
Bukharans Uzbeks, regardless of what language they spoke. In
Samarkand, Shiite Persian immigrants referred to themselves as
Irani but spoke an Uzbek dialect. Three-quarters of the residents
of Bukhara city in the mid-1920s considered themselves Uzbeks,
thereby identifying with the traditional ruling elite, although a majority
of them spoke Tajik. If linguistic identification was necessary, they
qualified themselves as either Tajik- or Farsi-speaking Uzbeks or
Turki-speaking Uzbeks.[3]

When the Russians insisted for purposes of the 1926 census that Bukharans declare their nationality (narodnost')—a concept totally alien to the overwhelming majority of the population—personal considerations often determined the choice and resulted in such anomalies as one brother identifying as an Uzbek and another as a Tajik, or the women of a family calling themselves Tajiks and the men declaring they were Uzbeks. Even after three decades of official promotion of the concept of nationality based on a common language, older forms of consciousness persisted in many areas. In 1959 a Soviet ethnographer discovered in Samarkand oblast two neighboring settlements inhabited by descendants of Uzbek nomads who retained their common identity as members of the Chaghatay tribe, despite the fact that one village spoke Tajik and the other Uzbek. Nor did this linguistic distinction prevent the surrounding Uzbek tribal groups from referring to the population of both settlements as Tajik.[4]

As of 1920, when the khanate was overthrown, none of the traditional groups in Bukhara had developed a national consciousness, that is, a shared sense of identity among individuals as members of an abstract group transcending ties of kinship and birthplace and based not on religion or social status but on a common historical experience and a common culture.[5] Such a sense of identity was restricted to the numerically insignificant modernist intelligentsia called Jadids and, later, Young Bukharans. At first, under the tutelage of Tatar reformers whose thinking ran along pan-Turkic and pan-Islamic lines, the Bukharan Jadids turned increasingly after 1905 toward the Young Turks of the Ottoman Empire for their model. They began to conceive of a Turkistan nation (millat) on the basis of a shared history and culture and a common national territory or homeland (vatan) embracing all of Russian Central Asia. Their political goal was a unified, autonomous Turkistan nation-state, Turkic and Muslim in character, democratic and liberal in structure. These aims were held in common by the Jadids of Bukhara and those of the government-general of Turkistan, all of whom recognized the arbitrary nature of the existing political boundaries in Central Asia.[6]

Stemming from the Uzbek-Tajik sedentary population, most of the modernist intelligentsia were bilingual but eventually opted for the transformation of Uzbek into a national literary language that would supplant the various Turkic vernaculars spoken by the great majority of Central Asians. Such a development was of particular interest to Abdalrauf Fitrat, a guiding intellect of the Central Asian Jadid movement. Fitrat, in fact, had begun his literary career by writing in Tajik, or, more accurately, Persian, a traditional literary language of Central Asia, later switching to Turki as his nationalist ideas developed.[7]

When the czarist regime collapsed in March 1917, the Jadids of
the khanate together with those of the government-general pressed
their claim for an autonomous Turkistan within a federation of nation-
states on the territory of the former Russian Empire. At the same
time they pressed the amir of Bukhara for a broad measure of political
and social reform, hoping to use him as a unifying symbol of Turkistan's
national regeneration and as a focus of popular loyalty during the
difficult period of cultivating and superimposing a Turkistan national
identity upon existing firmly rooted local and tribal identities.[8] The
events of the next three years betrayed many of the hopes of the
Central Asian nationalists. Neither the Provisional Government nor
its Bolshevik successors were sympathetic to their aims. Friction
between the government in Tashkent, as completely in Russian hands
as it had been under the czars, and the nationalists, joined with
xenophobic conservatives in an alliance against their common opponent,
ended in Tashkent's forcible suppression of the Kokand autonomous
regime in February 1918. The Young Bukharans' attempt to extract
reforms from the amir and use him for their own ends foundered on
the amir's conservatism, the strength of the ultraconservative clerical
zealots in the khanate, and the Russian Provisional Government's
inability or unwillingness to apply sufficient pressure. Tashkent's
ill-conceived and unsuccessful invasion of Bukhara in March 1918,
which the Young Bukharans supported, merely made outlaws of them
in their own country.[9]

The outlook for the Central Asian nationalist movement did not
improve until September 1920, when a well-planned Soviet invasion,
utilizing both Russian and indigenous troops, overthrew the amir and
put the Young Bukharans, led by Faizullah Khojaev, into power.
Prospects were still not entirely encouraging. The political sub-
division of Central Asia remained unaltered despite the changes in
governments and nomenclature: in place of the government-general
of Turkistan and the Khivan and Bukharan khanates there were now the
Turkistan Autonomous Soviet Socialist Republic (a part of the Russian
Soviet Federated Socialist Republic) and the Khivarazm and Bukhara
People's Conciliar Republics. Territorial unity was as distant as
ever. Worse yet, for those with hopes of independence, the Tashkent
government retained the character of a Russian colonial regime. And
the amir, a political refugee in Afghanistan from February 1921, had
become the divisive symbol of traditionalist resistance to the liberal
nationalist revolution rather than a unifying agent in the creation of
a Turkistan national consciousness among the populace. Even the
new people's republics, recognized by Moscow as sovereign states,
were bound to the Russian SFSR by treaties that, although less unequal
than those between the Russian and other soviet republics, gave
Moscow close control over defense, internal security, and economic

matters.[10] The brighter side of the picture was that, despite the qualified nature of Bukhara's independence, the nationalists now held power for the first time and were able to capitalize on all the historical associations and memories inspired by the name Bukhara, which had played a leading and often dominant role in Central Asia's history since the late ninth century. When the Young Bukharans spoke of a Bukharan nation and a Bukharan homeland, they were consciously manipulating these associations and memories to promote their concept of a Greater Bukhara or Turkistan, embracing all of Soviet Central Asia, although for the present they were compelled to limit their activities to the people's republic. The nationalist intelligentsia throughout Central Asia did in fact view the truncated but independent Bukharan republic as the herald of a Turkistan national renaissance.[11]

Although the Young Bukharans owed their power to the Red Army's invasion of the khanate in September 1920 and to its campaign in central Bukhara during the winter of 1920-21, and although the might of Soviet Russia hung over the new republic from the beginning like a sword of Damocles, there did seem reason to hope that the Young Bukharans would be allowed the opportunity to create a viable nation-state by fostering a new national consciousness among the populace at the expense of traditional local and tribal identities. Until 1923, in fact, despite periodic admonitions against "bourgeois nationalist deviation," Moscow did tolerate the nationalist orientation of the Young Bukharan regime. Bukhara was a useful exhibit to demonstrate to the world that Soviet Russia was not following in czarist Russia's imperialist footsteps but was a genuine patron of national liberation movements among eastern people. Closer to home, from the summer of 1921 until the fall of 1922 a threatening rebellion, that of the Basmachis, raged in central and eastern Bukhara, feeding on traditionalist support for the deposed amir among the clergy and lower classes and on nationalist sentiment among a section of the modernist intelligentsia, with hostility to Russia the common denominator. Moscow hesitated to add fuel to the fire by interfering too openly in Bukhara's affairs. Thus, at the Tenth Congress of the Russian Communist Party in March 1921, the People's Commissar for Nationality Affairs, Joseph Stalin, listed Bukharans and Khivans, along with Kazakhs, Uzbeks, Turkmens, and Tajiks, as Central Asian nationalities deserving help in developing and strengthening their statehood.[12]

Left largely to themselves, the Young Bukharans set about their task of nation-building. An important first step was the declaration of Turki as the official state language of Bukhara in March 1921 by a government in which Abdalrauf Fitrat, long an advocate of using language to foster national consciousness, was commissar (nazir) of education.[13] The length and difficulty of the road ahead became apparent during the republic's first year in connection with disaffection among the Turkmen minority along the Amu Darya (see ethnic maps of Bukhara, Figure 11.1). In the fall of 1920 Turkmen tribal chieftains led a revolt in Karki vilayet, in the course of which thousands of Turkmens fled into Afghanistan. In an attempt to win the Turkmens over to the Young Bukharan camp, the Bukharan Communist Party in February 1921 approved in principle the creation of special national sections (Russian: otdely) within the government to insure equal rights for minority nationalities (natsional'nosti).[14] Events in Khwarazm, where the traditional antipathy between the nomadic and seminomadic Turkmens and the sedentary Uzbeks had kept the country in continual turmoil since 1912, provided a further incentive and a specific model for solving the problem. In order to prevent civil war between Uzbeks and Turkmens in the fall of 1920, Tashkent intervened politically on the side of the latter, purged the Khwarazm Communist Party and government, and in May 1921 supervised the formation of a new government that affirmed the right of each nationality to local self-government, the use of its own language in local schools and courts, and equal access to land and water resources. Henceforth the Central Executive Committee (CEC) of the Khwarazm Congress of Soviets was to include a separate Turkmen section elected by a Turkmen congress.[15]

Two months later the Bukharan government convoked a Turkmen congress in Karki and in September established a Turkmen section within the CEC of the Bukharan republic. On this occasion, as in the following summer when Kazakh sections were formed in the CECs of both Khwarazm and Bukhara, Russian pressure is not to be ruled out. Nevertheless, the policy of the Young Bukharan regime in 1921-22 was clearly one not of separatism but of equal rights for all ethnic groups within a unitary democratic state, albeit with special provisions for the protection of minority interests. In an article published in June 1921 in preparation for the impending Turkmen congress at Karki, Faizullah Khojaev, the Bukharan premier, affirmed his dedication to "the unification of all the tribes and races that constitute the Bukharan republic" and to measures "for halting racial and tribal hostility among our people" and providing "every possibility to unite for the betterment of their situation and the satisfaction of their needs." Khojaev rejected the traditional policy of the amirs, who "divided the Bukharan people into Tajiks and Turkmens," that is sedentary folk and nomads, and renounced the "many false rumors" (presumably of separatism) to which the convocation of the Turkmen congress had given rise. The premier pledged his government to "the elimination of all racial subdivisions among the people" of the republic and to a policy of equal rights for all, recognizing "no differences between Sunnites and Shiites, Turkmens and Tajiks, between Muslims, Russians, and Jews."[16]

Whatever chances for success the program of the Young
Bukharans may have had were dispelled the moment Soviet Russia
adopted a hostile attitude. By the fall of 1922 the Basmachi revolt
was reduced to manageable proportions by a Red Army counter-
offensive in east-central Bukhara. Moscow now felt free to deal
decisively with the threat posed by the substantial number of Turkic
nationalists, in Central Asia and elsewhere, who had joined the Communist Party in 1918-19 in order to pursue, rather than the class
struggle for social justice, the cause of a Turkic national renaissance.
But one example of their attitude was the resolution passed in January
1920 by a conference of Muslim Communists of Central Asia, calling
for an "autonomous Turkic republic" in Turkistan under its own
autonomous Turkic Communist Party. At the time, Moscow had
responded merely by strengthening Russian control over the Tashkent
regime at the expense of the indigenous element.[17] In the spring of
1923, however, Stalin launched an all-out campaign against Turkic
nationalism, which he viewed as a dangerous threat to the unity and
goals of the Soviet state. In May he arrested his own lieutenant in
the Commissariat for Nationality Affairs, the Kazan Tatar Sultan
Galiev, chief among the leaders of the Turkic nationalist movement
within the Party.[18] At the same time Stalin withdrew his support for
the nationalist intelligentsia who were trying to develop the national
consciousness of the Bukharan populace. In the first half of 1923 the
Bukharan regime was several times attacked for nationalist deviations,
and at the Twelfth Congress of the Russian Communist Party in March
Stalin denounced the existence of "Uzbek chauvinism directed against
the Turkmens and the Kirgiz that is, [Kazakhs] in Bukhara and
Khivarazm."[19] Stalin renewed his charges of Uzbek chauvinism in
June at a conference in Moscow between the Central Committee of
the Russian Communist Party and leading Party members from the
national republics and regions. Khojaev, who was present, bravely
defended his government's policies and achievements and pressed for
Bukhara's admission to the newly formed USSR as an equal member
state, a step Stalin had himself envisioned only seven months earlier.[20]

Resistance to Moscow's new policy was foredoomed to failure.
Lacking any broad popular support for their program, the Young
Bukharans had already faced a choice between the Basmachis, behind
whom stood their old foe the amir, and Soviet Russia, which ostensibly
stood for national as well as proletarian liberation. Some, including
Osman Khoja, president of Bukhara in September-November 1921,
had opted for the Basmachis in late 1921 when the Young Turk adven-
turer Enver Pasha made his bid to supplant the amir as leader of the
rebellion on a platform calling for an independent Turkistan within
a pan-Turkic confederation.[21] This group had come to regard Russia
as an insuperable obstacle to the realization of their liberal and

nationalist program. The remaining Young Bukharans, led by Faizullah Khojaev, reaffirmed their belief that only in alliance with Moscow did their aims stand any chance of realization. This latter group, having chosen to depend on Russia, found themselves increasingly subordinate to Russia. Under Moscow's direction the Bukharan government and Communist Party had undergone a rigorous purge in the twelve months before Stalin declared open war on "nationalist deviationists" in Bukhara. After that declaration, in the summer of 1923 the purge was intensified, and claimed as its victims most of the remaining Young Bukharan leaders, including Fitrat, who was arrested and deported to Russia. Within a few weeks Lazar M. Kaganovich, who already occupied an important position in the Party under Stalin, was denouncing the very use of the term "Turkistan" as an intolerable manifestation "of a great-Turkic aspiration that ought to be eliminated as soon as possible from the Soviet vocabulary."[22]

Kaganovich's statement foreshadowed the dissolution of the Turkistan ASSR, just as Moscow's pressure on Bukhara to grant home rule to her minorities foreshadowed the dissolution of the Bukharan PCR. By October 1923 Khojaev was forced to abandon his policy of a unitary Bukharan state and accept at Moscow's dictation the formation of an autonomous Turkmen oblast, comprising Charjoy and Karki vilayets, to be governed by its own central executive committee. The following month an autonomous Kazakh national district (raion), centered on Nurata, was also formed.[23] Moscow had determined that the best guarantee against the threat of Turkistan nationalism, not yet a popular phenomenon but nevertheless a movement with strong support among the indigenous intelligentsia, including those who had joined the Communist Party, was to foster the development of half a dozen lesser nationalities in the area, according to the time-honored maxim "divide and rule." In place of the linguistic unity to which the Young Bukharans aspired, linguistic distinctions were to be emphasized. Hence the separation of the Kirgiz and the Karakalpaks from the Kazakhs, and the more difficult task of dividing the sedentary population into Uzbeks and Tajiks in defiance of their common history, culture, and economic interests and a considerable degree of geographic intermingling.

Totally dependent upon Russia for the support not yet forthcoming from the population he governed, Khojaev was too much the political realist to follow the Khwarazm government's policy of futile resistance to Moscow's policy of "national," that is, ethnic-linguistic delimitation. In February 1924 he reluctantly endorsed this policy but could not refrain from referring wistfully to an alleged past unity of all Turkic people, in what was a thinly disguised lament for the

abandoned attempt to develop a Turkistan national consciousness.*
By September 1924, when the new political order in Central Asia was
being formally ratified by the governments concerned, Khojaev was
already making the best of what for him was a disappointing turn of
affairs. Scheduled to be head of government of the new Uzbek republic,
he protested, too much to be entirely convincing, against the senseless
dreams of pan-Turkic unity, dreams that could not but founder on the
age-old hostility among the different Turkic peoples. The only solution
to this hostility, he now said, was the plan for ethnic-linguistic delimitation, which would allow the major nations (natsii) of Bukhara, the
(Kara-) Kirgiz, Tajiks, Turkmens, and Uzbeks to go their separate
ways, freed for the first time of subjection to one another and of the
mutual antagonism thereby engendered.[24]

Thus was the experiment in building a Turkistan nation cut short.
Turkistan national consciousness never did progress beyond the thin
stratum of modernist intelligentsia, although such a development would
not have been improbable under other, more favorable, political
circumstances. The power situation in Central Asia in the early 1920s
was such that Soviet Russia was calling the tune, and political considerations in Moscow determined that half a dozen minor nationalities, defined in ethnic and linguistic terms, rather than a single
major nationality, defined by a common historical experience and
culture, would be fostered in the area. The modernist intelligentsia
were caught fatally between their intellectual isolation from the
populace and their forced dependence on a great power that was,
despite all its talk about national self-determination, intent upon
subordinating nationalism to its own larger purposes. Even those
Turkistan or Bukharan nationalists like Faizullah Khojaev and
Abdalrauf Fitrat (set free in 1924), who survived in power by compro-
mising their beliefs and choosing to serve the newly defined Uzbek
nation, were victimized by Moscow in 1938 as "bourgeois nationalist
deviationists."

---

*The biographical sketch given in the 1970 edition of Khojaev's
selected works (I, 50) notes that his theses on the establishment of
the Uzbek SSR, approved in February 1924 by the Central Committee
of the Bukharan Communist Party, were generally correct, "with the
exception of the author's clearly mistaken affirmation about the past
national unity of all the people of Turkic origin."

15

THE TWO MODES OF
ETHNIC CONSCIOUSNESS:
SOVIET CENTRAL ASIA
IN TRANSITION?
Immanuel Wallerstein

By ethnic consciousness I mean the sentiment, shared by a group of people who define their boundaries in cultural terms (a common language, religion, color, history, style of life, and the like, or a combination of these), that they must seek to assert or extend their rights in the political arena in order to defend possibilities for their continued existence as a group and/or to maintain or improve their material conditions. Whether such a group prefers to call itself a nation, a nationality, an ethnic group, a tribe, a people, or any of the other sundry terms that are used is not very material to the substance of the fact that ethnic consciousness is an assertion in the political arena to defend cultural and economic interests.

Ethnic consciousness is eternally latent everywhere. But it is only realized when groups feel either threatened with a loss of previously acquired privilege or conversely feel that it is an opportune moment politically to overcome long-standing denial of privilege. For any particular group, this occurs periodically but not continuously.

Furthermore, the boundary lines of a group can only be perceived when it is ethnically conscious. It is the act of political assertion that defines the boundaries. Hence each periodic "act" may in fact be that of a group with somewhat different boundaries, even though over a long period of time the successive acting groups use the same name and seem to have largely similar defining characteristics.

I have started with this somewhat tedious definitional process in order to insist on a fundamental premise of my argument: any "ethnic" group exists only to the extent that it is asserted to exist at any given point in time by the group itself and by the larger social network of which it is a part. Such groups are constantly "created" and recreated; they also constantly "cease to exist"; they are thus constantly redefined and change their forms at amazingly fast rates. Yet through the physical maelstrom, some "names" maintain a long historical continuity because at frequent historical intervals it has been in the interests of the conscious elements bearing this "name" to reassert the heritage, revalorize the mythical links, and socialize members into the historical "memory."

Ethnic consciousness, being a political phenomenon, is a form of conflict. The conflict need not be violent, to be sure, though of course it often is. The nature of the conflict, however, may differ, and the form that ethnic consciousness may take may consequently differ as well. In the modern world-system there have been two quite distinct modes of ethnic consciousness occurring in two reasonably distinct arenas of the world-system.

The modern world-economy, within the framework of a single division of labor, contains core areas with a complex range of occupational activities, multiple social strata, a strong state machinery, and a relatively high over-all standard of living (except for the bottom strata). It also contains peripheral areas, which have a narrower range of economic tasks, fewer social strata, a weaker state machinery, and a low standard of living for all but a thin upper stratum. It is evident that the forms of social conflict to be found in these two areas are quite different.

In peripheral areas, the main activity is agricultural labor. Groups of these laborers sharing language, customs, and usually religion as well find themselves compelled by the world market and the local political machinery to engage in hard work for relatively little pay. Their major economic complaint is too high taxation by the government, and their major contemporary demand has been for more educational facilities for their children, seeing the educational system quite correctly as the only likely route of social mobility.

Finding themselves the majority of the people in the area in which they live, these laborers also find that quite often their political rulers come from another ethnic group. This is of course true in all colonial situations in the modern world where the administration has been in the hands of people of radically different culture and geographical origin. This is also true in many regions of noncolonial states of the periphery where the national political leadership is largely or exclusively in the hands of one ethnic group, which, from the perspective of given geographic regions, is a stranger group.

To the extent that the local area in question has educated cadres, whose own chances of advancement are in fact blocked by the absence of political autonomy of the particular area, these cadres may begin to agitate for greater self-rule. They begin to react against the arrogant style of cultural assimilation practiced by the politically dominant forces and reassert traditional cultural values and boundary lines, or invent them.

When economic and political circumstances are such that the
masses of the population respond positively to this agitation, we
usually call this phenomenon "nationalism." Because nationalism
has as its major slogan "self-determination," and to have self-
determination one must logically have a determinate unit, nationalism
tends to be attached to territorial units, either already in existence
or that can be seen as potential. However, because administrative
units, especially those already in existence, almost never correlate
perfectly with membership in linguistic, religious, or other cultural
groupings—because, that is, they are almost always to some extent
"artificial"—ethnically-conscious movements are normally faced
with a choice, especially as the moment of political realization of
aims draws near, between a territorial or a cultural definition of
ethnicity. And usually, despite the presumed cultural base of the
claims, they opt, out of realpolitik, for a territorial definition. This
means that, on cultural grounds, the resulting entity has cultural
minorities, which means that the problem remains, and the game can
go on and on.

It also means that one man's ethnic consciousness is frequently
another man's ethnic oppression. For territory is finite, and two
"groups" cannot both exercise sovereign control over the same area.
Yet quite frequently two groups can lay claims of fairly equal plausi-
bility to particular areas. At which point, more energy may be
devoted to pursuing these rival claims than in any attempt to change
the world-system that has maintained both "groups" and the entire
larger geographical area in peripheral status in the world-economy.

The ethnicity of core areas of the modern world is quite a
different affair. To be sure, there are certain surface similarities.
The ethnic consciousness is defined in cultural terms and emphasized
cultural renaissance. It has as an objective greater equality in the
political arena. And the underlying complaint is that of economic
deprivation. But there the similarities stop.

Core areas of the modern world-economy have been for the
past two centuries industrialized and urbanized areas. The role of
agriculture has constantly declined until today only a small minority
of the work force is involved in agricultural labor, and increasingly
that labor is in fact highly skilled work.

The cities of the industrial areas tend to be ethnic hodgepodges
in terms of the ancestry of the majority of the population. They are
usually of multiple religions. Often they speak various languages,
although the operation of the economy normally requires an official
language as a lingua franca.

Any particular ethnic group tends to be only a minority of the
population of the whole urban area, although they may be residentially
segregated into "ghettos." If anything, the politically dominant

ethnic group often constitutes the majority of the population, or the plurality, and comprises within it not only the political and economic elite but a large percentage of the professionals and of the most skilled workers. The multiple "minorities" are divided into those of higher status whose members are recruited into higher-status jobs, and those of lower status whose members are recruited into subproletarian positions (unskilled labor and lumpenproletarian, marginal, or criminal employment).

The ethnic consciousness of the higher-status minorities tends to be entirely defensive, activated partially to break down remaining discriminatory barriers but increasingly to prevent incursions into their privilege by lower-status groups. One major mode of defense is their own assimilation into the dominant ethnic group, and it is frequently pursued. The political meeting-ground of skilled workers of dominant ethnic group extraction and professionals and skilled workers of higher-status minority groups are institutions of the center-left (such as trade unions, "liberal" or "socialist" political parties, and the like).

Ethnic consciousness of the lower-status ethnic groups, however, is basically an urban phenomenon having strong roots in subproletarian elements. Since in the industrial urban areas education has usually been universal in recent years, these subproletarian elements are frequently joined by a stratum of so-called "unemployed intellectuals," that is, persons who have been educated for positions that either do not yet structurally exist because of the insufficient degree of economic development or from which they are excluded because of their low ethnic origin. When these elements reject assimilation, it is most frequently the assimilation of the center-left institutions of which they are thinking.

The organization of such subproletarian elements tends to take on a tone of more radical ideology than in the case of rural workers in peripheral areas who are led by urban educated elements that see separation as a mode of obtaining substantial personal benefits. In the latter case, agitation often leads to constitutional reform that meets the demands of the leadership, who thereupon can become more "conservative" in terminology.

In the subproletarian case, reform has a less promising outlook, largely because such elements confront in their demands not merely the upper privileged stratum of the society but a privileged middle stratum who already control the center-left "reform" institutions. Hence, there often occurs a process of "radicalization." If this ethnic movement has a firm territorial base, as in Quebec, it can lead to separatist demands, in which case, however, it involves sharing features of both forms of ethnic consciousness. If the territorial base is weak, as is the case with Blacks in the United States, the

movement tends to have a less focused immediate goal, which means
it is more difficult to organize but, once organized, more difficult to
satisfy.

How does all this apply to Soviet Central Asia? As the various
parts of Turkistan fell under Russian rule in the nineteenth century,
these areas were drawn into the periphery of the capitalist world-
economy. They were under colonial rule, which in Bukhara and Khiva
was of the so-called indirect variety. Among the educated elements
various forms of ethnic consciousness took root, for example the
jadid (reformist) movement, and by the early twentieth century there
flourished various overlapping and sometimes confused "nationalist"
sentiments: pan-Islamism, pan-Turanianism, Tatar nationalism,
greater Bukhara, and so on.

Central Asia was in turn part of Russia, herself part of the semi-
periphery of the world-economy. Faced in the late nineteenth century
with the prospect of going backward rather than forward in industrialization—relative to developments in Western Europe and North
America—Russia underwent the October 1917 revolution. This up-
heaval was in part the expression of a demand for a national leadership,
not tied to Western European capitalist forces, that could bring
about the industrial transformation of Russia, in part the expression
of Russian peasant protest against the peripheral role of Russian
agriculture (and their consequent exploitation), in part the expression
of Russia's urban classes (especially the proletariat of skilled workers) for an expansion of their opportunities, political, economic, and
cultural. It was, if you will, the expression of a class conflict in the
world-economy that took on heavily ethnic clothing (heavier than its
ideological leaders wished to admit at the time).

In ideological terms, Russia's colonies were an embarrassment
for the Communist leadership. In terms of their immediate collective
objectives, maintaining these "colonial" areas within the political
hegemony of Russia was, however, vital to the political economy.
The result was the uneasy compromise of the USSR. On the one hand,
the USSR was a federation of sovereign republics with the right of
secession, and the structure provided as well for a variety of lesser
forms of political autonomy. This presumably ended the colonial
status of the former outlying parts of the Russian Empire, insofar
as they were guaranteed the various cultural appurtenances of self-
government (especially language rights) and elected their own indigenous leadership. On the other hand, the USSR as such had a highly
centralized state structure and was a very tight political system involving the primacy of the Communist Party of the Soviet Union.
These two principles were not in perfect harmony. The evidence for
this is clear in the frequent campaigns conducted over the years by

the leadership of the CPSU against "bourgeois nationalism" in the various republics and other autonomous units.

In practice, the Soviet leadership sought a pragmatic compromise that would achieve the objective of territorial integrity and economic coordination at the lowest possible political price. The papers in this collection tend to show how successful this policy was over the first fifty years of the USSR.

The leadership of the CPSU very early adopted, in the dispute of Stalin with Sultan Galiev, an operational principle that has guided them ever since. They indicated that they were open to any suggestions about possible ethnically-defined administrative areas except those that would treat Central Asia (in any of its multiple versions) as a single entity. Evidently they felt that "Central Asianism" would inevitably escalate into separatist pressures. Instead, they encouraged the crystallization of five "nations" (in the official terminology) plus a few further "nationalities." Several of the studies in this collection argue that the CPSU leadership had to exert much energy to have these ethnic boundaries accepted. They also indicate that they had gained the support of large segments, but far from all, of the local cadres in this process of social definition.

Of course the central government demanded loyalty of the local leadership. They also demanded a certain sentiment of collective nationalism—Sovietism. And as an extra guarantee, they placed Russian personnel in number two positions of the various local Party organisms.

But in return, the central government pursued a policy of educational and agricultural development that was their boast and does them credit. Once again, the papers in this collection demonstrate the impressive degree to which educational and income gaps have been narrowed between Russia and Soviet Central Asia.

Soviet policy has consequently succeeded in two senses. The Central Asian areas of the USSR have manifested a remarkably low level of discontent, especially considering the fact that since 1917 all the rest of Asia has known so much nationalist turmoil and revolution. Secondly, nationalists in other parts of Asia (and elsewhere) have not for the most part considered Soviet Central Asia to be a "colonial area" where a national liberation movement should be encouraged.

Is there then no problem? The problem comes, ironically, from the inner contradictions of a capitalist world-system. The USSR has reached the level of a core industrialized nation in the world-economy, still a capitalist world-economy. If she is to maintain this status and not regress she must further transform her industry into one with a major export component, and she must export not merely industrial products but machinery and electronic equipment as well.

This requires the further industrialization and urbanization of European Russia. It also requires an expansion of population.

But European Russia is experiencing the kind of demographic slowdown that is precisely the consequence of the fact that an ever larger percentage of its population is going into the professions, or becoming highly skilled workers. There is in prospect a shortage of local people to fill the subproletarian positions in the economy. This is a situation that has faced every highly industrialized country in the world, especially since World War II. The only solution thus far found in Western Europe and North America has been widespread importation of laborers. Not being citizens, or at least being only second-class citizens, these laborers have had little political influence not only with the government but with the trade union movement as well, and have worked at relatively low wage scales and in poor working conditions.

Although their problem is basically a class problem, the fact that class in this case is almost perfectly correlated with ethnicity, combined with the fact that the presumed class-defense organizations (trade unions and left-liberal political organizations) are in the hands of the middle-income stratum of workers (of largely upper ethnic origin), has meant that the subproletariat has sought to organize to defend its class interests in ethnic organizations.

Once organized, this subproletariat of the industrialized nations has tended to become "radicalized" and to see parallels in its class-ethnic interests with those of the "proletarian" nations of the "Third World." Indeed, it has begun to use the appellations "Third World within," "internal colonies," and the like. At which point a certain international political solidarity has begun to manifest itself.

Is is possible that the USSR will come soon to face the development of such subproletarian ethnic strata? Where will the workers come from who will soon be needed to fill subproletarian positions in the occupational structure of European Russia? From Turkey? From Bulgaria? Or from Soviet Central Asia?

It seems plausible to assume that the government of the USSR would find it least disruptive to encourage increased internal migration within the USSR, and toward European Russia rather than away from it as heretofore—or rather toward it for unskilled workers, and away from it for the educated. And once large numbers of Central Asians find themselves located in the cities of European Russia, what will be the nature of their social relations with Russian workers? Will they organize themselves in ethnic associations? And what will be the class objectives of these ethnic associations, once formed? We can guess, by extrapolation from what has happened elsewhere, but we cannot be certain.

And should subproletarian ethnic strata in European Russia begin to make political demands, will they too consider themselves the "Third World within"? Will the "unemployed intellectuals" of the Soviet Central Asian republics join hands with the future educated segments of Central Asian extraction in European Russia who may sense "institutional racism," and will they begin to "radicalize," that is, attack the regime from the left? And if they do that, what will be the impact of such ideological currents on the undoubted remnants of more traditional "bourgeois nationalism" in Soviet Central Asia? Finally, how will the radical elements of the rest of Asia (and Africa and Latin America as well) react to this phenomenon? Will they feel sentiments of political solidarity toward such groups? Again, these are all questions that it is too early to answer.

What is clear, it seems to me, is that Soviet Central Asia is today at a turning point, and that any analysis of the "nationality question" must take into account the different ways in which ethnic consciousness and class consciousness intertwine, and hence the possible major shift in the political forms of expressing sentiments of "Central Asianism."

REVISED DRAFT OF SOME THESES PRESENTED TO
THE CONFERENCE ON THE NATIONALITY QUESTION
IN SOVIET CENTRAL ASIA, APRIL 7-8, 1972
Edward Allworth

The following set of THESES was drafted in preliminary form
mainly on the basis of discussions that took place in both the graduate
and faculty seminars on Soviet Nationality Problems, Columbia University, during the academic year 1971-72. The THESES were intended
to prompt and focus comments during the Conference on the Nationality
Question in Soviet Central Asia, April 7-8, 1972, held in New York
City. Included here in revised edition, they also have the purpose of
aiding continuing debate with respect to the definition and status of the
nationality question in a particular region of the USSR, as well as the
aim of providing an overview of the Central Asian situation in support
of the more specialized studies making up most of the present volume.
Many individuals, at the Conference and elsewhere, contributed helpful
remarks regarding the THESES, but these drafts remain entirely the
responsibility of the author.

Perhaps the most volatile, basic issue provoked by the THESES
revolved around the concept of discrimination, and the way that problem
has to be understood in the Soviet scene. Some persons are convinced
that ethnic discrimination does not occur in the USSR, defining such
discrimination strictly in terms of legally or officially sanctioned
disabilities, which they say are lacking, suffered by certain but not all
nationalities in the country. Others argue that the very "elder brother"
catchword, persistently employed in publicity or propaganda, with its
variants singling out the Russians and implying inferiority in the so-
called "younger" fraternal ethnic groups, typifies the nature of pervasive ethnic discrimination currently practiced against non-Russians.
Selective denial of civil or legal rights to the Crimean Tatars, Volga
Germans, or Meskhetian Turks deported to Central Asia and still
detained there since World War II, as well as the withholding of equal
protection for certain other ethnic groups, such as the Jews, under
Soviet nationality policy, has also been cited as evidence of actual
discrimination. If nothing else is taken into account, it may be pondered
whether the "tyranny of the majority," or even plurality, especially
in a country like the USSR where people are divided religiously according to ethnic affiliation, cannot help but inflict political, social, and

economic injury upon the minority (notably when it is fragmented into innumerable units). Unless that majority erects and rigorously maintains an effective structure of compensatory devices, polices its personal contacts constantly to stamp out a "we-they" polarity, and thoroughly denies itself advantages ordinarily accruing to size and power, the actual discrimination suffered by nationalities cannot be largely offset. That this equity has not been achieved in Soviet Central Asia so far, even if intended, which many deny, is borne out by a great deal of evidence, including much that has been adduced-regarding inequality in job-holding, education, real power sharing, and the like—for other purposes in the chapters of the present book by several scholars. Because the case against including discrimination as an important problem affecting the Soviet nationality question has yet to be persuasively made, the subject continues to find a central place in this revision of the THESES.

Within the USSR, Central Asia as a region exhibits a set of features unique to the area; (a) The population per arable acre is heavy, predominantly rural, and follows an extremely uneven pattern of distribution; (b) A substantial majority of the indigenous inhabitants are under 30 years of age, making it a remarkably youthful society; (c) The territory is and has been since the nineteenth century, at least, identified as a coherent region under names such as Turkistan, Central Asia, and the like; (d) Control of its cities and industrial centers has been preempted by outsiders through superior numbers and positions in employment, and remains primarily in their hands; (e) The area as a whole is collectively heir to a legacy of close internal religious, linguistic, cultural, and tribal kinship plus extensive interaction among its politicans, military forces, traders, entertainers, religious leaders, educators, and intellectuals; (f) The region possesses and has in the recent past enjoyed the presence of political units or administrative organization based upon multiethnic and multilingual mixtures of people; (g) A Central Asian variant of the new "Soviet" arts and culture is emerging. Bearing the earlier remarks as well as these traits in mind, these three groups of THESES are proposed:

Community

1. The special combination of traits peculiar to Central Asia imparts a distinctive character to the nationality question in that region.

2. Because traditional cultural community persists among some indigenous ethnic groups in the area, recent efforts by the authorities to promote a drawing-together (sblizhenie) remind the groups of the links between them, adding common modern elements that contribute to solidifying this ancient community. Such cultural community or

recently encouraged cultural drawing-together would have to super-
impose itself upon an identification recently fixed according to ethnic
linguistic principles, in a sense once more glossing over the variegated
ethnic designations long existing and currently employed in Central
Asia by Soviet politicians.

3. Present titular nationalities persist mainly as officially
promoted subdivisions of a larger community well aware of its latent
unity. A very small, select group within the indigenous population of
each Central Asian republic presently benefits from the political and
cultural segregation maintained between local ethnic groups. Current
divisions into the six republics mean little in the political and economic
sphere to most of the indigenous population. The concept of nationality
felt by Central Asians once differed basically from the well-known
European-style or Stalinist model of linguistic/ethnic "nation," and
may still support a latent identification strongly among people all over
the region. This could assist the Soviet government in its effort to
merge the population.

4. Now, as in the early 1920s, the pattern of distribution among
major indigenous ethnic groups in Central Asia remains virtually
unchanged, revealing that the imperfections in the partition of the
Bukhara People's Conciliar Republic, Turkistan ASSR, and other states
five decades ago still remain. With the rapid growth in population, the
political-administrative borders become less perfect in defining ethnic
territories, leaving a strongly mixed local population, especially in
the southern part of the area.

Equality

5. The social-class uniformity or homogeneity said to exist
among all groups in Central Asia does not bridge the significant distinctions between indigenous ethnic groups, generally agrarian, and the
main bodies of outsiders, who seem to function together as a dominant,
multiethnic, urban or industrial class in the Central Asian political,
military, and police establishment. This class of outsider operates
similarly with respect to each of the Central Asian nationalities by
imposing disabilities upon all.

6. Except for some local leaders (political, educational, management, intellectual) who may have thoroughly identified their own
interests with those of the dominant class of outsiders, among the
indigenous people consciousness of the general deprivation described
in Thesis 5, as well as specific discrimination experienced by qualified
Central Asians in various fields at the hands of non-Central Asians,
sharpens the self-awareness of indigenous groups and emphasizes the
general distinction between them and outsiders.

7. Achievement of economic equality among the ethnic groups in Central Asia has been hindered by the intensive immigration into the area from elsewhere, which continues to preserve skilled jobs and managerial responsibility in most fields for outsiders. So far as the nationality question is concerned, to talk only about general economic "equality"—if it has been achieved—for the ethnic groups in the region remains relatively meaningless in the absence of real possibilities for nationalities to make significant independent choices in economic, artistic, cultural, political, and social fields. Without independent responsibility and the possibility for each ethnic group in such a federation, true equality cannot exist.

8. Soviet policy for more than fifty years has claimed to work toward establishing political "equality" among the Russians and the nationalities of the USSR. The abstract or formal raising of the question of equality in general, including nationality equality, is typical of Soviet bureaucracy. Under the idea of equality among Soviet citizens in general, Soviet bureaucracy proclaims the formal or juridical equality of the Party with the non-Party man or woman, and the Russian with the non-Russian, to the great deception of the subjected classes or nationalities who accept those assertions.

Relations

9. Neither diverging (otdalenie) nor drawing together among Central Asian ethnic nationalities under present circumstances fundamentally alters the nationality question in the region, if that question is regarded as something other than a set of cultural relationships among the Central Asians (that is, Central Asian cultural community still sustains itself in either case, but Soviet politics normally do not function between nationalities but between the center and each nationality).

10. Local political decisions in Central Asia sometimes depend upon ethnic group/nationality factors in lobbying, and the like, so that such political decisions do not necessarily respond to the existence of the large cultural or social community overlaying the official ethnic divisions. This separation of the political from the cultural reflects a peculiar new stratification for Central Asian society, in which cultural ties and relations among the nationalities, and with outsiders, may differ from political links in important ways. Neither the term "drawing together" nor "merging" (sliianie) fits the political life in Central Asia accurately today.

11. Drawing together or merging, in the Soviet meaning of the terms, between Central Asians generally and outsiders—little evidenced recently in the region—has been retarded to a large extent by the discriminatory effect of economic and political practices of the

outsiders present in the area, and by strong Central Asian internal
cultural and ethnic attachments.

12. Diverging must proceed well beyond its present stage before
the communal cultural, linguistic, ethnic, and literary ties become
effectively cancelled as factors serving to maintain a consciousness
of some Central Asian unity. If that awareness becomes nullified, in
time each group's separate ethnic identity may be strengthened, with
the possible result that drawing together, between outsiders and in-
siders, becomes more feasible. But, rather than experiencing what
is known as drawing together or merging, the growing Central Asian
ethnic groups are now evidently subject to a further diverging, not only
from each other but from outsiders as well.

COMMENTARY UPON THE CONFERENCE SUBJECT
(an edited selection of remarks prepared
for Conference discussions)
Paula G. Rubel
Associate Professor of Anthropology,
Barnard College

One of the important factors that must be kept in mind in assessing the material presented in the chapters is that ethnic identity,
used interchangeably with nationality identity, is flexible as well as
situational. People who identify themselves as Uzbeks for certain
purposes on certain occasions may at other times identify themselves
as Tajiks or Bukharans. It is rare that there will be complete homogeneity of ethnic identity for people in a modern nation-state. Thus,
as in the William L. Hanaway, Jr., paper, the use of Bukharan national
identity in a political context should not be seen as inconsistent with
the use of identification as Uzbek or Tajik by the same people in other
contexts. The papers by Timur Kocaoglu and others also support
this point. Prior to 1925, when the Soviet government attempted to
"fix" ethnic identity by the establishment of new Central Asian republics, as well as subsequent to that time, ethnic identity was fluid
in terms of how individuals identified themselves in different situations. Furthermore, the usual or most frequent ethnic identity used
by people might shift over time. As was noted in discussion by Karl
H. Menges, more people identify as Tajiks now rather than Uzbeks,
indicating such a shift over time.

Another point that came out of the papers and the discussion
was the interpretation that may be placed upon the course and direction of Soviet literary policy. As described in the Robert J. Barrett
paper, such a policy can be seen as a process of creating cultural
symbols. It may be likened to the building of a new mythology or ideology. It should also be noted that this type of policy-making within
the political context of the Soviet Union, with its basic materialist
philosophy, may be seen as an acknowledgment that shifts in the
cultural symbols or myths of a society are one of the ways in which
to effect changes in that society.

The simple categorization in Thesis 4 between outsiders and
indigenous people, the former dominant and the latter suffering from
disabilities, seems not to allow for those indigenous Communists

who are able to move into positions of power in the political structures. [The revision has taken Paula Rubel's comment into account—ed.] With reference to the theses regarding community (1-4), it is recognized that Central Asia has been the focus of an Iranian- or Persian-Islamic-oriented tradition over the past centuries. This tradition has been dominant primarily in the urban centers. Other indigenous ethnic or cultural traditions such as Kazakh, Tajik, or Uzbek may be seen as "Little Traditions," related to, yet apart from, the "Great Iranian-Islamic Tradition." Though this categorization is somewhat simplistic, it can be used to represent this situation, since the Iranian tradition was really quite different from the others in terms of level of complexity and degree of sophistication. Furthermore, all of these traditions often coexisted. Through the centuries, political units have been established in this area, and have through time co-opted a variety of cultural identities at different levels of inclusiveness. Frequently, political hegemony has been established, after which came the task of building a cultural or "national" identity to fit the new state. This identity was usually built from pre-existing elements—as witness the data presented by William L. Hanaway, Jr., on the building of Bukharan identity 1909-24. The focus must be placed on ethnic identity- and nationality identity-building as a process, usually conscious, where attempts are made by leaders to promote the idea, using symbolic materials of a particular identity. This ties in with what the Soviets are trying to do in their literary policy. It further relates to the conceptualization of ethnic identity as fluid—even on the level of the individual, where people may use different identities in different contexts. The conceptualization of ethnic identity as a hard-and-fast ascription is not valid or useful as an explanatory device in the Central Asian context.

The process described above can be said to characterize the development of the Soviet Central Asian republics, since they are based upon particular identities that were used by people present in the area. To this is added the component of Communist culture, promulgated by the bureaucracy for adoption by the populace. Rather than a contrast between the Central Asian and European concepts of identity, as is the case in Thesis 3, the differences appear to relate to whether or not the ethnic identity is paralleled by the presence of a political structure clothed in that identity. If ethnic identity is associated, as in the latter instance, with a nation-state, then it is nationality. When it is not, it can be called ethnic identity. Different ethnic identities may coexist within a nation state that at the same time propounds a particular national identity. The large community-identity referred to in Thesis 3 is no more "authentic" than the present local ethnicities.

Jonathan Pool
Assistant Professor of Political Science, State
University of New York, Stony Brook

The papers presented at this conference, including the Theses
of Edward Allworth, have illuminated brightly a region that is usually
remote on the American academic map. At the same time these papers
have revealed, better than before, what we still do not know about the
Central Asian nationality question. The discussions following the
papers have also been revealing: they show some basic uncertainties
and controversies that we should be conscious of if we wish to understand each other—and our common subject.

Of the crucial problems facing the study of society in general,
let me in these comments briefly focus attention on four that particularly vex the study of the nationality question in Soviet Central Asia,
relying in a few cases on examples drawn from papers presented in
my own panel, Interdisciplinary Group 2.

Problem No. 1 is the definition of the problem. We should all
recognize something circular in a conference on the nationality question in Soviet Central Asia at which one of the main issues is the
question "What is the 'question'?" Yet, for reasons that need not be
enumerated now, this feature of our topic is, for the time being, in-
escapable. While we cannot avoid asking what we are asking about
even as we ask about it, we should also not minimize the consequence
of the answer. Immanuel Wallerstein, for example, has already com-
mented on our neglect of Central Asians living in parts of the Soviet
Union outside Central Asia, and indeed this neglect is mandated by
the words "in . . . Central Asia", of our topic title. What is not so
mandated, however, is the relative neglect of Russians—Russians as
a group—living in Central Asia, which has also been true of the scholarly work presented here. It is our definition of "nationalities" (as
opposed to the Soviet or any other definition) that will determine
whether we add what we know about the differences in the behavior of
Frenchmen in France and in Algeria, Americans in the United States
and in Vietnam, English Canadians in English Canada and in Quebec,
Russians in Russia and in Central Asia, and so forth, to our definition
and our understanding of the nationality problems in such areas of
cultural difference and domination.

Problem No. 2 is the definition of variables and of the single
properties that compose them. Social scientists have long flirted
with both objective and subjective, both observer-oriented and par-
ticipant-oriented, both "genotypical" and "phenotypical" definitions.
Neither is innately better than the other, but they are certainly different. Take two concepts central to our topic, nationality and equality,
for example. While the Soviet census and most of the scholars who

voiced relevant opinions at this conference prefer a subjective definition of nationality (e.g., a person has whatever nationality he thinks
he has), John Hanselman's research employed an objective definition,
based on a person's family name. Likewise, social equality is difficult to measure, and many prefer merely to measure subjective
equality (people's beliefs about whether they are treated equally).
Edward Allworth, on the other hand, adopted in his theses an apparently
objective definition that makes independence a prerequisite. This issue
raises the obverse of the question that Brown v. Board of Education
tried to answer in 1954: rather than asking whether it is possible for
a minority to be separate but equal, Allworth's definition implies, it
seems, the impossibility of being together but equal—if togetherness
includes political centralization. Especially because of their evalu-
ative connotations, we need to make clear our definitions of such concepts as identity and equality, as Allworth has done.

    The definitions of our variables have additional importance for
the theoretical utility of the observations we make in the Soviet Central Asian case. In concurrence with one of William K. Medlin's remarks, I must stress the need to study Soviet Central Asia using a
theoretically informed, comparatively oriented idiom. Otherwise
the instructive similarities and contrasts between nationality problems there and elsewhere will be lost. Yet how do we make Soviet
variables commensurate with those of other countries? This is a
frequent problem. M. Mobin Shorish, for example, presented some
cross-national comparisons of educational attainment; but what definition of "primary," "secondary," "higher," and similar educational
levels was used as a basis for comparing Soviet with non-Soviet at-
tainments? Given the major differences in educational systems, such
definitions could easily influence the direction, or at least the magni-
tude, of our comparative findings.

    Problem No. 3 is the discovery of motives and intentions. Shall
we presume to say not only what men do but also what they think and
feel, and, if so, how shall we know what to say? And even if motives
can be verifiably attributed to individuals, is the same true for col-
lectivities? This issue, bedeviling social analysis in general, is
especially troublesome in fields, such as our own, that are ideologically impregnated: fields in which findings of fact are taken as having
crucial normative and policy implications for intensely interested
persons inside and outside the field of scholarship itself. Immanuel
Wallerstein and many others here have contributed to the old debate
about the motives behind Russian and Soviet nationality policy: what
the motive has been, whether it has been constant or changing, and
whether it has been haphazard or has rationally dictated all policy.
Few, however, have said anything that would challenge the questionable assumption that there exists some unique definable motive for a

policy adopted by a state. Our experience suggests that policies are often adopted precisely when they happen to serve a large number of different policymakers' or groups' divergent motives. Given the existing evidence that czarist and Soviet leaders have often disagreed fundamentally on nationality policies and their goals, what do we mean by the "purpose" behind the policy at a given time? Is the impression of a purposive, rationally calculating, and carefully differentiated nationality policy that is conveyed by Ronald Wixman's paper, for example, documentably supportable in competition with less rationalistic interpretations?

By the same token, we must of course be careful in drawing motivational conclusions from facts about policy. When Barry M. Rosen noted that Russians were given incentives for outmigration from the RSFSR, or when Eden Naby informed us that official policy holds Western literature to be superior to Oriental, no single attitudinal source can be automatically deduced. A desire for expansion or a desire to relieve overcrowding? A belief in Russian supremacy or a belief in universalistic values that Western writers happen to express? The questions are important, but the answers are difficult—perhaps, in fact, impossible without a non-obvious definition of "becauseness."

Problem No. 4, finally, involves data. We hardly need to be reminded that data on Central Asia are limited. The limitations are especially frustrating when unusually complete nationality data have been collected and then have been released for secondary analysis in unusually incomplete form, as is the case with Soviet census statistics. And even when released without aggregation or falsification, data relevant to nationality are often problematic by virtue of being composed of mass responses to questions about hard-to-report facts of their behavior. Previous research has shown, for example, that individuals' ratings of their own ability in second languages are unreliable, and that responses to census takers' questions about nationality and language sometimes vary widely across time as incentives and awareness change. What can we then infer about actual abilities from Ronald Wixman's data on assimilation, based on the number of persons claiming a "good command" of another language?

Faults and shortages in data can, however, be overcome at times by innovative inferential techniques. Eden Naby has used artistic products, John N. Hazard has used legal texts, and Edward Allworth has used the contents and subjects of bibliographies as data about nationality problems that more conventionally-minded scholars might have overlooked. (Cf. Lieberson's use of Yellow Pages in Canada.) Others have made highly intensive analyses of data to compensate for their paucity. Ian M. Matley at this conference, and Robert A. Lewis elsewhere, are among those who have done so with census data. Numerous scholars, including Barry M. Rosen in his paper here, have searched the official press for signs of the inevitable discrepancy between policy and achievement, as well as relying on samizdat (independently published) and other less controlled media for such data. Official criticism, however, is a risky indicator, for the criticism of faults previously unmentioned may be a sign of either failure or success: it may mean either new faults or the overcoming of more important faults whose solution permits the quota of criticism to be directed at second-order ones.

The study of the nationality question in Soviet Central Asia shares, then, a number of the persistent problems of human affairs scholarship. But the topic of this conference bears even more than its share of four basic problems: the definition of the scholarly question, the definition of the key variables, the discovery of motivations and intentions, and the collection of useful data. By being aware of these problems and applying imaginative devices for dealing with them, we can increase the value of our contributions not only to the understanding of Soviet nationality problems, but, as well, to the panoply of scholarly fields, subfields, and hyphenated interdisciplinary fields to which our studies also belong.

John W. Strong
Associate Professor of History, Carleton University

Any conference or symposium that deals with a manifestation of the nationality question immediately encounters a serious problem of semantic definitions. What is a nation and does it differ from a nation-state? What is nationalism and is it the same phenomenon as national consciousness? What criteria are to be used in measuring national identity, and do they have universal application? Assuming that semantic difficulties can be overcome, one is then faced with more philosophical questions concerning nationality problems. For example: Do Western concepts of nationalism undergo subtle change when applied to a non-Western situation? Can national sentiments be encouraged, promoted, and at the same time harmonized within a multinational political unit? Is the concept of the nation-state any longer relevant in the shrinking global environment of the late twentieth century?

In dealing with nationality problems in the Soviet Union the difficulties are all compounded by the existence of a badly defined yet officially sponsored nationality policy and by a deliberate attempt on the part of the Soviet government to create artificial "nations" among some (but not all) of the ethnic groups within the USSR.

In the long run of history, nationalism is a relatively new idea even in the West, where it originated. Its export to the rest of the world is still more recent, and too often it has been applied in a highly

arbitrary manner. Imperial Russia brought the nationality idea to
Central Asia in the last half of the nineteenth century. One cannot
help but suspect that the resulting emergence of a national consciousness among the varied Central Asian people was the product more of
anti-Russian sentiment than of established ethnic, religious, linguistic,
or regional identifications. This process of national sentiment being
created in reaction to some form of Western imperialism is perhaps
natural, but nevertheless unfortunate. It is nationalism created for
negative reasons. The idea that "he who is against my enemy is my
brother" can produce only a weak bond of national unity. It contrasts
dramatically with, to take but one example, the unification of the
Italian people into an Italian nation-state.

In studying the over-all nationality question in Soviet Central
Asia the third interdisciplinary session of the Columbia conference
investigated, as a test case, the existence or nonexistence of a true
national consciousness in Bukhara around the year 1920. One could
ask, "But how is such a subject relevant to current Soviet nationality
problems?" To the historian, at least, the answer is obvious. Current
problems of all kinds have historical roots and can never be fully
understood without some knowledge of those roots. Five papers were
given in the conference session, and each approached the subject of
Bukharan nationalism from either a different discipline or a different
viewpoint.

Anna Procyk points to the literature of the Central Asians as
reflecting a genuine renewed interest in the peculiarities of their
historical background and the uniqueness of their cultural heritage.
If this trend continues, the indigenous nationality groups in Central
Asia will probably be drawn together again in some form of cultural
union. I feel that such a Central Asian regional nationalism, based
on a common cultural heritage, would have positive characteristics.
It would be a pity however if this type of nationalism then developed
negative political features based on anti-Russian, anti-Chinese, or
anti-Western sentiments.

William L. Hanaway, Jr. finds a form of Bukharan nationalism
in the early twentieth century based on the Bukharan intellectuals'
and writers' use of a consistent set of terms to express their relationship to the political entity of Bukhara and its people. This I think
raises an important sociological question. How important is the role
played by the intellectual in creating national consciousness among
people who might otherwise never learn to think in such terms? Further speculation could be directed to the question as to whether a
national consciousness created by the intelligentsia is not as artificial
as one created by government fiat.

Ian M. Matley's study of the ethnic and regional diversity of the Bukharan state in 1920 shows a population breakdown of 40 percent Uzbek, 40 percent Tajik, and 20 percent other. This population was unevenly divided geographically, and economically-socially divided between the agriculturalists, urban dwellers, and seminomads. In such a diverse demographic mosaic the development of a Bukharan nationalism was, at best, extremely weak, despite the unifying factors of ethnic and cultural identity that were present.

Timur Kocaoglu indicates the definite existence in 1920 of a Bukharan nationality based on common customs, culture, and on a unified economic community. This Bukharan identity was a conscious one, whereas ethnic identity (Uzbek, Tajik, Turkmen, and the like) was not consciously expressed. Mr. Kocaoglu feels that if the Soviets had permitted Bukharan nationalism to develop undisturbed it would have become the nucleus around which a Central Asian nationalism might have developed. Seeing this as a potential threat to their own authority, the Soviets acted quickly to block any such development, and in its place deliberately created artifical ethnic national groups in order to keep Central Asia a house divided against itself.

Seymour Becker's approach and conclusions are quite different. He finds little evidence of a real national consciousness among the people of Central Asia except among the local intelligentsia, who were seeking a unified autonomous state, Muslim and Turkic in character, democratic and liberal in structure. It was these aspirations of the intelligentsia that the Soviet government sought to frustrate by dividing Central Asia into ethnic regions based on linguistic differences. I would contend that a common language is a definite factor in any nation's identity; however, the subsequent, over-all development of nationality groups in Central Asia could not help but be branded with the "Made in Moscow" label.

In general, the conference session on Bukhara seemed to indicate that ethnic, linguistic, and religious identifications did exist in Central Asia in 1920. Among a few intellectuals these identifications were converging toward some form of Central Asian regional identification. However, a true national consciousness was at most only in the very earliest stage of formation. It is interesting that this was equally true in many other regions of Asia in 1920, not the least of which was China.

Today the nationality question in the Soviet Union is serious and deserves careful study, not only by Soviet citizens but by concerned scholars and politicians everywhere. Needless to say, the USSR is not the only country in the world facing a "nationality question" within its borders. Many countries share this troublesome set of problems. In dealing with them all countries, including the Soviet Union, should be able to profit from mutual consultation and shared experiences.

Ervand Abrahamian
Assistant Professor of Political Science,
John Jay College of the City University of New York

Robert Barrett's article raises the problem of the integration
of nationalities. Most modernizing societies face the same immediate
dilemma—how to integrate different traditional ties (ethnicity, tribal
links, region, language, and so on) into a broader sentiment toward
the state, usually by integrative moves or drastic acculturation. In
Russian policy perhaps the question is, what room is to be left for
existing cultural, ethnic, and other identification?

Warren W. Eason
Professor of Economics, Ohio State University

In Ralph Clems's analysis of job placement and ethnicity he has
to determine to what extent it can safely be inferred that there is real
ethnic discrimination in hiring, or how much it is true that indigenous
groups in Central Asia are actually less adequately prepared for the
urban or industrial work they seek.

Michael Rywkin
Professor of Russian Studies,
City College of the City University of New York

In Central Asia the basic national interplay occurs between the
indigenous Muslim Turkic nationalities and the European Christian
Slavic nationalities, and all other interplay is secondary.

Grey Hodnett
Associate Professor of Political Science, York University

Another dimension to nationality problems that has not received
the attention it should in theoretical writings is that of overt or covert
reality present in a situation such as that in Central Asia, a dimension
of dissimulation, the extent to which people are concealing their existence in multiple realities.

William K. Medlin
Professor of Continuing Education and
Community Development, University of Michigan

The social-cultural dominance of the outsiders in Central Asia
must be understood in terms of the agrarian revolution that brought

the outsiders there. In the battle of land use the European has imposed his technology; the Uzbeks as they mastered oasis agriculture achieved assimilatory power and are increasingly competitive outside their own area. There are also tendencies toward symbiotic relationships between the culturally dominant Slavs and the submissive indigenous systems: a coexistence at similar levels of cultural attainment of Central Asians and Russians without the Asians becoming a part of the Slavs.

David C. Montgomery
Assistant Professor of History and
Asian Studies, Brigham Young University

There seems to be a new self-confidence among young educated Central Asians; they have a better understanding of the Russians there than the Slavs do the Asians. Indigenous people are competing better now for higher education and employment than before, and this also seems to disquiet the Russians, who experienced little effective competition in these arenas previously.

Charles Issawi
Professor of Economics, Columbia University

The complex process by which Turkish, Arab, and Iranian national awareness evolved is interesting, because the main impulse creating these nationalities seemingly was their reaction against each other, not primarily against western imperialism. Such imperialism, I think, strengthened rather the "Muslim consciousness," and I wonder whether the reaction of Central Asians to the Russians would not primarily stimulate Muslim consciousness there, whereas difficulties between Turkmens, Uzbeks and Tajiks would stimulate local nationalism?

Karl H. Menges
Professor of Altaic Philology, Columbia University

Often there is a confusion in the delimitation between language and dialect, an objective confusion, and this is significant for the nationality question. Where are the beginnings of a language and when does it cease to be a dialect? Karakalpak was called merely a dialect of Kazakh by some Russian linguists, but by government decree in Soviet times Karakalpak was made into a separate language.

Though you had to wait a while before a genuine literature, not a translated literature, was produced in that language, it did appear.

Lowell Tillett
Associate Professor of History, Wake Forest University

Seymour Becker's definition of nationality is somewhat more restricted, conventional, and Western, whereas Timur Kocaoglu is apparently suggesting that there is an Asian mode of nation-forming. William L. Hanaway, Jr., would, it seems, side somewhat with Kocaoglu, saying that there was indeed a nationality awareness among Bukharans, but Hanaway confines this to the intelligentsia, which was a very small part of the whole population of Bukhara. This raises a serious question about the extent to which a very small intelligentsia can engender the nation-building process.

CHAPTER 1

1. Kirghiz Proverbs, collected and trans. to Turkish and English by Saniye and Azamat Altay (Paris-Munich and New York: typescript, 1967), entry No. 1194.

2. "K tebe, chitatel'-student," Komsomolets Uzbekistana, Sept. 15, 1971, p. 3; V. Gladilov, "Bol'shoi sovet druzei," Ibid., Oct. 13, 1971, p. 3.

3. Itogi vsesoiuznoi perepisi naseleniia. Uzbekskaia SSR (Moscow: Gosstatizdat TsSU SSSR, 1962), p. 14.

4. B. Vall; V. Ivanov, "Gizhduvanskie kontrasty. 3. Tish' da glad' . . . ," Komsomolets Uzbekistana, Sept. 16, 1971, p. 8; Ibid., "1. Pobeda, kotoruiu zhdali i ne zhdali," Sept. 14, 1971, p. 4.

5. "V TsK LKSM Uzbekistana. O tekh, kto okonchil shkolu," Komsomolets Uzbekistana, Aug. 31, 1971, p. 2.

6. S. Rakhimov; V. Poluianova, "'Ne ostavat'sia mertvoi bukvoi . . . '," Komsomolets Uzbekistana, Nov. 24, 1971, p. 2.

7. Ibid.

8. [Leonid Brezhnev], "Rech' tovarishcha L. I. Brezhneva," Komsomolets Uzbekistana, Oct. 20, 1971, pp. 1-2; "Uchit'sia, rabotat' i borot'sia po Leninu!" Ibid., Oct. 30, 1971, p. 2.

9. R. Alimov, "Dorogoi znanii," Komsomolets Uzbekistana, Nov. 13, 1971, p. 2.

10. B. Shubalov, "Soiuz nerushimyi," Komsomolets Uzbekistana, Dec. 31, 1971, p. 2; T. Murtazoyev, "Internatsionalizm—bayraqi mo," Komsomoli Tojikiston, March 21, 1971, p. 3; B. Jamg̈irchinov, "Lenindik ulut sayasaẗinïn saltanaẗi," Leninchil jash, Han. 30, 1971, p. 2. These and subsequent references to the Kirgiz and Tajik press have in the main been provided by Azamat Altay and Timur Kocaoglu. •

11. "Idi dūsẗi," Komsomoli Tojikiston, Sept. 10, 1971, p. 2; E. Sagalaev; S. Faniutin, "Prazdnik, kotoryi vsegda s toboi. Deviataia internatsional'naia vstrecha molodezhi Uzbekistana i Tadzhikistana," Komsomolets Uzbekistana, Sept. 21, 1971, p. 2.

12. "Taftishi hamdigar—yoru duston," Komsomoli Tojikiston, Aug. 11, 1971, p. 1; "Druzhba—eto znamia molodezhi. Dni internatsional'noi druzhby v Namangane. Festival posviashchen 50-letiiu SSSR," Komsomolets Uzbekistana, July 8, 1971, p. 3.

13. Nasir Fazilov, "Dostlikdä mä na kop," Shärq yulduzi No. 2 (1971), p. 9.

14. O. Panova; G. Lipshits, "Mudroe slovo aksakalov," Komsomolets Uzbekistana, Aug. 26, 1971, p. 4; Sanji Eginaliev, "Jakshï adamdar sharapattuu kelishat," Leninchil jash, Feb. 9, 1971, p. 4; Z. Toktobaeva, "Jemishin berüüdö," Ibid., Feb. 4, 1971, p. 4.
15. "Musohibai mo. Nakshaho va taraddudho," Komsomoli Tojikiston, Dec. 26, 1971, p. 3.
16. Sh. Rakhmanov, "Teatr 'Ësh Gvardiia'. Pervye itogi. V. Chto porodilo Kompromiss," Komsomolets Uzbekistana, Dec. 29, 1971, p. 3.
17. Ibid.; Sh. Rakhmanov, "Teatr 'Ësh Gvardiia'. Pervye itogi. 2. Nakhodki i poteri," Komsomolets Uzbekistana, Dec. 7. 1971, p. 4.
18. Ibid.
19. Sh. Rakhmanov, "Teatr 'Ësh Gvardiia'. Pervye itogi. 1. U istokov. Natsional'naia p'esa na stsene," Komsomolets Uzbekistana, Nov. 24, 1971, p. 4.
20. Joseph Castagné, "Le Turkestan depuis la revolution russe," Revue du Monde Musulman, Vol. L (June 1922), p. 69, cited also in Alexander Park, Bolshevism in Turkestan, 1917-1927 (New York: Columbia University Press, 1957), p. 140.
21. Sh. Rakhmanov, op. cit. [Note 19]
22. Sh. Rakhmanov, "Teatr 'Ësh Gvardiia'. Pervye itogi. III. V poiskakh repertuara," Komsomolets Uzbekistana, Dec. 23, 1971, p. 4.
23. "Qänatlär," Ozbekistan mädäniyäti, Oct. 28, 1969, p. 1.
24. S. Feniutin, "Tovarishch komsomol'skii sekretar'," Komsomolets Uzbekistana, Aug. 4, 1971, p. 3.
25. Ibid.
26. Cholpan Ergäsh, Tang yulduzi. She"rlär (Tashkent: "Yash Gvärdiyä Näshriyati, 1970), p. 19.
27. Turar Kojomberdiev, "Süyünchü," Ala-too, No. 12 (Dec. 1971), p. 27; Junay Mavlyanov, "Mezgil jana jashtardïn chïgar-machïligi," Ibid., No. 1 (Jan. 1971), p. 135.
28. Iakub Khaimov, " . . . No grazhdaninom byt' obiazan," Komsomolets Uzbekistana, Aug. 21, 1971, p. 3.
29. L. Beliavskii, "Obyknovennaia devushka. Delegat vsesoiuznogo sleta studentov," Komsomolets Uzbekistana, Oct. 13, 1971, p. 3.
30. "Respublikämiz ähalisi. Ozbekistan SSR ministrlär Soveti huzuriďägi märkäziy stätistikä bashqärmäsining äkhbarati," Sovet Ozbekistani, April 28, 1971, p. 2; "Sovettik Qazaqstan: Ösu örkendeu tsifrlarï. Qazaq SSR ministrler Soveti janïndaghï ortalïq statistika basqarmasïnïng khabarï," Sotsialistik Qazaqstan, June 10, 1971, p. 4; "Respublikanïn kalkï. Kïrgïz SSR ministrler

Sovetinin aldïndagï borborduk statistika bashkarmasïnïn bildirüüsü,"
Sovettik Kïrgizstan, May 5, 1971, p. 3; "Aholii respublikai mo.
Akhboroti upravleniyai markazi statistikii nazdi Soveti vazironi
RSS Tojikiston," Tojikistoni Soveti, May 6, 1971, pp. 1, 3;
"Türkmenïstanïng ilati. Turkmenistan SSR ministrler Sovetining
yanïndaki merkezi statistiki upravlenyäning khabari," Sovet
Türkmenistani, July 11, 1971, pp. 1-2.
    31. Robert A. Lewis, "The Mixing of Russians and Soviet
Nationalities and Its Demographic Impact," in Edward Allworth
(ed.), Soviet Nationality Problems (New York: Columbia University
Press, 1971), p. 146, Table 5.
    32. Hälimä Khudayberdievä, "Aq almälär pishgändä," Shärq
yulduzi, No. 12 (1971), pp. 67-68.

CHAPTER 2
    1. I. I. Groshev, Istoricheskii opyt KPSS po osushchestvleniiu
leninskoi natsional'noi politiki (Moscow: Izdatel'stvo "Mysl',"
1967), p. 307.
    2. Ibid., pp. 307-08.
    3. Ibid., p. 309; See also Umarali Narmatov, "Ädabiy alaqalar
imizning asasiy tendentsiyalari," Rus-ozbek adabiy alaqalari
tärikhi ocherkläri, (ed.) Gh. K Kärimov (Tashkent: V. I. Lenin
namidagi Tashkent Dävlät Universiteti, 1967), p. 217.
    4. Personal interview with Prof. Gogä Hidayätov, Chairman
of History Department, Tashkent State University, New York, N. Y.,
October 1971.
    5. Groshev, op. cit., p. 311.
    6. I. I. Groshev, op. cit., p. 329; and A. K. Valiev, "Nekotorye
osobennosti formirovaniia natsional'noi intelligentsii," Obschestvennye nauki v Uzbekistane, No. 1 (1971), pp. 6-7.
    7. Groshev, op. cit., p. 329.
    8. Groshev, op. cit., p. 311.
    9. E. Bagramov, "On the Nationality Question," Pravda, July
16, 1971, pp. 3-4, as quoted in The Current Digest of the Soviet
Press, XXIII, 28, p. 8.
    10. See Edward Allworth, "The Changing Intellectual and
Literary Community," in Central Asia: A Century of Russian
Rule, (ed.) Edward Allworth (New York: Columbia University
Press, 1967), pp. 386-87.
    11. "SSSR yazuvchiläri Soyuzigä," Ozbekistan mädäniyäti,
April 27, 1971, p. 1.
    12. T. Hamidov, "Milliy adabiyatlar ortäsidägi dostlik häqidä
lenincha ta″limat," Obschestvennye nauki v Uzbekistane, No. 4
(1971), p. 21.

13. For full comments, see G. M. Markov, "Soviet Literature in the Fight for Communism," Soviet Literature, No. 11 (1971), pp. 85-91.

14. "Ozbekistan yazuvchiläri Soyuzidä," Ozbekistan mädäniyäti, April 23, 1971, p. 1.

15. Kh. Daniyarov, et al., Ädäbiyat wä sän"ätda lenincha pärtiyävilik printsiplari (Tashkent: "Ozbekistan" Näshriyati, 1966), p. 181.

16. See Edward Allworth, Uzbek Literary Politics (The Hague: Mouton & Co., 1964), pp. 153-57; also T. Hamidov, op. cit., p. 21.

17. "Ädäbiyat wä sän"ät dekädälari," Ozbek sovet entsiklopediyäsi, Vol. I (Tashkent: Ozbek Sovet Entsiklopediyasi. Bash Redäktsiyäsi, 1971), p. 150.

18. Ibid.

19. Izzat Sultanov, "Yängi basqichdä," Mäharät mäktäbi: Ozbekistan yazuvchiläri äsärlärining SSSR yazuvchiläri Soyuzidä otkäzilgän muhakämäläri stenogrämmäsi (Tashkent: OzSSR Dävlät Bädiiy Ädäbiyat Näshriyati, 1962), pp. 621-22.

20. Sharaf Rashidov, "Yägonä ulugh ailädä," Mäharät mäktäbi: Ozbekistan yazuvchiläri äsärlärining SSSR yazuvchiläri Soyuzidä otkäzilgän muhakämäläri stenogrämmäsi (Tashkent: OzSSR Dävlät Bädiiy Ädäbiyat Näshriyati, 1962), p. 573.

21. "Khälqlärning buyuk bäyrämi," Ozbekistan mädäniyäti, Oct. 1, 1971, p. 1.

22. Ibid., pp. 1-2.

23. Ibid., p. 2.

24. Ibid.

25. "Dorogi i tseli u nas odni, ikh ozariaiut druzhby ogni," Pravda Vostoka, Oct. 1, 1971, p. 3.

26. Ibid.

27. For the details on the recent ouster of an Uzbek writer from the USSR Writers' Union, see "Ozbekistan yazuvchiläri Soyuzidä," Ozbekistan mädäniyäti Oct. 26, 1971, p. 4.

28. T. Hamidov, pp. 17.-19. Lenin's works quoted from Uzbek-language edition: "Amerikä jurnälistining sävallärigä jävab," Asärlär, Vol. 29, p. 539; "Rus tilini tazäläsh toghrisidä, Asärlär, Vol. 30. (No page given.)

29. Kh. Daniyarov, p. 163.

30. Läziz Qayumov, "Hayat qahramani wä mäharät," Shärq yulduzi, No. 9 (1971), pp. 52-54.

31. Georgie Anne Geyer, "A Quest for the Old Russia," Saturday Review, Dec. 25, 1971, pp. 14-17.

32. Ä" la Äshräpov, "Ulugh vätän urushidän keyingi tinch qurilish yilläridä rus-ozbek ädäbiy älaqäläri," Rus-ozbek ädäbiy älaqäläri tarikhi ocherkläri, ed. G. K. Kärimov (Tashkent: V. I. Lenin namidägi Tashkent Dävlät Universiteti, 1967), p. 200.

33. Umaräli Narmätov, "Ädäbiy älaqälärimizning äsäsiy tendentsiyäläri," Rus-ozbek ädäbiy älaqäläri tarikhi ocherkläri, ed. Gh. K. Kärimov (Tashkent: V. I. Lenin namidägi Tashkent Dävlät Universiteti, 1967), p. 217.

34. Ibid.

35. Ibid., p. 203.

36. Ibid. See also A. Muzäffarov, "Än änälär—dävr kozgusi," Ozbekistan mädäniyäti, Jan. 18, 1972, p. 1.

37. Umaräli Narmätov, pp. 205-06.

38. Otqir Hashimov, "Qälbinggä qulaq sal," Shärq yulduzi, No. 10 (1971), pp. 26-27.

39. Jämal Kämal, "Vätän," Shärq yulduzi, No. 12 (1971), p. 84.

40. Jämal Kämal, "Kun," Shärq yulduzi, No. 12 (1971), p. 86.

CHAPTER 3

1. As an example, see Robert A. Lewis, "The Mixing of Russians and Soviet Nationalities and Its Demographic Impact," Soviet Nationality Problems, ed. Edward Allworth (New York: Columbia University Press, 1971), 117-167.

2. See Edward Allworth, "Restating the Soviet Nationality Question," Soviet Nationality Problems, ed. Edward Allworth (New York: Columbia University Press, 1971), 1-21.

3. 1959 census data are drawn from Itogi vsesoiuznoi perepisi naseleniia 1959 goda (Moscow: Gosstatizdat, 1962-1963). 1970 data are from preliminary census reports as published in the Central Asian press: Kazakhstanskaia pravda, 9 June 1971, pp. 1, 3; Kommunist Tadzhikistana, 6 May 1971, p. 2; Pravda Vostoka, 28 April 1971, p. 2; Sovetskaia Kirgiziia, 5 May 1971. pp. 3-4; Turkmenskaia iskra, July 11, 1971, pp. 1-2. Also, these reports are translated into English and summarized in Soviet Geography: Review and Translation, XII, 7 (September 1971), 447-453. Data for 1970 percentage urban by oblast are from Narodnoe Khoziaistvo SSSR v 1969 g. (Moscow: Statistika, 1970), pp. 17-18.

4. Geoffrey Wheeler, The Peoples of Soviet Central Asia (London: The Bodley Head, 1966), p. 35.

5. J. William Leasure and Robert A. Lewis, "Internal Migration in Russia in the Late Nineteenth Century," Slavic Review, XXVII, 5 (September 1968), 375-394; George J. Demko, The Russian Colonization of Kazakhstan, 1896-1916 (The Hague: Mouton, 1969); T. V. Staniukovich, "Poseleniia i zhilishche russkogo, ukrainskogo i belorusskogo naseleniia sredneaziatskikh respublik i Kazakhstana," Etnografiia russkogo naseleniia Sibiri i srednei Azii, ed. G. S. Maslova and L. M. Saburova (Moscow: Nauka, 1969), pp. 221-227.

6. Richard A. Pierce, Russian Central Asia 1867-1917:
A Study in Colonial Rule (Berkeley: University of California Press,
1960), pp. 127-128, 137; Ian M. Matley, "The Population and the
Land," Central Asia: A Century of Russian Rule, ed. Edward
Allworth (New York: Columbia University Press, 1967), pp. 103-105.
7. Richard Pipes, The Formation of the Soviet Union (New
York: Atheneum, 1968), 2d ed., pp. 81-93, 172-184.
8. V. I. Perevedentsev, "Aktual'nye problemy territorial'nogo
pereraspredeleniia naseleniia SSSR," Naselenie, trudovye resursy
SSSR, ed. D. I. Valentei and I. F. Sorokina (Moscow: Mysl', 1971),
pp. 150-151.
9. Theodore Shabad, Basic Industrial Resources of the USSR
(New York: Columbia University Press, 1969), pp. 284-346.
10. I. Dudkin, "Etazhi rastut bystree," Kazakhstanskaia pravda,
12, March 1971, p. 1.
11. K. Kim, "Glavnyi prospekt," Kazakhstanskaia pravda, Feb.
7, 1971, p. 1.
12. For an example, see the much-noted Soviet study on the
ethnic composition of the work force at two major industrial
enterprises in Tajikistan in 1964: V. I. Perevedentsev, "On the
Influence of Ethnic Factors on the Migration Process," translated
in Soviet Anthropology and Archaeology, VI, 2 (1967), 16-17.
Original title: "O vliianii etnicheskikh faktorov na territorial'noe
pereraspredelenie naseleniia," Izvestiia Akademii Nauk SSSR,
Seriia geograficheskaia, No. 4 (1965), pp. 31-39.
13. Itogi . . . , Table 54, Republic volumes.
14. See: Narodnoe khoziaistvo srednei Azii v 1963 godu
(Tashkent: "Uzbekistan," 1964); Narodnoe khoziaistvo kirgizskoi
SSR v 1963 godu (Frunze: Statistika, 1964); Sovetskii Turkmenistan
za 40 let (Ashkhabad: Turkmenskoe Izdatel'stvo, 1964).
15. Narodnoe khoziaistvo srednei Azii, 324.
16. Itogi . . . , Table 57, Republic volumes.
17. T. A. Zhdanko and G. P. Vasil'eva, "Vliianie industrializatsii
i urbanizatsii na pereustroistvo byta narodov srednei Azii i
Kazakhstana," paper presented at the United Nations World
Population Conference, Belgrade, Yugoslavia (1965), p. 6; G. P.
Vasil'eva and B. Kh. Karmysheva, eds., Etnograficheskie ocherki
uzbekskogo sel'skogo naseleniia (Moscow: Nauka, 1969), pp. 292-
293.
18. S. Soskin, "Vybor puti," Kazakhstanskaia pravda, Jan. 14,
1971, p. 2.

CHAPTER 4
1. S. M. Abramzon, "Otrazhenie protsessa sblizheniia natsii
na semeino-bytovom uklade narodov srednei Azii i Kazakhstana,"

Sovetskaia etnografiia No. 3 (1962), pp. 18-34; See the translation of the above article: "Reflection of the Process of the Coming Together of Nations in the Family Life and Daily Habits of the Peoples of Central Asia and Kazakhstan," in Soviet Sociology I, 2, (1962), 41-52, especially footnote 2, p. 51. Subsequent citations refer to the translation.

2. Ibid., p. 42.

3. Ibid., p. 44.

4. Ia. R. Vinnikov, Khoziaistvo kul'tura i byt sel'skogo naseleniia turkmenskoi SSR (Moscow: Izdatel'stvo Nauka, 1969), p. 253.

5. Abramzon, op. cit., p. 48.

6. Vasil'eva and Karmysheva, (eds.), Etnograficheskie ocherki uzbekskogo sel'skogo naseleniia (Moscow: Izdatel'stvo Nauka, 1969), p. 225.

7. A. Kh. Margulan and V. V. Vostrov, Kul'tura i byt kazakhskogo kolkhoznogo aula (Alma Ata, Izdatel'stvo "Nauka" Kazakhskoi SSR, 1967), p. 224.

8. E. G. Gafferberg, Beludzhi turkmenskoi SSR, Ocherki khoziaistva, material'noi kul'tury i byta (Leningrad: Izdatel'stvo Nauka, 1969). p. 31.

9. Ibid., p. 165-169.

10. G. P. Vasil'eva, Preobrazovanie byta i etnicheskie protsessy v severnom Turkmenistane (Moscow: Izdatel'stvo Nauka, 1969), pp. 380-381.

11. Vasil'eva and Karmysheva, (eds.), op. cit., pp. 224-225.

12. Sh. Annaklychev, Byt i kul'tura rabochikh Turkmenistana (Ashkhabad: Izdatel'stvo "Ilim," 1969), p. 388.

13. Iu. V. Arutiunian, Sotsial'naia struktura sel'skogo naseleniia SSSR (Moscow: Mysl', 1971), pp. 81-82.

14. A. N. Dvoriadkina, "Znachenie migratsii naseleniia v formirovanii trudovykh resursov turkmenskoi SSR," Izvestiia Akademii nauk turkmenskoi SSR, Seriia obshchestvennykh nauk No. 2 (1971), pp. 40-42.

15. Ibid., p. 41.

16. Ibid., p. 39.

17. O. Musaev, "Nekotorye rezul'taty issledovaniia mezhnatsional' nykh brakov i semei v Turkmenistane," Izvestiia Akademii nauk turkmenskoi SSR, Seriia obshchestvennykh nauk No. 5 (1969), p. 20.

18. Ibid.

19. Vinnikov, op. cit., p. 254.

20. Annaklychev, op. cit., p. 288.

21. Abramzon, op. cit., p. 47.

22. A. V. Kozenko and L. F. Monogarova, "Statisticheskoe izuchenie pokazatelei odnonatsional'noi i smeshannoi brachnosti v Dushanbe," Sovetskaia etnografiia No. 6 (1971), pp. 112-118.

23. Ibid., p. 118.
24. Ethel Dunn, "The influence of religion in the Soviet rural community," The Soviet Rural Community, edited by James Millar, (Urbana: University of Illinois Press, 1971), p. 347.
25. B Saparmukhamedova, "Obshchestvennoe mnenie protiv religii," Nauka i religiia No. 11 (1971), p. 22.
26. S. Begmedov, "Osobennosti proiavleniia nekotorye religioznykh perezhitkov sredi gorodskogo naseleniia," Izvestiia Akademii nauk turkmenskoi SSR, Seriia obshchestvennykh nauk No. 3 (1968), pp. 34-40.
27. T. Bairov, "Formy proiavleniia religioznykh perezhitkov v sele (na materialakh kunia-ugrenchskogo raiona)," Izvestiia Akademii nauk turkmenskoi SSR, Seriia obshchestvennykh nauk No. 2 (1968), pp. 47-52.
28. T. Bairov, "K kharakteristike sovremennogo sostoianiia religioznosti sel'skogo naseleniia Severnogo Turkmenistana," Izvestiia Akademii nauk turkmenskoi SSR, Seriia obshchestvennykh nauk No. 2 (1969), pp. 33-36.
29. Stephen P. Dunn and Ethel Dunn, "Soviet Regime and Native Culture in Central Asia and Kazakhstan: The major peoples," Current Anthropology VIII, 3 (1967), 147-208.
30. See, for example, the articles by Ia. R. Vinnikov, "Novoe v semeinom bytu kolkhoznikov Turkmenistana," Sovetskaia etnografiia No. 6 (1967), pp. 32-41; and G. P. Vasil'eva, "Sovremennye etnicheskie protsessy v severnom Turkmenistane," Sovetskaia etnografiia No. 1 (1968), pp. 3-17.
31. See N. A. Akopian, "Sotrudnichestvo respublik srednei Azii v podgotovka kadrov na sovremennom etape," Obshchestvennye nauki v Uzbekistane No. 4, (1968), pp. 48-50.
32. See William Mandel," Urban Ethnic Minorities in the Soviet Union," a paper presented to the AAASS convention in Dallas in March 1972.

CHAPTER 5

1. T. Burmistrova, Teoriia sotsialisticheskoi natsii (Leningrad: Izdatel'stvo Leningradskogo Universiteta, 1970), p. 3.
2. Yusufjon Akobirov, "Sairi diruzu fardo," Sadoi Sharq, No. 4 (April 1971), p. 15; M. Nazarov, "Nash'ynamoi madaniyati khalqi Tojik," Tojikston Soveti, Jan. 29, 1971, p. 3.
3. Stephen P. Dunn and Ethel Dunn, "Soviet Regime and Native Culture in Central Asia and Kazakhstan: The Major Peoples," Current Anthropology, VIII, 3 (1967), 147-160.
4. Ann Sheehy, "Soviet Central Asia and the 1970 Census," Mizan, XIII, 1 (Aug. 1971), p.

5. Itogi vsesoiuznoi perepisi naseleniia 1959 goda. Tadzhikskaia SSR (Moscow: Gosstatizdat, 1963), pp. 116-120.

6. Tojikiston dar zarfi solhoi hokimiyati Soveti (Dushanbe: Nashriyoti Statistika, 1967), p. 15.

7. M. Khojaev, "Oyanda durakhshontar khokad shud," Maorif va madaniyat, Jan. 1, 1972, p. 2.

8. Narodnoe khoziaistvo srednei Azii v 1963 godu (Tashkent: Izdatel'stvo "Uzbekistan," 1964), p. 328.

9. Yusuf Rajobov, "Solho digarguniho," Tojikiston Soveti, March 27, 1971, p. 3; S. Shodova, "Zindagy khush budu khushtar gardad," Maorif va madaniyat, Jan. 1, 1972, p. 3.

10. A. Shukurov, "Nazorati durust ba samarai on," Maorif va madaniyat, Nov. 25, 1971, p. 2; A. Savdulloev, "Oila byudzhet ba maishat," Tojikston Soveti, Jan. 29, 1971, p. 4; "Khonanda, istihosolot Tajriba," Maorif va madaniyat, Oct. 9, 1971, p. 1.

11. Ann Sheehy, "Soviet Central Asia and the 1970 Census," p. 5.

12. "Tal"limi zaboni khalqi buzurg," Maorif va madaniyat, Nov. 23, 1971, p. 1.

13. V. I. Perevedentsev, "On the Influence of Ethnic Factors on Geographical Population Shifts," Soviet Anthropology and Archaeology, VI, 2 (Fall 1967), 16-20.

14. "O rabote TsK Kompartii Tadzhikistana po vypolneniiu reshenii XIII s'ezda KPSS," Partiinaia zhizn', No. 1 (Jan. 1969), pp. 4-5. George J. A. Murray provided an English translation of this article.

15. Ibid.

16. William K. Medlin, William M. Cave, and Finley Carpenter, Education and Development in Central Asia: A Case Study of Social Change in Uzbekistan (Leiden: E. J. Brill, 1971), p. 214.

17. Yanina Djyarnovskaya, "Khele dur az Varshava," Sadoi Sharq, No. 6 (June, 1971), pp. 108-109.

18. Teresa Rakowska-Harmstone, Russia and Nationalism in Central Asia. The Case of Tadzhikstan (Baltimore: The Johns Hopkins Press, 1970), pp. 94-141; Alec Nove and J. A. Newth, The Soviet Middle East: A Communist Model for Development (New York: Frederick A. Praeger, 1967), pp. 130-132.

19. "Prezidiumi Soveti Olii RSS Tojikiston," Tojikiston Soveti, June 2, 1971, pp. 1, 4.

20. Ibid., p. 3.

21. "Plenumi yakumi KM PK Tojikiston," Tojikiston Soveti, Feb. 20, 1971, p. 1.

22. Ruth Johnston, "New Approach to the Meaning of Assimilation," Human Relations, XVI, 3 (August 1963), 295-296.

23. "O rabote TsK Kompartii Tadzhikistana po vypolneniiu reshenii XIII s"ezda KPSS," p. 5; "Soviet Party Denounces Leaders of Tadzhik Republic and Demands Reforms," The New York Times, Jan. 14, 1969, p. 8.

24. Current Digest of the Soviet Press, XXI, 26, p. 27.

25. Zh. R. Rasulov, "Hisboti Komiteti Markazii Partiya Kommunistii Tojikiston," Tojikiston Soveti, Feb. 19, 1971, p. 4.

26. B. Nabiv, "Komitethoi jam"iyatii gishloqot," Tojikiston Soveti, Jan. 27, 1971, p. 3.

27. "O rabote TsK Kompartii Tadzhikistana po vypoleneniiu reshenii XIII s"ezda KPSS," p. 5.

28. U. Pulodov, "Arkheologiya va din," Kommunist Tojikistoni, No. 4 (July 1971), pp. 60-67.

29. "O rabote TsK Kompartii Tadzhikistana po vypolneniiu reshenii XIII s"ezda KPSS," p. 5.

30. S. Dodoboeva, Qurbon va zanon (Dushanbe: Nashriyoti Irfon, 1965), pp. 40-42.

31. "Dar borai ba modaroni serfarzandi sokini RSS Tojikiston dodani nomi fakhrii 'Qahramonmodar'," Tojikiston Soveti, June 26, 1971, p. 2.

32. S. Dodoboeva, "Ba"ze sababhoi darbaini zanon beshtat joi doshtani urfu odathoi dini," Kommunisti Tojikiston, No. 1 (Jan. 1971), pp. 60-67.

33. Kh. Shodikilov, "Fadeev va adabiyati Tojik," Maorif va madaniyat, Dec. 26, 1971, p. 3.

34. "Ba s"ezdi IV jurnalistoni Tojikiston," Maorif va Madaniyat, Oct. 30, 1971, p. 1.

35. Nizam Nurdzhanov, Tadzhikskii narodnyi teatr (Moscow: Izdatel'stvo Akademii Nauk SSSR, 1956), pp. 227-252.

36. Edward Allworth, Central Asian Publishing and the Rise of Nationalism (New York: New York Public Library, 1965), pp. 32-33.

37. Kholiq Mirzozoda, "Himoyai davlati markazi dar ash"ori Rudaki," Maorif va madaniyat, Nov. 18, 1971, p. 3.

38. Kudoi Sharifov, "Risolai qadimtarin roje"ba ilmi she"r," Sadoi Sharq, No. 6 (June, 1971), pp. 125-127.

39. Yusuf Akbarov, "Khoki vatan az takhti Sulaymon Khustar," Sadoi Sharq, No. 3 (March 1971), pp. 137-140.

40. Asadullo Sufiev, "Hofiz va fol'klor," Sadoi Sharq, No. 4 (April 1971), pp. 91-95; H. Rahim, "Hofiz va Kamol," Ibid., No. 4 (April 1971), pp. 84-90.

41. Sulton Safar, "Bevatan," Sadoi Sharq, No. 3 (March 1971), pp. 40-78.

42. Gulrukhsor, "Vatan," Sadoi Sharq, No. 3 (March 1971), p. 38.

CHAPTER 6

1. Vsesoiuznaia perepis' naseleniia 1926 goda (Moscow:
Izdanie Tsentral'nogo Statisticheskogo Upravleniia SSSR, 1929);
Itogi vsesoiuznoi perepisi naseleniia 1959 goda (Moscow: Gosstatizdat, Tsentral'noe Statisticheskoe Upravlenie SSSR, 1962-63);
"Naselenie nashei strany. Soobshchenie tsentral'nogo statisticheskogo upravlenie pri Sovete ministrov SSSR o vozrastnoi
strukture, urovne obrazovaniia, natsional'nom sostave, iazykakh i
istochnikakh sredstv sushchestvovaniia SSSR po dannym vsesoiuznoi
perepisi naseleniia na 15 ianvaria 1970 goda," Pravda, April 17,
1971, pp. 2, 3.

2. V. I. Kozlov, "K voprosu ob izuchenii etnicheskikh protsessov
u narodov SSSR (opyt issledovaniia na primere mordvy)," Sovetskaia
etnografiia, No. 4 (1961), p. 60.

3. Alexandre Bennigsen, "Islamic or Local Consciousness
Among Soviet Nationalities," Soviet Nationality Problems, Edward
Allworth (ed.) (New York: Columbia University Press, 1971), p. 169.

4. Joseph Stalin, Marxism and the National Question (New York:
International Publishers, 1942), p. 12.

5. Walter Kolarz, Russia and Her Colonies (London: George
Philip & Son, 1953), p. 297.

6. V. K. Gardanov, B. O. Dolgikh, T. A. Zhdanko, "Osnovnye
napravleniia etnicheskikh protsessov u narodov SSSR," Sovetskaia
etnografiia, No. 4 (1961), p. 14.

7. Theodore Shabad, "News Notes," Soviet Geography: Review
and Translation, XII, 9 (November, 1971), 635.

8. "Ba'ze mas"alahoi ta"limi zaboni Rusi," Tojikiston Soveti
(January 26, 1971), p. 4. This article was translated from tajik
for the author by Barry M. Rosen.

CHAPTER 7

1. Nicholas DeWitt, Education and Professional Employment
in the USSR (Washington, D.C.: National Science Foundation,
1961), p. 359.

2. Khojag'i khalqi Tojikiston dar sol 1958 (Stalinabad:
Nashriyoti Dovlati Tojikiston, 1959), p. 310; Narodnoe khoziaistvo
tadzhikskoi SSR v 1962 godu (Dushanbe: Gosstatizdat, 1963),
p. 346.

3. Narodnoe khoziaistvo SSSR v 1958 godu. Statisticheskii
ezhegodnik (Moscow: Izdatel'stvo "Statistika," 1959), and
corresponding volumes for 1959-1965 published 1960-1966.

4. M. Mobin Shorish, "The Place of Local Women in the
'Multi-Tiered' Culture of the Soviet Central Asia" (paper presented
at the Interdisciplinary Conference on Process of Change in
Contemporary Asian Societies, Champaign, Illinois, November 5,

1970); Ibid., "The Employment Opportunities of the Local Women
of the Soviet Central Asian Republics" (paper read at the Colloquium
on Education and Political Development, University of Chicago,
February 1970).

5. See O. Qosidov and A. Hodiboev, "Problemhoi migratsiiai
aholi dar Tojikiston," Kommunisti Tojikiston, No. 2 (February
1970), pp. 9-13; "Dar borai strukturai sinnu sol, darajai ma"lumot,
hayati milli, zabon va manbai daromadi aholii SSSR muvofiqi
baruykhatgirii umumittifoqii aholi to 15 ianvari soli 1970,"
Tojikistoni Soveti, April 18, 1971, pp. 3-4.

6. For 1959 figures see Itogi vsesoiuznoi perepisi naseleniia
1959 goda: tadzhikskaia SSR (Moscow: Gosstatizdat TsSU SSSR,
1963), pp. 116-117; Narodnoe khoziaistvo tadzhikskoi SSR v 1965 g.
(Dushanbe: Izdatel'stvo "Statistika," 1966), p. 11. For 1970
population see Narodnoe khoziaistvo SSSR v 1969 g. Statisticheskii
ezhegodnik (Moscow: Izdatel'stvo "Statistika," 1970), p. 690; "Dar
borai strukturai . . . " Tojikistoni Soveti, April 18, 1971, pp. 3-4;
Roman Szporluk, "The Nations of the USSR in 1970," Survey, XVII,
4 (Aug. 1971), 94; "Census Data: Age, Education, Nationality,"
Current Digest of the Soviet Press, XXIII, 16 (May 18, 1971), 14-18.
For data on higher education see Atlas tadzhikskoi sovetskoi
sotsialisticheskoi respubliki (Dushanbe-Moscow: Glavnoe
Upravlenie Geodezii i Kartografii pri Sovete Ministrov SSSR,
1968), p. 175.

7. Usmon Jum"aev, "Ghamkhori dar haqqi muthassisoni javon,"
Maorif va madaniyat, May 14, 1971, p. 1.

8. See Development of Higher Education, 1950-1967 (Paris:
Organization for Economic Cooperation and Development, 1970),
pp. 291, 329, 668, 728, and 797; and Demographic Yearbook, 1967
(New York: The United Nations, 1968), pp. 126-30.

9. See V. I. Perevedentsev, "The Influence of Ethnic Factors
on the Territorial Redistribution of Population," Central Asian
Review, XIV, 1 (1966), 48, 55.

10. See Usmon Jum"aev, op. cit.; "Dar borai strukturai . . . "
op. cit.; and "Aholii respublikai mo: Akhboroti Upravleniiai
Markazii Statistikii Nazdi Soveti Vazironi RSS Tojikiston dar borai
strukturai sinnu sol, darajai ma"lumot, hayati mi li, zabon va
manbai daromadi aholii RSS Tojikiston muvofiqu baruykhatgirii
umumiittifoqii aholii to 15 ianvari soli 1970," Tojikistoni Soveti,
May 6, 1971, pp. 1, 3.

11. Ibid.

12. For a brief discussion of the rationale for bride price in
Islam, see M. Mobin Shorish, "The Employment Opportunities,"
p. 20, n. 11. For a more detailed discussion of the custom in
Central Asia, see M. Ghafforova, Ba hayot tatbiq shudani ideiai
ozodii zanon (Stalinabad: Nashriyoti Davlatii Tojikiston, 1960).

13. "Qabuli studentoro alon menamoyad," Tojikistoni Soveti,
May 8, 1971, p. 4; Ann Sheehy, "Labour Problems and Employment
in Kazakhstan and Central Asia," Central Asian Review, XIV, 2
(1966), 164-65

CHAPTER 8
1. Of particular importance are the following two works:
Karl Deutsch, et al., "Political Community and the North Atlantic
Area," in International Political Community. An Anthology (Garden
City & New York: Anchor Books; Doubleday, 1966); Amitai Etzioni,
Political Unification: A Comparative Study of Leaders and Forces
(New York: Holt, Rinehart & Winston, 1965).
2. For Central Committee membership lists see: "Sostav
TsK KP Kirgizii, izbrannyi XV s'ezdom kompartii Kirgizii,"
Sovetskaia Kirgiziia, March 6, 1971, p. 1; "Sostav tsentral'nogo
komiteta kommunisticheskoi partii Uzbekistana, izbrannogo XVIII
s"ezdom," Pravda Vostoka, March 5, 1971, p. 1. For lists of
Supreme Soviet delegates see: "Spisok deputatov verkhovnogo
soveta kirgizskoi SSR," Sovetskaia Kirgiziia, June 17, 1971, pp. 3-4;
"Uspekha vam, izbranniki naroda!" Pravda Vostoka, June 17, 1971,
pp. 3-4.
3. The census results detailing the ethnic composition of
Kirgizia and Uzbekistan appeared in the following newspapers:
"Naselenie nashei respubliki," Pravda Vostoka, April 28, 1971,
pp. 2, 4; "Naselenie respubliki," Sovetskaia Kirgiziia, May 5, 1971,
pp. 3-4.
4. For a discussion about the application of the concept of
co-optation to Communist systems see: Michael P. Gehlen and
Michael McBride, "The Soviet Central Committee: An Elite
Analysis," and Frederic J. Fleron, Jr., "Co-optation as a
Mechanism of Adaption to Change: The Soviet Political Leadership
System," in The Behavioral Revolution and Communist Studies,
ed. Roger E. Kanet (New York: The Free Press, 1971), pp. 103-
151.
5. Teresa Rakowska-Harmstone, Russia and Nationalism in
Central Asia: The Case of Tadzhikistan (Baltimore: The Johns
Hopkins Press, 1970), pp. 94-146.
6. V. V. Pokshishevskii, "Urbanization and Ethnographic
Processes," Soviet Geography, XIII, 2 (1972), 113-120. This
article is a translation of V. V. Pokshishevskii, Problemy
urbanizatsii v SSSR (Moscow: Izdatel'stvo Moskovskogo
Universiteta, 1971), p. 53-62.
7. Narodnoe khoziaistvo srednei Azii v 1963 godu (Tashkent:
Izdatel'stvo "Uzbekistan," 1964), pp. 280, 284, 324.

8. For discussion of the concepts involved see: Lucian Pye, Politics, Personality and Nation Building (New Haven: Yale University Press, 1962); Herbert A. Simon, Administrative Behavior (New York: The Free Press, 1957); Stanley H. Udy, "Administrative Rationality, Social Setting, and Organizational Development," in A Sociological Reader on Complex Organizations, ed. Amitai Etzioni (New York: Holt, Rinehart & Winston, 1969), pp. 480-495; Ralph Braibanti, "External Inducement of Political-Administrative Development: An Institutional Strategy," and Warren F. Ilchman, "Productivity, Administrative Reform and Antipolitics: Dilemmas for Developing States," in Political and Administrative Development, ed. Ralph Braibanti (Durham, N.C.: Duke University Press, 1969), pp. 3-106, 472-526.

9. For this section of the study, the 1971 issues of the following Central Asians journals were also surveyed: Partiinaia zhizn' (Tashkent) and Kommunist (Frunze). Mr. Azamat Altay was the reader for the Kirgiz-language Kommunist.

10. T. U. Usubaliev, "Otchetnyi doklad tsentral'nogo komiteta KP Kirgizii XV s"ezdu kommunisticheskoi partii Kirgizii," Sovetskaia Kirgiziia, March 4, 1971, p. 3.

11. Ibid.

12. M. Altaev, "Rastit' internatsionalistov," Sovetskaia Kirgiziia, Oct. 23, 1971, p. 3.

CHAPTER 9

1. Stalin, Marxism and the National Question (New York: International Publishers, 1942), p. 12; T. Burmistrova, Teoria sotsialisticheskoi natsii (Leningrad: Izdatel'stvo Leningradskogo Universiteta, 1970), p. 3.

2. H. J. Janmatova, "Al-Kindiy muzikäsi," Fän vä turmush, No. 9 (1971), p. 36; Askarali Rajabov, "Girdovarii asosi san"at," Maorif va madaniyat July 24, 1971, p. 3.

3. "Ansambli 'Lola' ba Afghonistan meravad," Maorif va madaniyat, May 13, 1971, p. 1; "Hunarmandoni javoni hunaristonho," Maorif va madaniyat, Feb. 13, 1971, p. 3.

4. "Vaqeälär," Ozbekistan mädäniyäti, Dec. 7, 1971, p. 1.

5. A. Sokolova, "Hämishä nävgiron," Shärq yulduzi, No. 7 (1971), p. 160.

6. Nugzar Sharia, Soviet Georgian performer who recently acted in Tajik and Uzbek films, interviewed February 25, 1972, in New York.

7. H. Khojäev, "Ozbekfil'm Kharäzmdä," Ozbekistan mädäniyäti, May 14, 1971,

8. Sharia interview (See Note 6)

9. "'Asrori qabila' oshkor megardad," Maorif va madaniyat, July 29, 1971, p. 3.

10. Nahanov, "Ozbekfil'm," Ozbekistan mädäniyäti, Dec. 31, 1971, p. 4.

11. T. Saidov, "Kriditi banki davlati va kino," Maorif va madaniyat, Sept. 2, 1971, p. 4: "Yuksäk mäs'uliyät bilän, " Ozbekistan mädäniyäti, Dec. 24, 1971, p. 1.

12. M. Nazarov, "Repertuar oinai teatr ast," Maorif va madaniyat, Jan. 28, 1971, pp. 1, 3.

13. "Ansambli 'Lola' ba Afghonistan meravad," p. 1.

14. "'Läzgi'ning säfäri," Ozbekistan mädäniyäti, Dec. 21, 1971, p. 4.

15. Yanghin Mirza, "Royal' vä ghäzäl," Ozbekistan mädäniyäti, Nov. 26, 1971, p. 3.

16. I. Äbdullaev, "Mä" näsini nänini yegänlär chäqsin," Ozbekistan mädäniyäti, Nov. 26, 1971, p. 2.

17. Säyfi Jälil, "Istäklärim," Ozbekistan mädäniyäti, Nov. 26, 1971, p. 1.

18. R. Ghafurov; Q. Solenkov, "On chi khush nest, khush nemeoad," Maorif va madaniyat, Jan. 30, 1971, p. 3.

19. A discussion of the changes in traditional Central Asian instruments, the policy behind the action as well as some of its implications appears in Mark Slobin's "Conversations in Tashkent," Asian Music, II, 2 (1971), 10.

20. "Hunarnamoii mehmonon," Maorif va madaniyat, July 24, 1971, p. 3.

21. I. Hidoyatov, "Tuhfai san"atkoron," Maorif va madaniyat, Jan. 7, 1971, p. 3.

22. Edward Allworth (ed.), Soviet Nationality Problems (New York: Columbia University Press, 1971), p. 287; Theodore Shabad, "News Notes (Ethnic Results of the 1970 Soviet Census)," Soviet Geography: Review and Translation, No. 9 (1971), pp. 450, 452.

23. M. Nazarov, pp. 1, 3.

24. M. Bobojonov, "Malikai sahna," Maorif va madaniyat, June 10, 1971, p. 3.

25. B. Islamov, "Isyankanlär fajeäsi," Ozbekistan mädäniyäti, Dec. 21, 1971, p. 2.

26. "Works exhibited at the Second All-Union Water-colour Exhibition," Soviet Literature, No. 12 (1970), p. 192.

27. "Dar olami adab," Sadoi sharq, No. 1 (1970), p. 157; M. Nazarov, pp. 1, 3.

28. N. Nurjonov, "Jashni qasri san"at," Maorif va madaniyat, May 13, 1971, p. 4.

29. For examples see A. Afsazod; V. Samad, "Fajiai 'Khayyom' dar sahna," Maorif va madaniyat, Jan. 9, 1971, p. 3; "Asarhoi navi

'Tajikfil'm," Maorif va madaniyat, Feb. 16, 1971, p. 4; "Hunarnamoii san'atkoroni Afghonistan," Maorif va madaniyat, Dec. 14, 1971, p. 3.; Photo and caption, Ozbekistan mädäniyäti, Jan. 2, 1971, p. 4.

30. "Muziqi va nazariyai on," Maorif va madaniyat, May 13, 1971, p. 4.

31. "Kochma plenum," Ozbekistan mädäniyäti, Nov. 16, 1971, p. 1.

32. Sh. Sayfiddinov, "Ohang va changsozii Tajik," Maorif va madaniyat, Feb. 27, 1971, p. 1.

33. M. Nazarov, pp. 1, 3.

34. Ė. Dolgonosova, "Jilvai rangho," Sadoi sharq, No. 8, (August 1970), p. 115-119.

35. A. Nemirovskii, "Khushvakhti san"atkor," Maorif va madaniyat, March 10, 1971, p. 1: "Rassomoni javon namoish medahand," Maorif va madaniyat, July 22, 1971, p. 3.

36. "Rässamlär soyuzidä," Ozbekistan mädäniyäti, July 6, 1971, p. 3.

37. M. Nazarov, pp. 1, 3.

CHAPTER 10

1. Evidence has been drawn from recent—late 1960s and early 1970s—newspapers and journals both in Russian and in local languages, focusing primarily on the cultural developments in Uzbekistan, Kirgizia, and Tajikistan. Especially useful were the following: Ozbekistan mädäniyäti, Zvezda Vostoka, Obshchest-vennye nauki v Uzbekistane, Pamir, Sovet edebiyat'i, Ala-too, Druzhba narodov, and Radio Liberty Dispatches. I would like to express my gratitude to Machmud Maksud-Bek, Azamat Altay, and Aman B. Murat, my language consultants in the Uzbek, Kirgiz, and Turkmen-language press. For background information I have consulted the following: Edward Allworth, Uzbek Literary Politics (New York: Humanities Press; London, the Hague, Paris: Mouton, 1964); Alexandre Bennigsen; Chantal Lemercier Quelquejay, The Evolution of Muslim Nationalities of the USSR and Their Linguistic Problems (London: Central Asian Research Centre, 1961); Edward Allworth, ed., Central Asia: A Century of Russian Rule (New York: Columbia University Press, 1967).

2. A thorough analysis of literary developments in Uzbekistan is presented in Edward Allworth, Uzbek Literary Politics.

3. Alexandre Bennigsen, "Les peuples musulmans de l' U.R.S.S. et les Soviets: III. La campagne contre les epopées nationales, la résistance kirghize," L'Afrique et l'Asie, No. L (1953), pp. 13-30; Serge A. Zenkovsky, "Ideological Deviations in Soviet Central Asia," Slavonic and East European Review, XXXII, 79 (1954), 424-437.

4. On the arrest and persecution of people working in cultural fields in the Ukraine at the end of 1965, see Vyacheslav Chornovil, The Chornovil Papers (New York, Toronto, London, Sydney, Johannesburg, Mexico, Panama: McGraw-Hill, 1968).

5. A. Osman, "Ozbek ädäbii tilining bä"zi mäsäläläri" Sovet Ozbekistani, May 24, 1969, p. 3.

6. T. Tilegenov, Sotsialistik Kazakhstan, Jan. 7, 1971, Radio Liberty Dispatch, "A Recent Protest Against Poor Usage of Kazakh Language in Alma-Ata," January 27, 1971.

7. K. Zhitov, "Puteshestvie po gorodu 25 vekov," Zvezda Vostoka, No. 11 (1971), pp. 146-148.

8. "Mädäniy bayligimiz," Ozbekistan mädäniyäti, Dec. 30, 1969, p. 1; Kazakhstanskaia pravda, May 16, 1971, quoted in Mizan, (Oct. 1971), "The Central Asian and Kazakh SSRs in the Soviet Press, 1 May to 31 July 1971," p. 104; "Tarïkh jana madaniyat ëstelikterin korgoo koomunun s"ezdi," Sovettik Kïrgïzstan, March 24, 1971, p. 1; E. Moldobaev, "Baÿirkïlardï da barktayli," Sovettik Kïrgïzstan, Dec. 24, 1971, p. 4.

9. "Tärikhimiz shahidläri," Ozbekistan mädäniyäti, Jan. 21, 1962, p. 1; S. Hamoroeva, "Abidälär-khälq bayligi," Ibid.

10. Mukhtar Magauin, Kobyz i kop'e (Alma-Ata: Izd-vo "Zhazushy," review of a Russian translation by R. Berdibaev in Druzhba narodov, No. 10 (1971), p. 282.

11. Ibid.

12. Anaur Alimzhanov, Suvenir iz Otrara (Moscow: "Molodaia Gvardia," 1970), reviewed by V. Karpenko in Zvezda Vostoka, No. 9 (1971), pp. 217-218.

13. V. V. Barthold, A Short History of Turkestan (Four Studies on the History of Central Asia), trans. from Russian by V. and T. Minorsky (London: E. J. Brill, 1956).

14. A. Näsrullaev, "Prozamiz yutughi," Ozbekistan mädäniyäti.

15. Vitalii Korotych, "Kil'ka krokiv na skhid," Vitchyzna, No. 1 (1972), pp. 140-158; No. 2 (1972), pp. 118-135.

16. Ibid., No. 1, p. 147.

17. Ibid. No. 2, p. 128.

18. Pravda Vostoka, May 12, 1971, quoted in Mizan (Oct. 1971), "The Central Asian and Kazakh SSSRs in the Soviet Press, May 1 to July 31, 1971," p. 104.

19. See for example the January 18, 1972, issue.

20. Alexandre Bennigsen, "Islamic or Local Consciousness Among Soviet Nationalities," in Edward Allworth (ed.), Soviet Nationality Problems (New York and London: Columbia University Press, 1971), p. 181.

21. D. Rakhmatova, "Forum navoivedov" (A Forum of Nawaiy Scholars), Obshchestvennye nauki v Uzbekistane, No. 6 (1961), pp. 60-61.

22. K. Kurumbaev, "Ёdebi aragatnashïklarïmïzïng tarïkhïndan" Sovet ёdebiyat'i (Ashkhabad), No. 2 (1971), pp. 110-120.

23. Baydïlda Sarnogoev, "Salat saga," Ala Too, No. 2 (1970), p. 44.

24. Rakhmanqül Berdïbaev, "Tashkentte tughan oylar," Qazaq ädebieti, March 24, 1972, p. 4.

25. A. Muzaffarov, "Propaganda Against Religion in Settled Areas," Ozbekistan kommunisti, No. 7 (1970), quoted in Radio Liberty Dispatch, Feb. 17, 1971, "The Resurgence of Islam in Soviet Central Asia as Reflected in Soviet Media in the Summer of 1970" (from the Turkestan Quarterly, translated and edited by David Nissman).

26. D. Rakhmatova, op. cit.

27. Vitalii Korotych, op. cit., No. 2, p. 118.

28. Ibid., p. 126.

29. Ibid., pp. 130-131.

30. Gretchen S. Brainerd, "Soviets Intensify Propaganda to Moslem Nationalities in China," Radio Liberty Dispatch, Feb. 14, 1962.

31. Ibid.

CHAPTER 11

1. D. N. Logofet, Bukharskoe khanstvo pod russkim protektoratom (St. Petersburg: V. Berezovskii, 1911), I, p. 187, estimated 3 million; A. I. Dmitriev-Mamonov, Putevoditel' po Turkestanu i sredne-aziatskoi zheleznoi doroge (St. Petersburg: Ministerstvo Voennoe: Puti Soobshcheniia, 1903), p. 284, gave 2.5 million; V. I. Masal'skii, Turkestanskii Krai, in V. P. Semenov-Tian-Shanskii, ed., Rossiia: Polnoe geograficheskoe opisanie nashego otechestva (St. Petersburg: Devrien, 1913), XIX, p. 348, put the total at 2.5 million or not less than 2.25 million and probably not as high as 3 million; V. Suvorov, Istoriko-ekonomicheskii ocherk razvitiia Turkestana (Tashkent: Gosizdat UzSSR, 1962), p. 68, Table 4, gives 3.6 million in 1913-14; E. E. Skorniakov, Aziatskaia Rossiia (St. Petersburg: Pereselencheskoe Upravlienie Glavnago Upravlieniia Zemleustroistva i Zemledieliia, 1914), II, p. 245, combines Bukhara and Khiva for 3 million, giving Bukhara some 2.5 million.

2. M. Chokaiev, "Turkestan and the Soviet Regime," Journal of the Royal Central Asian Society, Vol. XVIII (1931), p. 410.

3. Alexander G. Park, Bolshevism in Turkestan 1917-1927 (New York: Columbia University Press, 1957), p. 99, note to Table 3.

4. M. Vakhabov, Formirovanie uzbekskoi sotsialisticheskoi natsii (Tashkent: Gosizdat UzSSR, 1961), pp. 104, 415, shows the

major ethnic groups around 1924, totalling 1,959,336, but excludes Russians and other non-Central Asians; M. Nemchenko, Natsional'noe razmezhevanie srednei Azii, (Moscow: Izdanie Litizdata NKID, 1925), map opposite p. 28, gives a total population of 2,029,512. Vakhabov's figures for ethnic groups agree with Nemchenko's. The data used may be inaccurate, but the estimates are probably closer to the truth than most; Seymour Becker, Russia's Protectorates in Central Asia: Bukhara and Khiva, 1865-1924 (Cambridge, Mass.: Harvard University Press, 1968), p. 346, footnote 10.

5. Vakhabov, p. 415, Table 11. The figure given for the Uzbek population also appears in S. P. Tolstov, et. al., eds., Narody srednei Azii i Kazakhstana (Moscow: Izdatel'stvo Akademii Nauk SSSR, 1962), I, p. 195. Vakhabov's figures agree with those in Nemchenko, Table on p. 22.

6. Ibid., pp. 398-399. Similar percentages are given in Istoriia uzbekskoi SSR (Tashkent: Izdatel'stvo "Fan" UzSSR, 1967), III, p. 379.

7. Vakhabov, p. 399; Istoriia uzbekskoi SSR, III, p. 379.

8. M. Nemchenko, "Natsional'noe razmezhevanie Srednei Azii," Mezhdunarodnaia zhizn', Nos. 4-5 (1924), p. 86. Becker, p. 7. Park, p. 88, gives a figure of 45.1 percent, based on Nemchenko's figures.

9. G. P. Vasil'ev and B. Kh. Karmyshev, eds., Etnograficheskie ocherki uzbekskogo sel'skogo naseleniia (Moscow: Izdatel'stvo "Nauka," 1969), pp. 40, 44.

10. B. A. Antonenko, Istoriia tadzhikskogo naroda (Moscow: Izdatel'stvo "Nauka", 1964), III, book 1, p. 153, quoting Revoliutsionyi Vostok, No. 16 (1934), p. 115; Istoriia uzbekskoi SSR, III, p. 379.

11. Nemchenko (1924), p. 86; Park, p. 88; Becker, p. 7.

12. Nemchenko (1924), p. 86; Becker, p. 7; Park, p. 88, gives a figure of 7.5 percent.

13. Istoriia turkmenskoi SSR (Ashkhabad: Izdatel'stvo Akademii Nauk TSSR, 1957), II, p. 249; Istoriia uzbekskoi SSR, III, p. 379.

14. Vasil'ev and Karmyshev, p. 44.

15. B. V. Andrianov, "Karta narodov srednei Azii i Kazakhstana," in T. A. Zhdanko, ed., Materialy k istoriko-etnograficheskomu atlasu srednei Azii i Kazakhstana, (Moscow: Izdatel'stvo Akademii Nauk SSSR, 1961), p. 20.

16. Logofet, I, p. 186.

17. Park, p. 88.

18. Andrianov, p. 21; O. A. Sukhareva, Bukhara XIX - nachalo XX v. (Moscow: Izdatel'stvo "Nauka," 1966), p. 168.

19. Sukhareva, pp. 150, 154.

20. Masal'skii, pp. 362, 405.

21. Ibid., pp. 362, 380, 392.
22. For comments on the tribal composition of the Uzbek and Tajik population see: Vakhabov, p. 413; Park, p. 94; Vasil'ev and Karmyshev, p. 40; Andrianov, pp. 18, 21.
23. Dmitriev-Mamonov, p. 284; Becker, p. 7, accepts these figures.
24. Logofet, I, p. 187.
25. Vakhabov, pp. 103-104.
26. Ibid., p. 104.
27. Becker, p. 7.
28. Edward Allworth, "The 'Nationality' Idea in Czarist Central Asia," in Erich Goldhagen, ed., Ethnic Minorities in the Soviet Union (New York: Frederick A. Praeger, 1968), p. 232.
29. V. K. Gardanov, B. O. Dolgikh, and T. A. Zhdanko, "Osnovnye napravleniia etnicheskikh protsessov u narodov SSSR," Sovetskaia etnografiia, No. 4 (1961), pp. 13-14.
30. In the period 1911-13 the population of the city of Bukhara was estimated at 80,000 to 100,000. See Logofet, I, p. 186; Masal'skii, p. 349. Sukhareva, p. 103, places it around 70-80,000.
31. Park, p. 89.

CHAPTER 12
1. 'Abd al-Ra'ūf Fitrat, Munāzara (Istanbul: Matba'a-i Islāmiyya-i Hikmat, 1327/1909-10).
2. Sadr al-Dīn 'Aini, Namūna-i adabiyyāt-i Tājik (Moscow: Chāpkhāna-i Nashriyyāt-i Markazī-i Khalq, 1926), p. 600. Avāz-i Tājik began publication in Samarkand on August 25, 1924.
3. Fitrat, Munāzara, p. 17.
4. Ibid., p. 2: "be towr-i muhāvara-i Bukhārā iān."
5. 'Aini, Namūna, pp. 550-551.
6. Bukhārā-i sharif, No. 50(9 May 1912), 1.
7. Fitrat, Munāzara, p. 2.
8. Ibid., p. 63.
9. 'Ainī, Namūna, p. 533.
10. Ibid., p. 535.
11. A'ina (Ayinä), No. 13 (18 January 1914), 215-216. This journal was published in Samarkand from August 1913 to October 1915. See 'Ainī, Namūna, p. 551.
12. 'Ainī, Namūna, p. 552.
13. Ibid., pp. 578-579.
14. Ibid., p. 581.
15. Ibid., pp. 583-584.
16. Ibid., pp. 584-585.
17. Ibid., pp. 585-586.
18. Fitrat, Munāzara, Epilogue, p. 3.

19. [Fitrat], Hindistandä bir farangi ilä Bukharali bir
mudarrisning bir nechä mas' alälar ham usul-i jadidä khususidä
qilgan munazaräsi muharriri Fitrat, trans. to Turki by Hajji
Mucin ibn Shukrullah Samarqandi (Tashkent: Turkistan Kutub-
khanäsi, H. 1331/1913).

20. Täjik, "Maẓmūn sokhanhä hamagī yak ast va likin libāsi
shän mokhtalif ast," Rahbar-i dänish No. 7 (10), (July 1928), p. 34.

21. See his Divän (Moscow: Idära-i Nashriyyät be Zabänhä-i
Khäriji, 1946), pp. 289-290.

CHAPTER 13

1. Alexandre Bennigsen, "Islamic, or Local Consciousness
Among Soviet Nationalities?," Soviet Nationality Problems
Edward Allworth, ed. (New York: Columbia University Press,
1971), pp. 168-82.

2. For more details about nationality consciousness among
the Kazakhs and Turkmens, see Edward Allworth, "The 'Nationality'
Idea in Czarist Central Asia," Ethnic Minorities in the Soviet
Union, Erich Goldhagen, ed., (New York: Frederick A. Praeger,
1968), pp. 229-50.

3. Ian Murray Matley, "The Population and the Land," Central
Asia: A Century of Russian Rule, Edward Allworth, ed., (New
York: Columbia University Press, 1967), p. 94.

4. Mukhtar Bakir, Turkistan tarikhi (Tashkent: n.p., 1918):
in Persian version as Turkistan, trans. by Sayyid Rizä cAlïzäda,
(Lahore: Nashriyät-i Shïr Muhammad, 1927), pp. 297-300; Shakir
Ya cqub-Sä cid Akhrari, Bukhara jäghrafiyäsi (Old Bukhara:
Bukhara Khälq Shuralar Jumhuriyätining Dävlät Näshriyati, August
1924), pp. 20-21.

5. Mukhtar Bakir, Turkistan, p. 297.

6. Abdurrauf Fitrat-i Bukhariy, "Täziyäna-yi ta' dib," Ayinä,
No. 13 (Jan. 18, 1914); cited in Edward Allworth, Central Asia:
A Century of Russian Rule, p. 425.

7. Fitrat Bukharets, Spor bukharskago mudarrisa s evropeitsem
v Indii o novometodnykh shkolakh (Tashkent: Elektro-Parovaia
Tipografiia-Litografiia, Shtabs Okruga, 1911).

8. Fitrat-i Bukhäräyï, Munäzara (Istanbul: Matba cä-yi
Islämiya Hikmat, 1327/1909), p. 67.

9. Ibid., p. 2.

10. Letters from the Bukharan emigrants, Dr. Naim Oktem
(b. 1900), dated March 8, 1972, and Nadir Ricaloglu (b. 1914), dated
February 28, 1972.

11. Baymirza Hayit, Some Problems of Modern Turkistan
History (Dusseldorf: East European Research Institute, 1963), p.
32.

12. Ibid., p. 32.

13. Sadriddin Ayniy, Tārikh-i amirān-i manghitiya-yi bukhārā (Tashkent: Mustaqil Bukhara Khālq Shuralar Jumhuriyäti Maᶜarif Näzaräti Näshriyati, 1923), pp. 39, 149.

14. Sadriddin Ayniy, Bukhara inqilabi tärikhi uchun mäteriyällär (Moscow: SSSR Khälqlarining Märkäz Näshriyati, 1926): reprinted in same author's Äsärlär (Tashkent: OzSSR Dävlät Adäbiyat Näshriyati, 1963), I, p. 239-240.

15. Edward Allworth, "The 'Nationality' Idea in Czarist Central Asia," p. 244.

16. Ziya Säᶜid, Ozbek vaqtli mätboᶜati tärikhigä mäteriyällär, 1870-1927 (Samarkand-Tashkent: Ozbek Dävlät Näshriyati, 1927), p. 107; Zeki Velidi Togan, Bugunku Turkili (Turkistan) ve yakin Tarihi (Istanbul: Arkadash Ibrahim Horoz ve Guven Basimevleri, 1942-47), pp. 505, 508, 510.

17. Memorandum of Osman Khoja, President of the Bukharan Republic, to the government of Afghanistan on April 20, 1922; see in A. Receb Baysun, Turkistan Milli Hareketleri, (Istanbul: n.p., 1945), p. 137.

18. Zeki Velidi Togan, Hatiralar (Istanbul: Hikmet Gazetecilik Ltd., Tan Matbaasi, 1969), pp. 362-66.

19. Ozbekistan SSR tärikhi (Tashkent: Ozbekistan SSR Fänlär Äkädemiyäsi Näshriyati, 1958), II, p. 235.

20. Shakir Yaᶜqub-Säᶜid Akhrari, Bukhara jäghrafiyäsi, title page.

21. Sadriddin Ayniy, Tārikh-i amirān-i manghitiya-yi bukhārā, title page.

22. Ozbekistan SSR tärikhi, II, p. 235.

23. Letters of Dr. Naim Oktem and Nadir Ricaloglu.

24. Osman Kocaoglu, "Buhara Cumhuriyeti," Yeni Turkistan, No. 39 (Istanbul, Sept. 1931), pp. 1-2.

CHAPTER 14

1. For a brief description of the history and structure of the Bukharan khanate, see Seymour Becker, Russia's Protectorates in Central Asia: Bukhara and Khiva, 1865-1924 (Cambridge, Mass.: Harvard University Press, 1968), pp. 4-9.

2. Alexandre Bennigsen and Chantal Lemercier-Quelquejay, Islam in the Soviet Union (New York: Frederick A. Praeger, 1967), pp. 20, 23.

3. Ol'ga A. Sukhareva, Bukhara XIX—nachalo XX v. (Moscow: Nauka, 1966), pp. 125-128, 153.

4. Ibid., pp. 122-129, 143, citing findings by B. Kh. Karmysheva.

5. On the problem of national consciousness, nationality, and nationalism, see Karl W. Deutsch, Nationalism and Social

214   NATIONALITY QUESTION IN SOVIET CENTRAL ASIA

Communication, 2nd ed. (Cambridge, Mass.: MIT Press, 1966);
Carlton J. H. Hayes, Nationalism: A Religion (New York: Macmillan,
1960); Frederick Hertz, Nationality in History and Politics (London:
Routledge & Kegan Paul, 1944); and Hans Kohn, The Idea of
Nationalism (New York: Macmillan, 1944).

6. Hélène Carrère d'Encausse, Réforme et révolution chez
les musulmans de l'Empire russe, Bukhara 1867-1924 (Paris:
Armand Colin, 1966), pp. 136, 143, 179, 186-187; Bennigsen and
Lemercier-Quelquejay, pp. 47-48.

7. Edward Allworth, Uzbek Literary Politics (The Hague:
Mouton, 1964), pp. 49-50; Serge A. Zenkovsky, Pan-Turkism and
Islam in Russia (Cambridge, Mass.: Harvard University Press,
1960), p. 74.

8. Bennigsen and Lemercier-Quelquejay, pp. 69, 72, 78-79,
134; Carrère d'Encausse, pp. 175, 178, 220, 222-223, 232.

9. Ibid., pp. 228-229; Bennigsen and Lemercier-Quelquejay,
pp. 73, 84-85.

10. Becker, pp. 297-300.

11. Carrère d'Encausse, p. 256.

12. Iosif V. Stalin, Sochineniia (Moscow: Gosudarstvennoe
Izdatel'stvo Politicheskoi Literatury, 1946-51), V, 23.

13. Carrère d'Encausse, p. 256.

14. Atabai I. Ishanov, Bukharskaia narodnaia sovetskaia
respublika (Tashkent: Izdatel'stvo "Uzbekistan", 1969), pp. 242,
260, 272; Faizulla Khodzhaev, Izbrannye trudy (Tashkent: Akademiia
Nauk uzbekskoi SSR, 1970-), I, 421, 427.

15. Becker, pp. 301-302.

16. Khodzhaev, I, 321-325.

17. Carrère d'Encausse, pp. 241-243; Bennigsen and Lemercier-
Quelquejay, pp. 89-90, 99-100, 103.

18. Ibid., pp. 110, 116-117, 124-125, 155-156.

19. Khodzhaev, I, 46; Carrère d'Encausse, pp. 268-269; Stalin,
V, 189.

20. Khodzhaev, I, 47.

21. Alexander G. Park, Bolshevism in Turkestan, 1917-1927
(New York: Columbia University Press, 1957), p. 51; Carrère
d'Encausse, pp. 262-264.

22. Quoted in Carrère d'Encausse, p. 272.

23. Khodzhaev, I, 47.

24. Ibid., I, 273-275, 278, 358-361.

SELECTED LIST OF RECENT (1951–71) BOOKS IN ENGLISH
ABOUT CENTRAL ASIA
AND THE GENERAL SOVIET NATIONALITY QUESTION

Allworth, Edward (ed.). Central Asia: a Century of Russian Rule. New York: Columbia University Press, 1967.
_____. Central Asian Publishing and the Rise of Nationalism: An Essay and a List of Publications in The New York Public Library. New York: New York Public Library, 1965.
_____. Nationalities of the Soviet East: Publications and Writing Systems. A Bibliographical Directory and Transliteration Tables for Iranian- and Turkic-Language Publications, 1818-1945, Located in U.S. Libraries. New York: Columbia University Press, 1971.
_____. (ed.) Soviet Nationality Problems. New York: Columbia University Press, 1971.
_____. Uzbek Literary Politics. The Hague: Mouton, 1964.
Aspaturian, Vernon V. The Union Republics in Soviet Diplomacy: A Study of Soviet Federalism in the Service of Soviet Foreign Policy. Geneva: Droz, 1960.
Bacon, Elizabeth E. Central Asians Under Russian Rule: A Study in Culture Change. Ithaca, N.Y.: Cornell University Press, 1966.
Becker, Seymour. Russia's Protectorates in Central Asia: Bukhara and Khiva, 1865-1924. Cambridge, Mass.: Harvard University Press, 1968.
Bennigsen, Alexandre and Chantal Lemercier-Quelque jay. Islam in the Soviet Union. New York: Praeger Publishers, 1967.
Caroe, Olaf. Soviet Empire: The Turks of Central Asia and Stalinism. New York: St. Martin's Press, 1953, 2d ed. 1967.
Chadwick, Nora, and Victor Zhirmunsky. Oral Epics of Central Asia. London: Cambridge University Press, 1969.
Coates, William P., and Zelda Coates. Soviets in Central Asia. London: Lawrence and Wishart, 1951: 2d ed., New York: Greenwood Press, 1969.
Conquest, Robert. The Nation Killers: The Soviet Deportation of Nationalities. London: Macmillan, 1970.
_____. (ed.) Soviet Nationalities Policy in Practice. (New York: Praeger Publishers 1967).
Demko, George J. The Russian Colonization of Kazakhstan, 1896-1916. Bloomington: Indiana University Publications, 1969.
Eckmann, Janos. Chagatay Manual. Bloomington: Indiana University Publications, 1966.
Goldhagen, Erich (ed.). Ethnic Minorities in the Soviet Union. New York: Praeger Publishers, 1968.

Hambly, Gavin (ed.). Central Asia. New York: Delacorte Press, 1969.

Hofman, H. F. Turkish Literature, a Bio-Bibliographical Survey. Section III: Moslim Central Asian Turkish Literature. Utrecht: Library of the University of Utrecht, 1969.

Holdsworth, Mary. Turkestan in the Nineteenth Century: A Brief History of the Khanates of Bukhara, Kokand and Khiva. London: Central Asian Research Center, 1959.

Hostler, Charles Warren. Turkism and the Soviets: The Turks of the World and Their Political Objectives. New York: Praeger Publishers, 1957.

Inoyatov, Khamid. Central Asia and Kazakhstan Before and After the October Revolution: Reply to Falsifiers of History. Moscow: Progress Publishers, 1966.

Kaushik, Devendra. Central Asia in Modern Times. A History from the Early 19th Century. Moscow: Progress Publishers, 1970.

Kolarz, Walter. Russia and Her Colonies. New York: Praeger Publishers, 1955.

Krader, Lawrence. Peoples of Central Asia. Bloomington: Indiana University Publications, 1963.

Loewenthal, Rudolf. The Turkic Languages and Literatures of Central Asia, a Bibliography. 's-Gravenhage: Mouton, 1957.

Medlin, William K., William M. Cave, and Finley Carpenter. Education and Development in Central Asia: A Case Study on Social Change in Uzbekistan. Leiden: E. J. Brill, 1971.

Menges, Karl. Turkic Languages and Peoples: An Introduction to Turkic Studies. Wiesbaden: Harrasowitz, 1968.

Nove, Alec, and J. A. Newth. The Soviet Middle East: A Model for Development? London: Allen & Unwin, 1967.

Park, Alexander G. Bolshevism in Turkestan, 1917-1927. New York: Columbia University Press, 1957.

Pierce, Richard A. Soviet Central Asia: A Bibliography. Berkeley: Center for Slavic and East European Studies, University of California, 1966.

_____. Russian Central Asia, 1867-1917: A Study in Colonial Rule. Berkeley: University of California Press, 1960.

Pipes, Richard. The Formation of the Soviet Union: Communism and Nationalism, 1917-1923. Cambridge, Mass.: Harvard University Press, 1954. 2d ed., 1964.

Rakowska-Harmstone, Teresa. Russia and Nationalism in Central Asia: The Case of Tadzhikistan. Baltimore: The Johns Hopkins Press, 1970.

Rywkin, Michael. Russia in Central Asia. New York: Collier Books, 1963.

Schlesinger, Rudolf (ed.). The Nationalities Problem and Soviet
    Administration. London: Routlege and K. Paul, 1956.
Tillett, Lowell. The Great Friendship: Soviet Historians on the
    Non-Russian Nationalities. Chapel Hill: University of North
    Carolina Press, 1969.
Vaidyanath, R. The Formation of the Soviet Central Asian Republics:
    A Study in Soviet Nationalities Policy, 1917-1936. New Delhi:
    People's Publishing House, 1967.
Wheeler, Geoffrey. The Modern History of Soviet Central Asia.
    New York: Praeger Publishers, 1964.
    _____. The Peoples of Soviet Central Asia: A Background Book,
    London: The Bodley Head, 1966.
    _____. Racial Problems in Soviet Muslim Asia. London: Oxford
    University Press, 1962.
Winner, Thomas G. The Oral Art and Literature of the Kazakhs of
    Russian Central Asia. Durham, N. C.: Duke University Press,
    1958.
Zenkovsky, Serge A. Pan-Turkism and Islam in Russia. Cambridge,
    Mass.: Harvard University Press, 1960.

EDWARD ALLWORTH, Ph.D. in Slavic and Central Asian literature, Columbia University, is Professor of Turco-Soviet Studies in the Department of Middle East Languages and Cultures, and Director of the Program on Soviet Nationality Problems, in Columbia University. He has traveled and conducted research in the USSR (including Central Asia), Turkey, and Europe, and he knows Turkish, Uzbek, and other Central Asian languages, and Russian. His publications include "The 'Nationality' Idea in Czarist Central Asia," in Erich Goldhagen (ed.), Ethnic Minorities in the Soviet Union (New York: Praeger Publishers, 1968), pp. 229-250, and "Bilim ochaghi 'The Source of Knowledge', a Nationalistic Periodical from the Turkistan Autonomous Soviet Socialist Republic," Central Asiatic Journal, Vol. X, No. 1 (March 1965), pp. 61-70. Additional writings by him and the other authors are included in the "Selected List of Recent Books . . ." at the end of this volume.

ROBERT J. BARRETT received a B.A. from the University of Texas in 1958. He is Assistant Professor of Russian Language and Literature, Department of Germanic and Slavic Languages, Bernard Baruch College, The City University of New York. He is currently a Ph.D. candidate in the Department of Middle East Languages and Cultures at Columbia University, majoring in Central Asian literature and language. He has traveled extensively in Central Asia and the USSR and knows Uzbek and other Turkic languages, as well as Russian.

SEYMOUR BECKER, Ph.D. in History, Harvard University, is Associate Professor in the Department of History at Rutgers University. He speaks Russian and was an exchange scholar at Moscow State University in 1967-68.

RALPH SCOTT CLEM received his M.A. in Geography from Columbia University in 1972. He is currently a Ph.D. candidate in the Department of Geography at Columbia University, majoring in the population geography of the Soviet Union. He knows Russian and some Ukrainian. He has written Assimilation of Ukrainians in the Soviet Union, 1959 (M.A. Thesis, Columbia University, 1972).

ETHEL DUNN, M.A. in History, Columbia University, is Executive Secretary of the Highgate Road Social Science Research Station, Inc.

STEPHEN P. DUNN, Ph.D. in Anthropology, Columbia University, is lecturer in anthropology at the Monterey Institute of Foreign Studies. Their publications on directed culture change in the Soviet Union include "Soviet Regime and Native Culture in Central Asia and Kazakhstan: the Major Peoples," Current Antropology, Vol. 8, No. 3 (June 1967), pp. 147-208. Stephen Dunn is the editor of Soviet Anthropology and Archeology and Soviet Sociology, and his publications include Cultural Processes in the Baltic Area under Soviet Rule (Berkeley: Institute of International Studies, University of California, Research Series No. 11, 1966). Both Ethel and Stephen P. Dunn use Russian and have spent time in the USSR.

WILLIAM L. HANAWAY, Jr., Ph.D. in Iranian Studies, Columbia University, is Assistant Professor of Persian Language and Literature at the University of Pennsylvania. He has traveled in the Middle East and knows Tajik, Persian, Turkish, and Russian. His publications include "Formal Elements in the Persian Popular Romance," Review of National Literatures, III (1971), pp. 139-160.

JOHN HANSELMAN received an A.B. from the University of Michigan in 1967. He is currently a Ph.D. candidate in the Political Science Department at Columbia University, majoring in comparative politics. He speaks Russian and is the Program Assistant for the Program on Soviet Nationality Problems at Columbia University.

TIMUR KOCAOGLU received his B.A. from Istanbul University in 1971. He is currently a Ph.D. candidate in the Department of Middle East Languages and Cultures, Columbia University, majoring in Central Asian cultural history. He knows Tajik, Uzbek, and other Central Asian languages, Turkish, Persian, and some Russian.

IAN M. MATLEY, Ph.D. in Geography, University of Michigan, is Professor of Geography at Michigan State University. He speaks Russian, and has spent time in the Middle East. His publications include "The Population and the Land," "Agricultural Development," and "Industrialization," in Edward Allworth (ed.), Central Asia: A Century of Russian Rule (New York: Columbia University Press, 1967), pp. 92-131, 266-309, and 309-349, and "The Golodnaya Steppe: A Russian Irrigation Venture in Central Asia," Geographical Review, Vol. 60, No. 3 (July 1970), pp. 328-346.

EDEN NABY received her M.A. in Persian Literature from Columbia University in 1971. She is currently a Ph.D. candidate in the Department of Middle East Languages and Cultures at Columbia University, majoring in Central Asian cultural history. She served in the Peace

Corps in Afghanistan, has traveled in the Middle East, and knows Tajik, Uzbek, Persian, and some Russian. She has written Gowar Murad: A Persian Playwright (M.A. Thesis, Columbia University, 1971).

ANNA PROCYK received her M.A. in History from Columbia University in 1967. She is currently a Ph.D. candidate in the Department of History at Columbia University, majoring in the history of Russia, the Soviet Union, and East Central Europe. She knows Russian, Ukrainian, and Polish, and has traveled to the Soviet Union. She has written The Ukrainian Treaty of Brest-Litovsk, February 9, 1918 (M.A. Thesis, Columbia University, 1967), and The Nationality Policy of the White Movement (Ph.D. Dissertation, Columbia University, 1973).

BARRY ROSEN received his M.A. in Political Science from Syracuse University in 1967. He is currently a Ph.D. candidate in the Department of Middle East Languages and Cultures at Columbia University, majoring in Persian cultural history and language. He served in the Peace Corps in Iran, has traveled extensively in the Middle East and Soviet Central Asia, and knows Tajik, Persian, and some Uzbek and Russian. He has written The Religio-Political Thought of Maulana Mawdudi and the Jama'at-i-Islami of Pakistan (M.A. Thesis, Syracuse University, 1967).

M. MOBIN SHORISH, Ph.D. in Education and Social Order (Comparative Education), University of Chicago, is an Assistant Professor of Comparative History and Philosophy of Education at the University of Illinois and Director of the Office of International Programs in Education. He speaks Tajik, Uzbek, and other Central Asian languages, and Russian. His writings include "The Role of Local Women in the 'Multi-Tiered' Society of Soviet Central Asia," a paper delivered at the Interdisciplinary Conference on Processes of Change in Contemporary Asian Societies, November 5, 1970, Champaign, Illinois.

IMMANUEL WALLERSTEIN, Ph.D. in Sociology, Columbia University, is Professor of Sociology at McGill University. He is President of the African Studies Association. His publications include The Road to Independence: Ghana and the Ivory Coast (Paris: Mouton, 1964) and Africa: The Politics of Unity (New York: Random House, 1967).

RONALD WIXMAN received his B.A. in Russian Language and Geography from Hunter College in 1968, and his M.A. in Geography from Columbia in 1972. He has written Assimilation of Ethnic Groups of the Caucasus Which Lack Native Ethnic Institutions (1926-1959) (M.A. Thesis, Columbia University, 1972). He is currently a Ph.D.

candidate in the Department of Geography at Columbia University, majoring in the population and cultural geography of the Soviet Union. He has traveled in the Middle East and the USSR and knows Russian and some Azeri.